AF652134

Linguistic Issues In Encoding Sanskrit

Linguistic Issues In Encoding Sanskrit

PETER M. SCHARF
MALCOLM D. HYMAN

MOTILAL BANARSIDASS PUBLISHERS
PRIVATE LIMITED • DELHI

First Edition: Delhi, 2012

© 2011 by The Sanskrit Library.
All Rights Reserved.

ISBN: 978-81-208-3539-9

MOTILAL BANARSIDASS
41 U.A., Bungalow Road, Jawahar Nagar, Delhi 110 007
8 Mahalaxmi Chamber, 22 Bhulabhai Desai Road, Mumbai 400 026
203 Royapettah High Road, Mylapore, Chennai 600 004
236, 9th Main III Block, Jayanagar, Bangalore 560 011
Sanas Plaza, 1302 Baji Rao Road, Pune 411 002
8 Camac Street, Kolkata 700 017
Ashok Rajpath, Patna 800 004
Chowk, Varanasi 221 001

Printed in India

By Jainendra Prakash Jain at Shri Jainendra Press,
A-45 Naraina, Phase-I, New Delhi 110 028
and Published by Narendra Prakash Jain for
Motilal Banarsidass Publishers Private Limited,
Bungalow Road, Delhi 110 007

Foreword
by GEORGE CARDONA

Questions surrounding the encoding of speech have been considered since scholars began to consider the history of different writing systems and of writing itself. In modern times, attention has been paid to such issues as standardizing systems for portraying in Roman script the scripts used for recording other languages, and this has given rise to discussions about distinctions such as that between transliteration and transcription. In recent times, moreover, the advent and general use of digital technology has allowed us not only to replicate with relative ease details of various scripts and to produce machine searchable texts but also to reproduce images of manuscripts that can be viewed and manipulated, a true boon to philologists in that they are thus enabled to consult and study materials with all the details found in original manuscripts, such as different hands that can be discerned and clues to modifications made due to features of different scripts. At the source of such endeavors lie the facts of language: phonological and phonetic matters that scripts portray with various degrees of fidelity.

India can justifiably lay claim to being the home of what is doubtless the most thorough and sophisticated consideration of speech production, phonetics, and phonology in ancient times. The preservation of Vedic texts and their proper recitation according to the norms of various groups of reciters led to the early analysis of continuously recited texts (*saṁhitāpāṭha*) into constituents — called *pada* — characterized by phonological alternations that appear at word boundaries, including boundaries before particular morphemes within syntactic words. A text that includes such elements is termed *padapāṭha*. At least one such analyzed text predates the grammarian Pāṇini, the padapāṭha to the *Ṛgveda* by Śākalya. The padapāṭha related to any saṁhitāpāṭha obviously derives from the latter, its source. On the other hand, the separate padas of the padapāṭha can be viewed theoretically as the source of the continuously recited text, gotten by removing pauses at boundaries and thereby applying phonological rules that take effect between contiguous units. This is, in fact, the theoretical stance taken by authors of texts called *prātiśākhya*, which formulate phonological rules modifying padas in contiguity with other padas. Thus, phonological alternations within Vedic texts were objects of concern by at least the early sixth century B.C. Pāṇini himself — who can hardly be dated later than around 500 B.C. — composed a generalized grammatical work, his śabdānuśāsana, which includes both a set of rules, called *Aṣṭādhyāyī*, serving to account through a derivational system for the accepted usage of his time and place as well as certain dialectal differences and features particular to earlier Vedic. One of the appendices to the *Aṣṭādhyāyī* is an inventory of sounds — referred to as the *akṣarasamāmnāya* by early students of Pāṇini's work — that is divided into fourteen sets, each set off from the others by a final consonantal marker (*it*), which serves to form abbreviatory terms (*pratyāhāra*) referring to groups of sounds with respect to phonological rules as formulated in the *Aṣṭādhyāyī*.

The order of sounds in Pāṇini's akṣarasamāmnāya shows properties best explained as due to its being a reworking of an earlier source. The five sets of stops in such earlier inventories, moreover, show an obvious phonetic ordering, from velar to labial, that is, an order based on the production of sounds, from the back of the oral cavity to the front. Moreover, prātiśākhyas not only state rules of phonological replacement but also describe the production of sounds, a topic which is dealt with in works on phonetics (*śikṣā*) such as the *Āpiśaliśikṣā* of Āpiśali. Accordingly, scholars are justified in maintaining that early Indian texts reflect a sophisticated investigation of Sanskrit phonology and phonetics.

Scholars have also frequently debated whether or not writing played a role in the composition and transmission of such early works as the prātiśākhyas and the *Aṣṭādhyāyī*. There can be no doubt whatever that the latter was later transmitted orally. It is also most plausible that Pāṇini himself composed and transmitted his work orally. Thus, Pāṇini formulates a group of rules identifying certain sounds as markers, given the class name *it*, and provides that such sounds are unconditionally deleted before any other operations apply. Had he transmitted his work in writing, thus being able to make use of script particularities such as placing given sounds above or below a line, Pāṇini would not have needed such rules. That works such as Pāṇini's were transmitted orally does not mean, however, that the society in which Pāṇini lived was not literate. To the contrary, he lived in a part of the subcontinent — Śalātura in the extreme north-west — that at his time was under Persian control, and the Achemenid rulers had inscriptions recorded. Nevertheless, a literate society does not imply necessarily that compositions must be put in writing and thus transmitted; later Indian traditions, for example, stress the oral transmission, though writing was clearly known then. The earliest attested written documents on the subcontinent, nevertheless, come several centuries after Pāṇini. These are the inscriptions of the emperor Aśoka in the third century B.C., which for the most part employ two scripts: Brāhmī everywhere except the northwest, where Kharoṣṭhī is used; in the extreme-north-west, one finds also Aramaic and Greek used.

Peter M. Scharf and the late Malcom D. Hyman have written a valuable work, *Linguistic Issues in Encoding Sanskrit*, in which Sanskrit and its systems of description and transmission serve as a background to more general discussions concerning encoding of language. The authors explain the need for a work such as this and set forth their general aims in the introduction (p. 2) as follows:

> Today people use computers to manipulate linguistic and textual data in sophisticated ways; yet current encoding systems tend to reflect visual and orthographic design factors to the exclusion of more relevant information-processing principles. Thus these systems reproduce deficiencies inherent in the traditional orthographies themselves. In this book we examine some fundamental issues in the coding of natural language texts. We consider above all the relation the information selected for encoding bears to natural language structure. We focus on Sanskrit, which is characterized by an extensive oral tradition, a highly phonetic orthography, and a copious literature. We survey various Sanskrit encoding schemes in past and present use and investigate their suitability for particular applications. We conclude by advancing some concrete proposals.

Although this book centers on Sanskrit, it covers a great many important issues and history relative to the general subject of encoding. The second and third chapters take up different coding systems. A brief sketch of the history of Indian printing serves as a background to presenting coding systems, including Roman transliterations, keyboard arrangements, and Unicode. These are subjected to a critique that centers on issues of ambiguity and redundancy consequent to their being based on Devanāgarī and Roman transliteration. The fourth chapter may well be the most important one from a theoretical viewpoint. Here the authors take up what they deem to be the basis for encoding. Their discussion is organized around three axes, as follows (p. 47): Axis I: Graphic–phonetic: Is the basic unit of the encoding a written character or a speech sound? Axis II: Synthetic–analytic: Are units encoded as a single Gestalt? Or are they decomposed into distinctively encoded features? Axis III: Contrastive–non-contrastive: Are codepoints selected only for units that contrast minimally (graphemes or phonemes)? The sixth and seventh chapters deal with the basic issue of encoding elements of speech or writing. The discussion of distinctive elements in chapter six is particularly wide ranging and includes succinct presentation of issues in areas such as generative grammar and historical linguistics. Given that the principal emphasis throughout is on Sanskrit, it is appropriate that these discussions are preceded, in chapter five, by considerations of Sanskrit phonetics and phonology. These include both presentations of what was said in various prātiśākhyas and śikṣās — including treatments of these statements by modern scholars — and feature analysis (section 5.2.6).

In the eighth and final chapter, the authors emphasize that, since computers now are used to carry out many tasks in addition to displaying data, this can no longer be considered the primary factor in determining a scheme for encoding. Instead, "... language should be encoded in such a way as to facilitate automatic processing, to minimize extrinsic ambiguity and redundancy, and to ensure longevity (p. 113)." Scharf and Hyman then go on to discuss what they call dynamic transcoding as well as possibilities concerning text-to-speech and speech-recognition and higher-level encoding.

The main text is complemented by a series of appendixes, four of which directly concern encoding. The first of these contains thirteen tables, in which are treated not only Sanskrit phonetic and phonological features but also, interestingly, reconstructions of Proto-Indo-European phonology according to different scholars. The second, third and fourth appendixes concern encoding schemes developed within the context of the Sanskrit Library established as a website by Scharf: the Sanskrit Library Phonetic basic encoding scheme, the Sanskrit Library segmental encoding scheme, and the Sanskrit Library phonetic featural encoding scheme.

Even this brief overview should show that *Linguistic Issues in Encoding Sanskrit* is a rich and varied work that deserves the serious attention not merely of Sanskritists but of scholars working in several areas related to language encoding.

George Cardona
February 19, 2011

Preface

The current generation is witnessing a transition in the dominant medium of knowledge transmission from print to electronics. The transition began in America and Western Europe but is quickly spreading around the world. Naturally due to the region of its origin, conventions in the new digital medium have been dominated by the conventions of modern Western European languages. While these conventions are making some adjustments to suit the diversity of the world's cultures, the world is likewise quickly adapting to prevalent standards, and these standards are quickly becoming entrenched. That which doesn't fit the standards is in danger of being left behind. History has shown that in previous media transitions the knowledge that fails to adapt to the new medium recedes from public view to the restricted domain of the endeavoring antiquarian research scholar or becomes irretrievably lost. Yet the digital medium is flexible and powerful; it has the potential not only to adequately mimic the printed medium but to exceed it by innovative software design and interactivity. The current book — and indeed much of the work of the authors including the Sanskrit Library itself — is motivated by the desire to minimize the loss of access to the knowledge of the vast heritage of ancient India in the current media transition, to facilitate innovation in the digital medium to make that knowledge more readily accessible, and to inspire those who discover it to integrate that knowledge into the dominant stream of education and culture. We believe that the insights we have gained working to make Sanskrit more accessible should be of use in making other major culture-bearing languages of the world more accessible as well. Some of these insights should be useful in the communication of knowledge in the digital medium in general.

Sanskrit text has been moving into the digital medium. Recent decades have witnessed the growth of machine-readable Sanskrit texts in archives such as the Thesaurus Indogermanischer Text-und Sprachmaterialien (TITUS), Kyoto University, Indology, and the Göttingen Register of Electronic Texts in Indian Languages (GRETIL). The last few years have witnessed a burgeoning of digital images of Sanskrit manuscripts and books hosted on-line. For example, the University of Pennsylvania Library, which houses the largest collection of Sanskrit manuscripts in the Western Hemisphere, has made digital images of two hundred ninety-seven of them available on the web. The Universal Digital Library, and Google Books have made digital images of large numbers of Sanskrit texts accessible as part of their enormous library digitization projects. Digitized Sanskrit documents include machine-readable text and images of lexical resources such as those of the Cologne Digital Sanskrit Lexicon project (CDSL), and the University of Chicago's Digital Dictionaries of South Asia project (DDSA).

As oral, manuscript, and print media that have conveyed the knowledge embodied in the ancient Sanskrit language make their transition into digital media, a number of scholars have begun collaborating in the Sanskrit Computational Linguistics Consortium which has organized several symposia since 2007. Members include linguists finding new challenges in formalizing the syntax of a free-word-order language, computer scientists drawn to model techniques of generative grammar used by the ancient India grammarian Pāṇini, philologists using digital methods to assist in critical editing, and scholars collaborating to build corpora, databases, and tools for the use of academic researchers and commercial enterprises. The authors of the present volume have actively participated in and fostered this growing collaboration.

Since 1999, we have worked together to facilitate the entry, linguistic processing, and display of Sanskrit texts both in print and on the Web. Our collaboration began with the preparation of the web and print publication of Scharf's (2002) *Rāmopākhyāna* and the launch of The Sanskrit Library website[1] in 2002, and continued with the International Digital Sanskrit Library Integration project at Brown University under grants from the National Science Foundation (NSF) 2006–2009. In July 2009 we began the project Enhancing Access to Primary Cultural Heritage

[1] <http://sanskritlibrary.org/>.

Materials of India under a grant from the National Endowment for the Humanities, and in July 2010 we began the project Sanskrit Lexical Sources: Digital Synthesis and Revision. Struggling to overcome the lack of adequate encoding for Sanskrit led us to tackle the issue both practically and theoretically. With colleagues worldwide, we prepared a proposal to extend the Unicode Standard to allow adequate encoding of Vedic Sanskrit. Simultaneously, we engaged in a thorough review of the fundamental principles of encoding. We reviewed encoding principles not just for Sanskrit and not just in digital character encoding, but considered the question broadly in terms of the means that humans communicate knowledge through speech, writing, print, and electronic media. The present volume is a result of these investigations. While the linguistic material discussed is drawn primarily from Sanskrit, the questions addressed are relevant to linguistic encoding in general and should be of interest to scholars of linguistics.

On the fifth of September 2009, I received a call from my colleague and co-author Malcolm Hyman's wife informing me that he had passed away suddenly the night before. It is regrettable that he did not get to see the publication of this book that has been nearly complete for two years and that he himself was primarily responsible for typesetting. It is far more regrettable that the fruitful collaboration that we have undertaken in the past decade has come to an end, and that the potential contributions he had to make will not materialize. Malcolm had a comprehensive view of digital humanities and prescient vision of productive directions for research. I am grateful for what I have learned from him in the course of our work together – even in being forced to learn TeX to bring this book to completion. In tribute to him and in the hope that others may find his work instructive and inspiring, his complete curriculum vitae is included in Appendix E of this volume.

Part of this work was supported by the NSF under grant no. 0535207. Any opinions, findings, and conclusions or recommendations expressed are those of the authors and do not necessarily reflect the views of the NSF.

Contents

Illustrations

Abbreviations

A.	Pāṇini's *Aṣṭādhāyī*
ĀŚ.	*Āpiśaliśikṣā*
APr.	*Atharvaprātiśākhya*
ASCII	American Standard Code for Information Interchange
BCDIC	Extended Binary Coded Decimal Interchange Code
CA.	*Caturādhyāyikā*
CCITT	Comité Consultatif International Télpéhonique et Télégraphique
DhP.	The Pāṇinian *Dhātupāṭha*
MBhK.	Kielhorn's edition of Patañjali's *Mahābhāṣya*
PIE	Proto-Indo-European
R̥Pr.	*R̥kprātiśākhya*
R̥V.	*R̥gveda*
TPr.	*Taittirīyaprātiśākhya*
VPr.	*Vājasaneyiprātiśākhya*
Vyā. Pa.	*Vyāḍi Paribhāṣāvr̥tti*

Chapter 1

Introduction

Human beings express knowledge in various modes: through images in visual art; through movement in dance, theatrical performance, and gestures; and through speech in spoken language. Each of these means of expression includes means to encode knowledge, and each is used to express knowledge originally encoded in one of the others. Poetry describes depicted scenes, while epics narrate the events depicted there. Manuscript images depict scenes from the epics the texts they decorate narrate, while Kathakali enacts the epics in performance. Certain media dominate as the primary methods for the transmission of detailed information at different times and places. Oral tradition dominated the tradition of Sanskrit in India in the first and second millennia B.C.E. Writing overtook orality in the first millennium C.E. and dominated until replaced gradually by printing beginning in the 15th century in Europe and in the 19th century in India. Since the invention of digital electronic transmission in the 19th century, the digital medium has slowly expanded its domain and now is replacing printing as the dominant means of knowledge transmission. In order to rescue the enormous body of literature extant in print, writing, and living memory from being marginalized and becoming extinct, it is vital to reflect on the nature of transitions in knowledge transmission in order to understand the nature of the present transition from the printed to digital now taking place. Consciousness of the nature of the transition taking place will allow deliberate steps to maximize the preservation of inherited learning. Such consciousness will additionally open avenues of research not previously practicable without features of the digital medium.

Today people use computers to manipulate linguistic and textual data in sophisticated ways; yet current encoding systems tend to reflect visual and orthographic design factors to the exclusion of more relevant information-processing principles. Thus these systems reproduce deficiencies inherent in the traditional orthographies themselves. In this book we examine some fundamental issues in the coding of natural language texts. We consider above all the relation the information selected for encoding bears to natural language structure. We focus on Sanskrit, which is characterized by an extensive oral tradition, a highly phonetic orthography, and a copious literature. We survey various Sanskrit encoding schemes in past and present use and investigate their suitability for particular applications. We conclude by advancing some concrete proposals.

1.1 Technologies for representing spoken language

Problems that arise in current encoding schemes stem from a long history of adaptation in technologies for the visual representation of language. The history of these technologies reveals a recurrent tendency to imitate the appearance of earlier technologies and the possibility of information loss at each transition (cf. Waller 1988, 262; Hockey 2000, 25).[1] Recent developments in text processing lead us to reconsider the fundamental purpose of text encoding.

Writing emerged gradually as a technology for representing spoken human language.[2] Social and economic factors led at certain times and in certain places to an increase in the frequency of writing and the number

[1] "No revolution in communications media succeeds without a transitional period during which it simply imitates the old system. [...] For example, early printed books imitated manuscripts, and early cinema used fixed cameras in imitation of the fixed viewpoint of the theatre-goer" (Waller, 1986, 74).

[2] The earliest "proto-writing", attested in the ancient Near East, is associated with economic and administrative functions; it is related only loosely to spoken language (Damerow, 1999). For further remarks on proto-writing, see: Boltz 2006; Hyman 2006.

FIGURE 1.1: Some of Gutenberg's ligatures and abbreviations (from left to right): *pp/pop, ppe, prae, pre/pri, pri, prop, qua/qui, quoque*

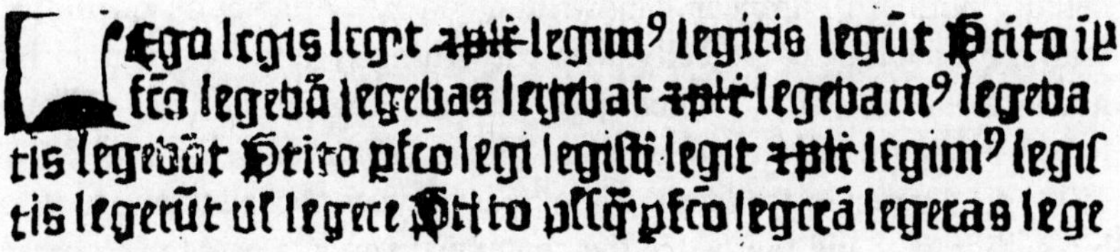

FIGURE 1.2: Printed text with paradigm of the Latin verb *lego* 'read', ca. 1445

of literate individuals. Historians distinguish three stages: (1) *scribal literacy,* in which the technology is restricted to a specialized group of users; (2) *craftsman's literacy,* in which a majority of skilled craftspeople use writing; and (3) *mass literacy,* in which the technology of writing is known to nearly everyone (Harris, 1989).

An invention in fifteenth-century Germany — the printing press — came to have a profound and worldwide effect on the dissemination and production of documents (Eisenstein, 1980). It is in the context of this technology that mass literacy was achieved in Europe and other parts of the world in the nineteenth and twentieth centuries (Vincent, 2000). Printing with movable type closely followed the conventions of scribal writing (Füssel, 2005, 18–19).[3] Gutenberg's 42-line Bible of 1455 employed a font of almost 300 characters, including a large number of lig-

[3] "The earlier printers, in their anxiety to compete successfully with manuscript books, adopted the existing written letter forms and did not question their entire suitability as shapes for reproduction into metal types. Nor did either printer or founder, for many years until printing had been recognized for its own sake, make any attempt to seek or create letter forms better adapted to type reproduction than the written characters" (Ghosh, 1983, 12).

atures, alternate letterforms, accented letters, and abbreviations (Steinberg 1961, 20, 30; Walden Font 1997; Füssel 2005, 17–18); see FIGURE 1.1. These had arisen in response to the demands of manuscript copying. Gutenberg's characters were modeled upon a style of gothic script current in the Germany of his day (Gill 1936, 32–33; Sampson 1985, 112; Kapr 1993, 20–22; Haralambous 2004, 367–368); see FIGURE 1.2. In its general layout, the printed Bible also resembled a fifteenth-century northern European handwritten codex.[4] Adaptation of printing with movable type to radically different writing systems was neither fast nor without difficulty.[5] When the Venetian Gregorio de Gregorii published an Arabic-language Book of Hours (*Kitāb ṣalāt as-sawāʿī*) in 1514, his attempt to produce the hundreds of types needed to imitate Arabic calligraphy and reproduce the contextual variants of Arabic characters resulted in an un-aesthetic and partly unreadable publication (Lunde 1981, 21; Roper 2002). Arabic printing only achieved a mature form with the types cut by Robert Granjon in the 1580s.[6]

The Industrial Revolution of the nineteenth century led to increased mechanization in the production of printed materials and the transformation of basic techniques. The Mergenthaler Linotype (1886) and Lanston Monotype (1889) allowed the keyboarding of text to replace the process of manual composition, in which types were picked one by one from a wooden typecase, as in FIGURE 1.3 (Steinberg 1961, 286; Schlesinger 1989; Kahan 2000).[7] The layout of the keyboards on these machines,

---

[4]The British Library has made digital images of its two complete Gutenberg Bibles available: <http://www.bl.uk/treasures/gutenberg/homepage.html>. See also the Ransom Center's Digital Gutenberg Project: <http://www.hrc.utexas.edu/exhibitions/permanent/gutenberg/>.

[5]On the earliest printing in Greek and Hebrew, see Füssel (2005, 101–104, 107–109). Aldus Manutius, who published the first volume of an edition of Aristotle in Greek in 1495, closely imitated calligraphic style in his type, and made use of numerous ligatures and abbreviations. Ingram (1966), who provides an extensive guide to ligatures and abbreviations in early Greek typography, remarks that when he first encountered Renaissance Greek printing, "I saw little resemblance between the Greek I had learned in school and this peculiar, cramped typeface which I could not read and which often contained only an occasional letter I could recognize" (Ingram, 1966, 371).

[6]On the early history of Arabic typography in Europe, see Roper (2002).

[7]Automation began to be introduced into type composition and casting considerably earlier in the nineteenth century. Notable early systems were devised by William Church (1822) and by James Young and Adrian Delambre (1840–1841) (Schlesinger 1989; Kahan 2000, 1–2).

FIGURE 1.3: Newspaper composing room with workers setting text manually from typecases, 1892

however, resembled at first the older typecases; with time, they became simplified and more ergonomic (AbiFarès, 2001). Another late nineteenth century technology, the typewriter, was first commercially manufactured in the United States in the 1870s.[8] The typewriter greatly expanded the mechanical production of texts and allowed mechanical technology to be used for the creation of even ephemeral documents. Typewriters reproduced many aspects of printing technology, but with several accommodations: a greatly reduced inventory of characters, monospacing, and the elimination of many possibilities for aesthetic refinement.

Teletype machines, which originated around 1907, allowed for the remote transmission and printing of text; they led eventually to standards for information encoding, most notably ASCII (American Standard Code for Information Interchange) in the 1960s (Bemer, 1963; Smith, 1964; Mackenzie, 1980; Gaylord, 1995).[9] Current digital computer keyboards evolved from teletype keyboards, and the first documents created using computers resembled typewritten documents. Digital typesetting emerged in the 1970s and made possible the creation of high-quality documents that incorporated aspects of traditional typography (Syropoulos, Tsolomitis & Sofroniou, 2003). The desktop publishing revolution of the 1980s and 90s brought these capabilities to an international public that continues to expand today.

---

[8] Manufacture by Remington of the typewriter designed by Christopher Latham Sholes and Carlos Glidden began in 1873 (Beeching, 1990; Bukatman, 1993; Kahan, 2000).

[9] We may look even earlier, to the five-bit code for telegraphy patented in 1874 by Baudot (Gillam, 2002, 43). A later rearrangement of the code was standardized in 1931 as CCITT #2 by the Comité Consultatif International Télpéhonique et Télégraphique (now renamed ITU-T) and extensively used by teletype machines (Mackenzie, 1980, 6, 62–64). As a matter of historical curiosity, we may note that the ultimate antecedent of the Baudot code was Francis Bacon's so-called "bi-literal" cipher, first published in 1623 (Strasser 1988, 88–9; Kahn 1996, 882–3).

ASCII became an American (ASA) standard on June 17, 1963. Although ASCII is generally thought of as a seven-bit code, it was actually designed as an eight-bit code with the eighth bit unassigned (Bemer, 1963, 35). When ASA (American Standards Association) became ANSI (American National Standards Institute), ASCII was officially designated ANSI X3.4-1968 (Mackenzie, 1980, 8). On the relation of ASCII to ISO 646 see Gaylord (1995).

An interesting predecessor of character encoding is the Linotype, which redistributed its matrices in accordance with a seven-digit binary code assigned to each type, "although [Mergenthaler] probably did not realize the mathematical significance" (Kahan, 2000, 206).

With each shift in technology, we observe the survival of elements from earlier technologies. To varying degrees, writing *represents* spoken language (Gibson, 1972, 13); printing *represents* writing; the typewritten text *represents* the printed text; and the first texts created with digital computers *represent* their typewritten forbears. The representation of speech in writing involves a fundamental change of medium from aural to visual, while the representation of writing in print, printed text in typed text, and typed text in digitally produced printed text all occur within visual media. Yet even the latter involve deliberate information recoding. Decisions are made in the selection of a limited repertoire of certain fixed shapes to represent in print the multiplicity of variously formed characters written with the free hand. Similar decisions are made in the further reduction of the relatively large number of print types to the relatively small number of types used in a typewriter, and in the design of patterns to represent characters in a dot-matrix. The issue of character coding emerges as a problem with the technological shift from traditional manual instruments such as pen, stylus, and brush to mechanized technologies: movable type, the typewriter, and the digital computer. Whereas the earlier manual technologies allowed complete flexibility in the final shape of characters, printing fixed the repertoire of possible shapes into sets of *types* (τύπος: that which is *struck* or *impressed;* but also a *type* as opposed to a *token* — cf. Plato *Republic* 396e). With the possibility of *data transmission,* it was necessary to ensure that characters on one machine were mapped accurately to characters on another.

At present, the digital computer offers exciting possibilities and challenges. There is great flexibility in how a text may be displayed or printed — designers can even draw upon calligraphic principles that were not possible within the confines of traditional printing technologies. At the same time, *display* is only one of numerous functions that computers can perform. Computers can exchange textual data over space and time; they can perform linguistic processing, such as spell-checking, machine translation, content analysis and indexing, and morphological and syntactic analysis.[10] Display for a human reader should no longer be

[10]Computers led first to advances in the culture of calculation. Their application to text and language processing followed at first only slowly, although we find already in 1949 the first electronic text project in the humanities, namely, Roberto Busa's computer-generated concordance *Index Thomisticus* (Hockey, 2000, 5). Today the *Index Thomisticus* lives on as the *Index Thomisticus Treebank,* a morphologically and syntactically annotated

considered as the primary determinant of an encoding scheme. Rather, language should be encoded in such a way as to facilitate automatic processing, to minimize extrinsic ambiguity and redundancy, and to ensure longevity. Traditional orthographies — which have led time and again to scribal corruption, readers' misunderstandings, and entire industries of textual criticism — are clearly not optimal. The need to encode Sanskrit, which has for its entire history been associated with an extremely sophisticated tradition of phonetic and linguistic analysis, provides us with an exceptional opportunity to rethink some fundamental issues of language encoding. Traditional orthographies for Sanskrit exhibit a number of infelicities in their design that should not be carried over into computer encodings.

1.2 The Sanskrit language

Sanskrit is the primary culture-bearing language of India, with a continuous production of literature in all fields of human endeavor over the course of four millennia. Middle Indo-Aryan languages (Prākrits Pālī, Apabhraṁśa, etc.) and New Indo-Aryan languages (regional languages such as Tamil, Malayalam, Marathi, Hindustani, etc.) served as the media of literary composition as well since about the third century B.C.E. Yet the extent and diversity of literature produced in Sanskrit, the long temporal span of its use, and the breadth of the use of the language throughout the Indian subcontinent and Southeast Asia are unparalleled. Indeed, extant literature in Sanskrit constitutes the largest body of literature in the world prior to the invention of the printing press. The cultural heritage of Sanskrit is extant in some thirty million manuscripts and serves as an object of study in academic institutions. The language persists in the recitation of hymns in daily worship and ceremonies, as the medium of instruction in centers of traditional learning, as the medium of communication in selected academic and literary journals and academic fora, and as the primary language of a revivalist community near Bangalore. Preceded by a strong oral tradition of knowledge transmission,

---

corpus that will be invaluable in the construction of new NLP tools for post-classical Latin (see <http://gircse.marginalia.it/~passarotti>). Lamentably, the increasing availability, and decreasing cost, of computer equipment has led (perhaps paradoxically) to an atavism that fetishizes display.

records of written Sanskrit remain in the form of inscriptions dating back only to the first century B.C.E. — two centuries *after* the oldest inscription in one of the Middle Indo-Aryan languages descended from Sanskrit (Bühler 1896; Salomon 1998, 17, 46, 86).[11] While the oldest Sanskrit inscriptions are in the Brāhmī script, texts are mostly written in the many Brāhmī-derived scripts used today in South and Southeast Asia. Most of the twenty-two officially recognized languages of India also use writing systems derived from Brāhmī, and these writing systems have been used for writing Sanskrit and Prākrits as well as regional languages. The most common script today for writing and printing Sanskrit is Devanāgarī. While the following discussion therefore selects Devanāgarī as exemplar, the issues raised with regard to Devanāgarī pertain to the other Brāhmī-derived writing systems as well. In the nineteenth century, European philologists adapted Roman script to represent Sanskrit. Most computer encoding schemes for Sanskrit are based on either Devanāgarī script or Romanization.

1.3 The Devanāgarī script

Devanāgarī, like the majority of the scripts of South and Southeast Asia, is derived from the ancient Brāhmī script (of which the first attested inscriptions date from the third century B.C.E.; see FIGURE 1.4). The Brāhmī script is related to another ancient Indian script, Kharoṣṭhī,[12] which appears to be adapted from Aramaic (Salomon, 1995; Scharfe, 2002; Voigt, 2005). Brāhmī developed into a number of regional varieties, partly in response to differing technologies of writing; the Proto-Nāgarī style originated in Rajasthan toward the end of the sixth century C.E. (Dani, 1963; Sharma, 2002). By the eleventh century Devanāgarī had become important for the transcription of Sanskrit literature (Singh 1991; Salomon 1998, 41). Today Devanāgarī is used for writing Hindi, as well as Marathi, Nepali, and at least twenty-four other languages (Unicode Consortium, 2006).

[11] The preference for oral rather than written transmission of texts in India has often been remarked upon. In the late seventh century the Chinese Buddhist pilgrim Yijing noted that "The Vedas have been handed down from mouth to mouth, not transcribed on paper or leaves" (Takakusu, 1896, 182).

[12] Kharoṣṭhī is now encoded in plane 1 of Unicode (`U+10A00–U+10A5F`).

FIGURE 1.4: Fragment of Aśoka's 6th pillar edict, written in Brāhmī script, 238 B.C.E.

Devanāgarī, like other scripts derived from Brāhmī, has attributes of both *alphabetic* and *syllabic* writing systems (Patel 1995; Salomon 1998, 15; Ishida 2002; Vaid 2002). Consonantal graphs imply an inherent short /a/ vowel, unless another vowel is explicitly indicated, or the absence of a vowel is made explicit by the virāma sign (्). With the exception of word-initial vowels, for which independent characters exist, vowels are indicated by means of dependent (diacritic) signs. Dependent vowel signs are placed above, below, before, or after the character (or characters) that represent the preceding consonant sound (or sounds). Thus Devanāgarī differs on the one hand from a pure alphabetic system such as Greek, which has independent letters to indicate vowel sounds, and on the other from the Japanese syllabaries (Hiragana and Katakana). Greek vowel characters α ⟨a⟩, ι ⟨i⟩, υ ⟨u⟩, etc. are as independent as consonant characters β ⟨b⟩, γ ⟨g⟩, δ ⟨d⟩. Japanese Katakana syllable symbols カ ⟨ka⟩, キ ⟨ki⟩, and ク ⟨ku⟩ are not related to each other in any systematic fashion even though they represent syllables that have the consonant /k/ in common.

The basic unit of Devanāgarī writing is sometimes known as an *orthographic syllable* (or *orthosyllable*): that is, a sequence of any number of consonant characters plus a vowel diacritic, optionally accompanied by a sign for the nasal *anusvāra* (ं) or release of breath, *visarga* (:). Although modern languages written in Devanāgarī make less use of complicated ligatures, sequences of up to five consonants are permissible and occur in Sanskrit, and in Sanskrit loanwords in modern Indic languages:

- Sanskit: दङ्क्ष्ण्वोः *daṅkṣṇvoḥ* GEN/LOC DU M/F of दङ्क्ष्णु *daṅkṣṇu* 'mordacious'
- Hindi < Sanskrit: तात्स्थ्य *tātsthya* 'metonymy'.

A symbol for a velar fricative [x] (*jihvāmūlīya*) or bilabial fricative [ɸ] (*upadhmānīya*) (usually written ≍) may occur instead of the visarga. Thus, letting *C* stand for any consonant graph, *V* for any vowel graph, and *X* for the anusvāra or visarga (or jihvāmūlīya, upadhmānīya) graph, we may describe an orthographic syllable by means of the regular expression $C^{0-5}VX^{?}$.[13] Because all consonant graphs imply an inherent vowel, a sequence of multiple consonants (consonant cluster, *saṁyoga*) must be rendered with a single ligature, in which the shape of constituent graphs can vary considerably. The shape of the ligature is a function of the shapes of the constituent consonant graphs. Generally, all consonants are rendered in partial form except the last (the prevocalic one). Consonant graphs that have a vertical bar to the right are usually stacked horizontally; round-bottomed consonant graphs, by contrast, are stacked vertically. Sequences involving /r/ are especially complex: when /r/ occurs as the initial element of a consonant cluster, it is written as a diacritic above the line (र्क ⟨rka⟩ = र् + क); elsewhere it takes the form of a diagonal bar slanted down to the left, attached near the bottom of the graph that represents the (phonetically) preceding consonant (क्र ⟨kra⟩ = क् + र).

---

[13]Notation: e^{0-5} denotes a concatenation of from zero to five occurrences of *e*; $e^{?}$ is equivalent to e^{0-1}.

Psycholinguistic research suggests "that orthographic representations are organized into syllable-like units independently from phonological influences" (Ward & Romani, 2000, 654). Cf. Caramazza & Miceli (1990); Badecker (1996, 60 n. 5, 67). For further discussion with reference to Indic scripts see Sproat (2006); Kompalli (2007). The regular expression given above formalizes one of the two criteria of orthographic legality: "how many consonant letters you may have in a row before you must have a vowel" (Ward & Romani, 2000, 654). Knowledge of orthographic legality also involves knowledge of orthotactic constraints on sequences of consonant characters (i. e., is a particular sequence of characters legal or illegal?).

Some ligatures (e. g., क्ष ⟨kṣa⟩ = क् + ष) have idiosyncratic forms that are opaque in terms of their constituent analysis, and may thus be considered "graphic idioms" (Ivanov & Toporov, 1968, 35).[14] Traditional Sanskrit orthography requires glyphs for representing more than a thousand consonant clusters, and it is not uncommon for there to exist four or more distinct styles for representing a single cluster (Wikner, 2002). Agenbroad (n.d.) illustrates difficulties in unifying consonantal characters in single ligatures. Shaw (1980, 28) reports that traditionally Devanāgarī fonts required 500–800 types for conjunct consonants.

An examination of the visual characteristics of Devanāgarī script helps to explain its graphotactic properties. Hamp (1959, 2) uses the term 'graphotactic' for the combination of graphic units by analogy with the term 'phonotactic'. The two most obvious visual features of Devanāgarī are the headstroke (*śirorekhā*) that runs horizontally across the top of a sequence of Devanāgarī consonant graphs,[15] and the vertical bar that appears at the right of many characters. The portion of the character that is densest in information (in information-theoretic terms) is below the

[14] Voigt (2005, 34) argues that ⟨क्ष⟩ originally was not a ligature, but rather was derived directly from Aramaic ⟨ṣ⟩ and was used to represent [ts] (possibly with the final component glottalized: [ts']).

[15] This feature arose from the technology of calligraphy (Ghosh, 1983, 16). The headstroke developed from an earlier head mark, which evolved in turn from the triangle of ink formed by the first placement of the pen at the start of drawing a character (Salomon 1998, 31–81; Shaw 1980, 28).. In typographic terms, the headstroke in Devanāgarī is the equivalent of the *baseline* in scripts such as Latin and Greek (cf. Katsoulidis 1996).

Ivanov & Toporov (1968, 35) offer a doubtful functional explanation of the *śirorekhā*. They write:

> The continuity of the phonetic stream is reflected in the continuity of the graphic chain: separate syllabic symbols in a word and separate words themselves are connected by an uninterrupted horizontal line. This feature of the Indian writing can be explained not only by its phonetic character but also by the specific character of the word in Sanskrit where a significant role is played by long compound words which are sometimes functionally analogous to entire syntagms.

Such an explanation cannot be accepted because there is no correlation between the phonetic unity and the graphic unity of strings united by a headbar or separated by a gap in the headbar. There is no greater phonetic unity in *tasmātkaroti* than in *anyo 'gacchat* even though the latter breaks the headbar between words, and the former forms a conjunct consonant running the headbar across two words. Moreover, manuscripts write entire sentences uninterrupted regardless of word boundaries.

headstroke and to the left of the vertical bar.[16] In only a few signs (थ ⟨tha⟩, ध ⟨dha⟩, and भ ⟨bha⟩) is the headstroke broken. Visually, we can establish three major classes of (consonant) characters:[17]

1. Characters with a vertical bar at the far right (ख ग घ च ज ञ ण त थ ध न प ब भ म य व श ष स)

2. Characters with a vertical bar at the center (क फ)

3. Characters that hang from a small stem attached to the headstroke (छ ट ठ ड ढ द ह); most of these characters have round bottoms.

The character ⟨jha⟩ may belong either to group 1 (if it takes the shape झ) or to group 2 (if it takes the shape भ). The character ⟨la⟩ may belong either to group 1 (if it takes the shape ल) or group 3 (if it takes the shape ल). The character र does not readily fit into this typology. The following basic script behaviors are explicable with reference to the above categories:

1. Ordinarily, the vertical bar at the right of a consonant character is deleted when the consonant appears as the non-final member of a cluster. (e g. ग्म = ग् + म)

2. But consonant characters with a vertical bar at the right that do not extend all the way up to the headstroke are often stacked vertically, sharing a single vertical bar. (e g. व्व = व् + व)

3. Characters with a vertical bar at the center lose their rightmost portion when they appear non-finally in a cluster. (e. g. क्प = क् + प)

4. Round-bottom characters are typically stacked above the graph for the following consonant in a cluster. (e. g. ट्ट = ट् + ट)

   (a) A consonant that follows /d/ is drawn using the tail of द ⟨da⟩ as its right vertical bar. (e. g. द्ब = द् + ब)

---

[16]Within-character information density may be expected to vary between different writing systems (Shimron & Navon, 1980).

[17]Cf. Mohanty (1998); Bansal & Sinha (1999); Govindaraju, Setlur, Khedekar, Kompalli, Farooq & Vemulapati (2004).

(b) A consonant that follows /ɦ/ is drawn within the open circle that comprises the lower half of the ह, utilizing the roof and right of this circle as its upper horizontal or right vertical bar. (e. g. ह्ल = ह् + ल)

Vowels are mostly written in Devanāgarī with diacritics, which may appear above, below, to the left, or to the right of the onset of the orthographic syllable. For example, diacritics for the vowels /e/ and /o/ are written above (के कै), below (कु कू कृ कॄ कॢ), to the left (कि), or to the right (का की को कौ) of the consonant character क ⟨ka⟩. Utterance-initially, however, independent vowel characters are used. This practice seems to reflect the influence of Semitic scripts (Scharfe 2002; Voigt 2005, 44). In Semitic writing, words do not begin with a vowel; this is a consequence of Semitic word structure, in which only consonants are allowed in word-initial position (Miller, 1994, 56).[18] Two consonant symbols, *aleph* (representing a glottal stop) and ʿ*ayin* (representing a pharyngeal or epiglottal voiced continuant) (McCarthy, 1994), that are frequent word-initially in Semitic are likely not to have been recognized as representing consonant sounds by speakers of languages that lacked the phonemes represented (cf. Driver 1976, 154–155, 178–179; Miller 1994, 46).[19] Thus the Brāhmī characters that developed into Devanāgarī अ/आ derive from the Aramaic *aleph* (for which the Aramaic name was *ālaph*), and the characters that developed into ए/ऐ derive from the Aramaic ʿ*ayin* (for which the Aramaic name was ʿ*ēn*). The characters ऋ ॠ ओ औ are secondary developments from अ. Characters for independent *r̥* and *au* are not attested until the second half of the first millennium C. E. (Scharfe, 2002, 393). In Kharoṣṭhī initial vowels are formed from attaching the dependent vowel signs to a character derived from *aleph*. Although Indian grammarians do not include the glottal stop in their phonologies, we may conceive of the independent initial vowel signs (अ आ इ ई उ ऊ ऋ ॠ ऌ ए ऐ ओ औ) as representing glottal stop + vowel,[20] an idea apparently anticipated already by Lepsius (see Whit-

[18] For the Arabic grammarians' treatment of this fact, see Hadj-Salah (1971, 74); Al-Nassir (1993, 22).

[19] A number of Middle and Modern Aramaic dialects show ʿ*ayin* having weakened into the glottal stop [ʔ] (Kaufman 1984, 93 n. 40; Hoberman 1985, 224).

[20] In Kharoṣṭhī initial consonants are formed from attaching the dependent vowel signs to a character derived from *aleph* (Scharfe, 2002, 393).

ney 1861, 328).[21] The independent vowel signs appear word-internally in the rare (Salomon, 1998, 15 n. 26) Sanskrit lexical items that contain a sequence of vowels in hiatus, e.g. प्रउग *praüga* 'front part of the shafts of a chariot', and in compounds, e. g. मनआप *manaāpa* 'gaining the heart, attractive, beautiful'.

Nasalization and pitch accents are written in Devanāgarī with additional diacritics. Nasalization is written by a half-moon plus dot (*candrabindu*) over the vertical bar of the nasalized sound (e. g. ताँश्च *tā̃śca*). The accentual systems of Vedic schools vary. The most widely used, the Ṛgvedic accentual system, generally places a horizontal stroke beneath the CV portion of an orthographic syllable that includes a low-pitched vowel (*anudātta*) (e. g. क॒), and a vertical stroke above the CV portion of an orthographic syllable that includes a circumflexed vowel (*svarita*) (e. g. क॑). Short and long aggravated svaritas (*kampa*) use the numerals 1 and 3 in addition (न्य॑१॒; प्यो॑३॒). The high pitch (*udātta*) is left unmarked. Other accentual systems employ additional diacritics, including various signs above, below, to the left, to the right, through the middle of, and around the CV portion of an orthographic syllable that includes a circumflexed vowel; within a given system, various signs differentiate particular types of circumflex accent. Diacritics added to the visarga symbol indicate high pitch, low pitch, or circumflex.[22]

---

[21] Owing to sandhi, initial independent vowel signs will be written only (1) in hiatus, i. e. the environment V##V; or (2) in pausa (initially in a major phonological phrase). Although the glottal stop is not a phoneme of English, it commonly occurs in inter-word hiatus, e. g. *heavy oak; steady awning* — N. B. that the glottal stop is not ordinarily realized as full glottal closure (Hillenbrand & Houde, 1996); cf. Hadj-Salah (1971, 73 n. 63). Similar phonetics is likely to obtain in Sanskrit. Note that inter-word hiatus is often considered exceptional — careful authors of ancient Greek prose, for example, avoided it entirely (Benseler, 1841). Many languages typically eliminate *within-word* hiatus (Clements, 1990, 301) or disallow it entirely (Romani & Calabrese, 1998, 102).

[22] Cardona 1997, li–lxiv; Witzel 1974.

1.4 Roman transliteration

As Sanskrit studies became important in the West, European scholars devised methods to transliterate Sanskrit text in Roman script. The early history of efforts to standardize such methods are described in the preface to the dictionary of Monier-Williams (1872). The eminent Sanskritist William D. Whitney made some comments in 1880 in the *Proceedings of the American Oriental Society* (Whitney, 1880). Whitney accords Western scholars great license, writing, "the language is written in India, to no small extent, in whatever alphabet the writers are accustomed to employ for other purposes; and there is no reason why we may not allow ourselves to do the same" (Whitney, 1880, li). He considers questions of how to mark vocalic quantity in Romanized Sanskrit, examines the question of how the diphthongs should be presented, prefers *ṛ* (or Lepsius' *r̥*) to *ṛi* (likewise *ḷ* or *l̥* to *lṛi* — characterized as "that monstrous absurdity"), and devotes considerable discussion to the matter of anusvāra. He concludes, "To sum up briefly: the items to be most strongly urged, as involving important principles, are the use of *ṛ* and *ṣ* for the lingual vowel and lingual sibilant respectively; of next consequence, for the sake of uniformity, is the adoption of the signs *c, j, y, ç* for the palatal sounds; the designation of long vowels, of the diphthongs, of the nasals, are minor matters, which will doubtless settle themselves by degrees in the right manner" (Whitney, 1880, liii).

Of particular importance as regards standardization of the schemes used by European scholars was the Geneva Oriental Congress of 1894 (Wujastyk, 1996). Contemporary schemes for Romanizing Sanskrit are quite similar to those employed in the nineteenth century and are characterized by the following conventions:

1. Sanskrit sounds that correspond to normal values for Roman letters are represented by those letters (e. g. *b* = [b]).

2. The letter *h*, which by itself indicates a phoneme /ɦ/, is used also to indicate the aspirate series of stops in digraphs such as *bh*.

3. The retroflex consonants are indicated with an underdot (e. g. *ṭ*).

4. A macron indicates a long vowel (e. g. *ā*).

5. The palatal nasal is written *ñ*; the velar, *ṅ*.

6. The palatal sibilant is written *ś* (formerly, *ç*).

7. Vocalic/syllabic *l* and *r* are written with an undercircle or underdot (*ḷ r̥*).

8. The anusvāra is written *ṃ* or *ṁ;* the visarga, *ḥ;* jihvāmūlīya and upadhmānīya, *ẖ* and *ḫ*, respectively.

9. Acute and grave accent marks indicate the udātta and independent svarita accents, respectively (*yé, kvà*); the dependent svarita (*ī* in *agním īḷe*) and the anudātta (*naḥ*) accent are usually left unmarked.

Several published standards relate to the Romanization of Sanskrit text written in Devanāgarī or other scripts. These include the Library of Congress transliteration (Barry, 1997, 186–7) and ISO 15919 "Transliteration of Devanagari and related Indic scripts into Latin characters".[23] Unicode, as part of its CLDR (Common Locale Data Repository) project released Unicode Transliteration Guidelines in 2008.[24] In the case of Indic scripts, these guidelines closely follow ISO 15919. The intent is that native script representations and transliterations be round-trippable.

It is important to distinguish between strict *transliteration* and *Romanization.* The former refers to a mapping at the graphic level: some character or characters in one script (e. g. Roman) are substituted for some character or characters in another (e. g. Devanāgarī). The transliteration reflects idiosyncrasies of the source orthography. Thus in Russian the name *William* is sometimes transliterated as Уиллям, despite the fact that the second ⟨л⟩ has no phonetic significance in Russian. A Romanization, on the other hand, renders linguistic content using the letters of the Roman alphabet; these letters stand for sounds of the source language. In designing a Romanization, one does not consider the non-Roman orthography of the source language.

Romanizations often suffer from the problem that the phonetic inventory of the source language differs considerably from (and is larger than) the set of sounds conventionally indicated by Roman characters. Three solutions get around this problem: (1) the use of digraphs, trigraphs, or "polygraphs"; (2) the use of diacritic marks; and (3) the creation of new

[23] ISO documents are available from the International Organization for Standardization (website: <http://www.iso.ch/>).

[24] <http://www.unicode.org/cldr/transliteration_guidelines.html>.

letters (Jones, 1942, 2–3). Each of these solutions has its weaknesses. Bartholomew Ziegenbalg in his Tamil grammar of 1716 spells the pre-palatal affricate (a unitary phoneme) of Tamil as ⟨ytsch⟩ (Firth, 1936, 34). Even today, it is customary in Germany to render with the heptagraph ⟨schtsch⟩ the phoneme written in Cyrillic as ⟨щ⟩. Clearly the use of "polygraphs" can be uneconomical. The use of diacritics can present extraordinary challenges to the typesetter, as when one wishes to indicate in a Romanized text that a Sanskrit vowel is long (macron), nasalized (tilde), and accented; in this case three diacritics must be stacked. The creation of new characters is always an option; but after one has added enough new characters, one has a new script — no longer Roman.[25]

1.5 The All-India Alphabet

The British linguist J. R. Firth served as professor at the University of Punjab in Lahore from 1920 to 1928 and returned to India in the late 1930s to spend a year studying Gujarati and Telugu (Anderson, 1985, 177). During his time in India, Firth became extremely interested in the development of a new orthography for Indian languages. This interest led to the creation of Firth's All-India Alphabet, intended as writing system for the languages of the Indian subcontinent. The All-India Alphabet is an adaptation of the Roman alphabet, with a number of additional modified letters; a few letters borrowed from other scripts, such as Cyrillic and Greek; and several symbols borrowed from the International Phonetic Alphabet (IPA). Upon occasion, Firth, rather grandiloquently, spoke of his scheme as "World Orthography" (Firth, 1936).

Firth's Alphabet aimed at addressing the problem of mass illiteracy in colonial India (Jones, 1942, 1). In addition, British intellectuals in India considered that a national orthography would contribute to national unity. In the words of Daniel Jones, "For the promotion of an All India mind, a sound All India Alphabet developed from the world-wide Roman alphabet would be a powerful implement" (Jones, 1942, 4). Firth claimed that the Alphabet was "designed on linguistic principles for the main languages of India entirely from the Indian point of view" (Harley, 1955,

[25] Yet even the Romans themselves proposed the addition of new characters to their alphabet (Ryan 1993; Desbordes 1990). On more recent created characters for the Latin alphabet, see Abercrombie (1981).

x). The Alphabet was also associated with progress in communication technologies: "the adoption of a Romanic system [...] would enable Indians to bring into use for their own languages such modern devices as the teleprinter and tape machine, with consequent great advantage to the Indian Press" (Jones, 1942, 17).[26]

Despite the ambitions of Firth, the Alphabet was scarcely used. Several textbooks made use of it, including A. H. Harley's *Colloquial Hindustani* (Harley, 1955) and T. Grahame Bailey's *Teach Yourself Urdu* (edited by Firth and Harley, and originally entitled *Teach Yourself Hindustani*) (Bailey, Firth & Harley, 1956). The Alphabet comprised a core set of characters, with extensions added for sounds present only in specific Indian languages. Firth worked out orthographies based on the Alphabet for Hindustani (Hindi and Urdu), Marathi, Gujarati, Tamil, Telugu, and Sinhalese (the last devised by Jones and Perera) (Jones, 1942, 13), as well as Burmese and Persian (Firth, 1936). Occasionally Firth's orthography appeared in the publications of linguists associated with the School of Oriental and African Studies (SOAS) at the University of London, for instance Allen (1951).

Although the All-India Alphabet seems not to have been used for Sanskrit, Firth included symbols for spelling Sanskrit words as they appear in Hindi. Moreover, W. Sidney Allen adapted the Alphabet for Sanskrit (Allen, 1953). The Alphabet was designed as a scientific orthography, "an alphabet that embodies all the latest findings of phonetics, linguistics and psychology, and which satisfies the demands of the typographer, the typewriter, and the calligraphist" (Jones, 1942, 10). The Alphabet tends to represent phonological rather than phonetic distinctions (Firth, 1936, 539). Surface morphophonological alterations and phonetic differences are not supposed to be represented in the orthography (Jones, 1942, 5–6). On the whole Firth aims at representing single sounds with single characters, but he departs for various reasons, employing at times digraphs and even trigraphs (e. g. **phw**[27] for a bilabial aspirated stop with velar co-articulation in Burmese) (Firth, 1936, 543). The design of the Alphabet is motivated by ease of reading (legibility

[26]Such arguments were once made also for China and Japan (Ramsey 1989, 143–154; Trigger 1998, 41). They are clearly vitiated by the high levels of literacy current in these countries as well, of course, as the tremendous economic growth.

[27]Text in the All-India Alphabet is conventionally printed in boldface.

and distinctness) as well as ease of writing (Jones, 1942, 10–11). Diacritic marks are eschewed, as they hinder reading and cause additional problems for printers. The inventory of characters is kept small, to make typesetting and typewriting more convenient.

Most stop consonants are represented in the All-India Alphabet as they are in conventional Romanizations. Aspirated stops are represented by digraphs **kh, ch,** etc. Retroflex sounds are indicated with a "tail", as **ʈ, ɖ, ʂ.** The palatal sibilant is indicated by **ʃ** (capital form **Σ**). The basic vowels of Hindi are represented by **ə** [ə], **a** [a], **y** [ɪ], **i** [i], **w** [ʊ], **u** [u], **e** [ɛ], **əy** [e], **o** [ɔ], **əw** [o] (IPA equivalents are given here in brackets for reference). Nasalization of vowels (anunāsika, **ənwnasyk**) is indicated by **ŋ** following the basic vowel graph (**əŋ** etc.). The All-India alphabet is duo-case, with distinct upper- and lower-case letterforms.

In Allen's use of the Alphabet for Sanskrit (Allen, 1953), the oral stops are represented as described above for Hindi. The nasals are indicated by **ŋ, ɲ, ɳ, n, m.** Here Allen follows Firth's design for Marathi, where **ŋ** is preempted for the velar nasal, and **ɱ** becomes the marker of nasalization (Jones, 1942, 13). Allen uses **h** for both the voiced phoneme /ɦ/ and the (voiceless) visarga. The symbols **a, i, ṛ, ḷ, u** are used for the Sanskrit vowels. Allen follows Firth's orthography for Tamil in representing the long vowels through doubling: **aa** etc. (Jones, 1942, 15). The long vocalic *r̥̄* is indicated by **rṛ**. The diphthongs are represented conventionally by **e, ai, o, au.**

Chapter 2

Existing encoding systems for Sanskrit

2.1 A brief history of Indian printing

The Jesuits introduced printing to India, when a printing press (apparently *en route* to Abyssinia) came to stay at Goa in 1556.[1] In 1578, Tamil types were created, and St. Xavier's *Doutrina Christã* was printed in Tamil, in sixteen pages. By the end of 1577 João Gonçalves had prepared a repertoire of about 50 pieces of Devanāgarī type, but these languished after his death in the subsequent year. During this period, books were predominantly published in European languages such as Portuguese. The press at Goa functioned until 1674. "Printing in the *Devanāgarī* characters in Goa started only in the second half of the nineteenth century" (Priolkar, 1958, 27).

The earliest printing of Devanāgarī took place in Europe. In the seventeenth century, works such as Athanasius Kircher's *China Illustrata* (Amsterdam, 1667) reproduced Devanāgarī by the technique of engraving (see FIGURE 2.1). The *Orientalisch- und Occidentalischer Sprachmeister* of Johann Friedrich Fritz and Benjamin Schulze (Leipzig,

[1] This paragraph is based on Priolkar (1958, 3–27). On the international spread of printing at this time see Füssel (2005, 70).

FIGURE 2.1: Engraved plate illustrating the Devanāgarī script from Athanasius Kircher, *China Illustrata*, 1667.

6 1 3 5 4 *

अजरामरवत् प्राज्ञो विद्यामर्थंच चिन्तयेत् ।

ajarāmaravat prājnō vidyām arthaṅcha chintayēt

FIGURE 2.2: *Hitopadeśa* Introduction 2ab excerpted from Charles Wilkins, *A Grammar of the Sanskrĭta Language*, 1808 (set with Devanāgarī type of the author's design).

1748) included two hundred translations of the Lord's Prayer in various languages and writing systems, Indian ones among them (Firth, 1936, 519). The first movable types for Devanāgarī were successfully cast in the 1740s in Rome for the press of the Congregatio de Propaganda Fide (Glaister 1979, 134; Shaw 1980, 29).[2]

The first important book printed in an Indic script is commonly held to be the Bengali grammar of Nathaniel Brassey Halhed (1751–1830), published in 1783, with type cast by Charles Wilkins (b. 1749–1750; d. 1836) (Smith 1885, 211, 242; Priolkar 1958, 51–53; Diehl 1968; cf. Firth 1946, 119–120), who later designed the first truly serviceable Devanāgarī type (see FIGURE 2.2) (Diehl, 1968, 335–336). Printed Devanāgarī in India appears as early as 1789, with *The New Asiatick Miscellany* published by the Chronicle Press of Calcutta (Shaw, 1980, 29).

In 1804 the English shoemaker and Baptist missionary William Carey published a Sanskrit reader at Serampore, thus making, in the words of H. T. Colebrook, the "first attempt to employ the press in multiplying copies of Sanscrĭt books with the Dévanagarí character" (Windisch, 1917, 28). A Devanāgarī font subsequently produced (in 1806) under the supervision of Carey contained nearly a thousand character combinations (Smith 1885, 243; Priolkar 1958, 59, 63, 65). Carey's Devanāgarī

[2] On the early history of Devanāgarī typography in Europe, see Windisch (1917, 70, 78–79); Glaister (1979, 134–136); Shaw (1980).

was used not only for setting Sanskrit, but also for vernacular languages such as Marathi, Hindi, Nepali, and Gujarati (Shaw, 1980, 30).

Hot-metal typesetting came to India in the 1920s when the Mergenthaler Linotype Company started shipping Indic fonts for its linecasters (Ross, 2002). The Monotype Corporation cut a 12 point Devanāgarī font for hot-metal typesetting as early as 1923 (Shaw, 1980, 28). Hot-metal technology, however, necessitated "severely restricted character sets, the lack of kerning, and the inability to position the subscribed or superscribed vowel signs" (Ross, 2002).[3] The Indologist W. Norman Brown (1892–1975), founder of the first South Asia area studies program in the United States (at the University of Pennsylvania), served as consultant to the Merganthaler Linotype Company in the 1930s and subsequent decades. Brown considered script reform measures that would ease the transition to modern technologies such as hot-metal typesetting.[4] The Devanāgarī script reform committee of Uttar Pradesh made several recommendations (1940), including:

1. to abandon the practice of vertical stacking of characters in conjuncts; instead characters with a vertical bar should form conjuncts using their combining form (without the vertical bar), and conjuncts involving other consonants should be indicated by means of the virāma;

2. to eliminate the exceptional directionality of certain characters: ⟨i⟩ is to be written with a new symbol that *follows* the consonant, ⟨r⟩ in clusters is to be replaced by a new symbol that does not disrupt the linear order;

3. to indicate anusvāra by a small circle at the right (Brown, 1953, 4).

The aim of these reforms was to reduce the number of pieces of type needed to set Devanāgarī. (Traditionally, Devanāgarī type required four

[3] "The Linotype mechanism put constraints on type face design because the machine could not emulate all the features of manuscript; in particular, where adjacent elements overlap vertically" (Kahan, 2000, 190). See also Ghosh (1983, 10).

[4] Politicians of course had their say in the matter. Jawharlal Nehru for some time considered the benefits that might follow from adopting the Roman alphabet. Gandhi sought to replace the independent vowel signs of Devanāgarī with the sign अ, together with the dependent vowel signs.

typecases, compared to the two needed for Roman.) The proposal of the committee required only 110 types (Brown, 1953, 5):

full consonant forms and independent vowel forms	42
half forms of consonants	26
special conjunct forms	1
dependent vowel forms	14
punctuation	8
numerals	10
miscellaneous signs	9

Several Hindi newspapers adopted certain of the committee's suggestions, although none adopted all (Brown, 1953, 5).[5]

2.2 Legacy systems: before standards

Modern text-processing technology arose in the English-speaking world and assumed as a norm the use of the Roman alphabet with few or no diacritics. CCITT #2, BCDIC version 2, and the original version of ASCII, as well as the original ISO 7-bit code, for instance, reserved three code positions for national use, in order to accommodate Western European orthographies such as Danish, German, Finnish, Norwegian, and Swedish, which require (assuming only a single case, rather than separate lower- and upper-case sets) only three characters with diacritics (e.g. Ä-Ö-Ü or Æ-Ø-Å) (Mackenzie, 1980, 64, 90, 238, 411–418, 450–451).[6] While the typewriter was an efficient instrument for composing English text, its adaptation to some non-Western scripts required considerable effort and compromise (Krishna, 1991). A number of keyboard layouts were designed for Hindi use. Such typewriters provided an early model for computer text processing, and their design is still reflected in some computer keyboard layouts.

Examining a typical Hindi typewriter keyboard (FIGURE 2.3)[7] reveals that many keys when struck without the *shift* modifier generate the

[5]For discussion of similar orthographic reforms in the Middle East, see Mahmoud (1979).

[6]See for instance the German code DIN 66003-1967, Informationsverarbeitung 7-Bit Code.

[7]For some other Hindi typewriter layouts, see Beeching (1990, 58). See also Bhatia (1974).

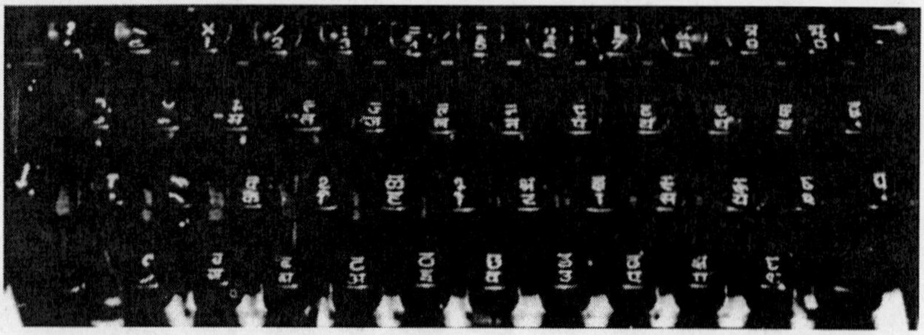

FIGURE 2.3: Hindi typewriter keyboard

full forms of consonants, while the same keys struck with *shift* depressed generate the half-forms used in the construction of ligatures. Certain individual graphs can only be typed with a combination of keystrokes. For instance the aspirate फ ⟨pha⟩ must be typed as: (1) प ⟨pa⟩ and (2) the loop that appears to the right of the vertical bar. Thus the Devanāgarī typewriter decomposes characters into their visual constituents.[8] Of course, many of the conjunct forms and diacritics traditionally used in high-quality Sanskrit typography simply cannot be reproduced with such a typewriter.

Text processing software on the digital computer brought the possibility of an expanded character repertoire and the possibility of shifting the burden of tedious composition processes from human to machine. Yet in the absence of standardized encodings and text layout software adequate to meeting the challenges of complex scripts, the first generation of Devanāgarī fonts made use of completely proprietary, non-standard encodings, were not able to unify non-distinctive glyph variants under a single grapheme,[9] and required that text be stored (and, often, typed) in

[8]Similarly, the typewriter keyboard designed by the Arabic script reformer Ahmed Lakhdar-Ghazal uses three symbols as the *appendices* of word-final Arabic letters; traditionally, the combination of letterform and appendix has been considered a variant form of a single grapheme (Mahmoud, 1979, 111).

[9]The term *grapheme* denotes a minimal distinctive unit of visual language; cf. Pulgram 1951; Hamp 1959. The term has been used in various ways by (psycho-)linguists. This

display order rather than *phonetic* order.[10] In the absence of specialized software, the end-user was often required to deal manually with such tedious issues as choosing which alternate shape for a dependent vowel aligned most harmoniously with a particular consonant graph.

The Devanāgarī typewriter and the first generation of Devanāgarī fonts provided solutions that were more or less adequate for the display and printing of texts. But these systems did not adequately address such problems as: the robust electronic interchange of data, facilitation of searching and collation, linguistic applications (e. g., spell-checking, morphological analysis, machine translation), and automatic transliteration and transcoding. By the end of 2009, India had about eighty-one million Internet users, which represents approximately 7% of the population.[11] Even so, many Indian-language web pages still require fonts with non-standardized, idiosyncratic encodings that severely impede many of the benefits commonly associated with the World Wide Web (Mujoo, Malviya, Moona & Prabhakar 2000; Singh 2006). Authors working for a UNESCO study on linguistic diversity on the Web note the need for the adoption of standards:

> Although there exist national standards, hardware vendors, font developers and even end-users have been creating their own character code tables which inevitably lead [sic] to a chaotic situation. The creations of so called exotic encoding scheme [sic] or local internal encoding have been accelerated particularly through the introduction of user-friendly font development tools. Although the appli-

usage has been studied by Henderson (1985), who identifies a Sense 1: the grapheme is "the minimal contrastive unit in a writing system" (135); and a Sense 2: the "grapheme is comprised of a letter or letters that refer to or correspond to a single phoneme in speech" (135). Throughout we follow Henderson's Sense 1; thus grapheme is parallel to phoneme, allograph to allophone, and graph to phone. It is worth remarking here that even the term "letter" has traditionally led to some confusion; see Abercrombie (1949).

[10]While the directionality of Devanāgarī is generally left-to-right, the short /i/ vowel is written to the left of the onset consonant(s) in its orthographic syllable; thus *-nti* is written न्ति. Moreover, in a sequence of /r/ + consonant(s), the /r/ is written above the *final* constituent of the orthographic syllable: धर्म्य *dharmya* 'suitable, legitimate, virtuous', कर्त्री *kartrī* 'female agent'.

Primary users of Devanāgarī, however, sometimes find the visual order of graphs "natural" (in as much as it is the order that they follow when writing by hand) and become confused if they are required to input the /i/ (for example) in its phonetic position (Joshi, Ganu, Chand, Parmar & Mathur, 2004).

[11]<http://www.internetworldstats.com/asia/in.htm>.

> cation systems working in these areas are not stand-alone systems and are published widely via the Web, the necessity for standardization has not been given serious attentions [sic] by users, vendors and font developers (Mikami, abu Bakar, Sonlert-lamvanich, Vikas, Pavol, abdul Rozan, János & Takahashi, 2005, 99).

2.3 UPACCII

In the early part of 1983 Pijush K. Ghosh was a guest of the digital typography project at Stanford University. Ghosh worked to create fonts that would allow Indic languages to be set using Donald Knuth's TEX system. Ghosh (1983, 23) recognized the need for "[t]he design of efficient internal codes for the characters of a script for information processing, storage and transmission." The solution was a Universal Phonetic Atom Code Chart for Information Interchange (UPACCII), based on ASCII (Ghosh, 1983, 26). Ghosh includes the control characters at their normal ASCII positions (000–037).[12] He largely maintains the ASCII characters at 040–077 in their normal positions, substituting only the candrabindu at 044 for ⟨$⟩, the anusvāra at 046 for ⟨&⟩, and the danda at 056 for ⟨.⟩. From 0100–0107 he places the visarga, accent marks, punctuation, the avagraha, and the short vowel ⟨अ⟩. The consonants ⟨क⟩ through ⟨ध⟩ are positioned at 0110–0132. The ASCII sequence is preserved from 0133–0140. The consonants ⟨न⟩ through ⟨ह⟩ are at 0141–0156. The vowels (save ⟨अ⟩) follow at 0157–0170: ⟨आ⟩, ⟨इ⟩, ⟨ई⟩, ⟨उ⟩, ⟨ऊ⟩, ⟨ऋ⟩, ⟨ए⟩, ⟨ऐ⟩, ⟨ओ⟩, ⟨औ⟩. At 0171 Ghosh places the virāma, at 0172 a BREAK character to prevent ligation (parallel to ZWNJ U+200C in Unicode). Normal ASCII values continue from 0173–0177.

Ghosh rightly makes his code independent from input (keyboarding) and output (printing). For the former, he proposes an ergonomic keyboard layout inspired by the Dvorak layout; for the latter he proposes a print code chart (Ghosh, 1983, 28, 31). UPACCII is basically phonetic in nature, so that there are not (as in ISCII and Unicode) separate characters for independent vowels and for dependent vowel mātras. Ghosh's encoding is intelligent and possesses some strengths in comparison with contemporary encodings that are widespread, but it was never adopted as

[12] Character codes are indicated here in octal notation, like that used for constants in the C programming language.

a standard or used in other projects. The code is inadequate for Sanskrit, since it provides no way to represent r̥̄, l̥, etc.

2.4 ISCII

The Indian Script Code for Information Interchange (ISCII) is an Indian national standard; the first version was published by the Indian Department of Electronics (DOE) in 1983 (Bhatt, n.d.). More recent versions have been published in 1986, 1988, 1991, and 1998. ISCII is designed to support Devanāgarī as well as nine other Brāhmī-derived scripts: Gujarati, Panjabi, Assamese, Bengali, Oriya, Telugu, Tamil, Malayalam and Kannada. These scripts are the primary means of writing for the twenty-two nationally recognized languages of India, with the exception of those that are primarily written in Perso-Arabic script, viz. Urdu, Kashmiri, Sindhi (Singh, 1997).

ISCII employs a single set of codepoints for ten distinct scripts. Thus the syllable ⟨ka⟩ is encoded identically whether it is written in Devanāgarī, Gujarati, or Malayalam. The general structural principles of ISCII are based on those of the Brāhmī-derived scripts. In general:

- Consonants imply /a/, unless overridden by either an explicit vowel or the HALANT character (= virāma, i.e. the Ø vowel).
- Separate codepoints exist for independent and dependent vowel signs.
- Characters are encoded in *logical* (phonetic) rather than *visual* order.

ISCII is an abstract encoding that does not specify the particular glyphs used to represent the underlying character stream. Proper rendering of ISCII-encoded text requires knowledge of the script behaviors for a particular writing system. ISCII-1991 (IS 13194:91) defines three important control characters (Bureau of Indian Standards, 1992):

1. INV: an abstract "invisible" consonant allows for the rendering of diacritic signs which would normally have to be positioned with respect to a particular consonant graph.

2. `EXT`: introduces extensions, including the Vedic extensions (31 symbols) specified in Annex G: special signs for jihvāmūlīya, upadhmānīya, and visarga; special signs for anusvāra; diacritics for accents (varieties of udātta, anudātta, svarita, and kampa); and an abbreviation sign and filler mark. These symbols do not exhaust the repertoire employed by the various Vedic schools.

3. `ALT`: prefixes a character or script attribute code that allows for character styles such as *boldface* or *italic* and for Indic script selection such as Bengali or Gujarati.

2.5 Unicode: Indic scripts

The Unicode Standard is an evolving character encoding designed to provide support for a great many of the modern and ancient languages of the world (Unicode Consortium, 2006). Many code blocks in Unicode are based on existing national or international standards; the Devanāgarī block of Unicode is based on ISCII-1988. Unicode differs from ISCII in that it provides separate blocks, isomorphic with one another to the greatest degree possible for each script, for eight other Indic scripts covered by ISCII. By design, Unicode encodes *plain text* and leaves non-distinctive character styles such as *boldface* or *italic* to a higher-level protocol. By employing separate blocks for distinct Indic scripts and by encoding only plain text, Unicode needs no equivalent for the ISCII `ALT` character. Version 5.0 of Unicode did not support characters needed for the adequate representation of Vedic texts. It did not include the Vedic character extensions in ISCII Annex G. The authors of the present volume drafted a joint proposal in collaboration with Michael Everson, the Irish representative to ISO 10646 (Universal Character Set), R. K. Joshi and Alka Irani of the Centre for Development of Advanced Computing (C-DAC) in Mumbai, Swaran Lata of the Department of Information Technology in the Ministry of Communications & Information Technology of the Government of India, New Delhi, and other scholars. The Unicode Technical Committee and International Standards Organization accepted sixty-eight new characters for Vedic and historical Indic which became part of Unicode Standard 5.2, and amendment 6 of ISO/IEC 10646:2003 in the Fall of 2009. The new characters are included in two code pages:

Devanagari Extended, and Vedic Extensions. Details of the proposal and its history are available on the Vedic Unicode page of the Sanskrit Library website (<http://sanskritlibrary.org/VedicUnicode/>). The Technical document specifying Vedic character context and usage there links to the Vedic Unicode Character Phonetic Value Table which correlates most of the new characters with the Sanskrit Library Phonetic encoding (SLP1) and demonstrates which are used in which of the various Vedic traditions.

A fundamental principle of Unicode is the *character-glyph model* (Gillam, 2002, 44–7).[13] Unicode generally distinguishes between distinctive units of textual *content* (called "characters") and displayed tokens (called "glyphs"), although the distinction may at times be contentious, and certain compromises have been made (Jenkins, 1999).[14] To put it differently, a *glyph* is a typographic symbol considered primarily as a visual object; a *character* is a linguistically- or logically-based archetype (Haralambous, 2002).[15] Characters frequently stand in a one-to-many relation to their glyph realizations. Consider the following examples:

- The sequence of Roman characters *f* + *i* may be displayed as two glyphs (*fi*) or as a single-glyph ligature (*ﬁ*).
- The Arabic letter *nūn*, a single character, may be realized as one of four different glyphs, depending on its context:

ن	isolated	
نـ	word-initial	نبت *nabata* 'to sprout'
ـنـ	word-medial	بنت *bint* 'girl'
ـن	word-final	تبن *tibn* 'straw'.

- The Devanāgarī sequence of क ⟨ka⟩ + HALANT + क ⟨ka⟩ may be realized as (1) a single glyph with two components stacked vertically

[13]A thorough discussion is to be found in ISO/IEC TR 15285:1998(E) "Information technology — An operational model for characters and glyphs".

[14]Frequently, inconsistencies are inherited from earlier encoding standards.

[15]The distinction resembles that sometimes drawn in the theoretical literature on writing between *inscriptions* and *characters*, where the latter are categorical in nature and presuppose an equivalence class (Tolchinsky, 2003, 17).

(क्क), (2) a single glyph with two components stacked horizontally (क्‍क), or (3) ⟨ka⟩ + *virāma* + ⟨ka⟩ (क्‌क).

A number of criticisms of Unicode, with reference to Indic scripts, can be found (Hellingman, 1998; White, 2002). We focus here on those features that may be perceived as anomalous from the point of view of the Sanskritist:

1. As Yannis Haralambous writes, Unicode is (for historical reasons) "quite awkward: it is partly logical and partly graphical" (Haralambous & Plaice, 2002). Separate versions of vowels (e. g. /ā/) exist for the independent (आ) and dependent (ा) forms. But the distribution of these vowel forms is entirely complementary.

2. In order to code the isolated consonant /k/, it is necessary to use the sequence U+0915 (क) U+094D (्) (DEVANAGARI LETTER KA + DEVANAGARI SIGN VIRAMA). Here a character is needed to encode the zero-vowel, whereas in U+0915 (क) (DEVANAGARI LETTER KA) *no* distinct character encodes the vowel /a/.

   (a) Shaping engines are supposed to provide a suitable ligature for क ⟨ka⟩ + virāma + क ⟨ka⟩ (= क्क); in order to prevent ligature formation, a special character ZWNJ (U+200C: ZERO-WIDTH NON-JOINER) is needed: U+0915 (क) + U+094D (्) + U+200C (ZWNJ) + U+0915 (क) → क्‌क. Similarly, to form the horizontally stacked conjunct, the special character ZWJ (U+200D: ZERO-WIDTH JOINER) is needed: U+0915 (क) + U+094D (्) + U+200D (ZWJ) + U+0915 (क) → क्‍क. These two format characters correspond to nothing either *visual* or *linguistic*.

2.6 CS (Classical Sanskrit) and CSX (Classical Sanskrit Extended)

In 1990 a group of scholars at the 8th World Sanskrit Conference in Vienna agreed on an 8-bit encoding for transliterated Sanskrit called CS (Wujastyk, 1990). A superset of this standard, CSX (Classical Sanskrit Extended), was also devised, which allowed for characters used in the

transliteration of Vedic and Tamil. The CS and CSX standards are based on IBM CP 437 (an 8-bit codepage with the lower half corresponding to ASCII, and an upper half containing accented characters for European languages and additional symbols). The CS standard replaced 32 codepoints in CP 437 with upper- and lower-case characters used in Sanskrit transliteration (but not used for modern Western European languages). CSX replaced an additional 22 codepoints. A fundamental design principle of CS and CSX was to depart as little as possible from CP 437. A superset of CSX, CSX+, also exists, which adds an additional 28 characters used in Indic transliteration and specified in ISO 15919; four other characters for general-purpose typography are also added. One character (*á*) has been moved, since its codepoint is reserved in Windows character sets for a non-breaking space.

Although a number of fonts supporting the CS family of standards exist (including fonts released under free licenses such as the GPL[16]), CS/CSX/CSX+ are not registered with any international standards authority and lack any general OS- or application-level support. Packages providing support for CS in TEX are available, however (Pandey, 1998).

2.7 TITUS Indological 8-bit Encoding

TITUS (*Thesaurus Indogermanischer Text- und Sprachmaterialen*), directed by Prof. Dr. Jost Gippert at the Johann Wilhelm von Goethe Universität, Frankfurt am Main, holds a significant collection of digitally-accessible texts for the investigation of proto-Indo-European (PIE) linguistics. Among this collection is found a large number of Indic texts (Old Indic, Middle Indic, and Modern Indic). The collection of Old Indic (Sanskrit) texts is one of the largest in the world. Historically, TITUS made these texts available in the *TITUS Indological 8-bit Encoding,* which is based on the legacy IBM CP 437 codepage used by the PC-DOS variant of MS-DOS. Nowadays, the publically-accesible version of the texts is available in Unicode via a Web interface. Still, the TITUS Indological 8-bit Encoding is primarily used in private work with the documents, in which the WordCruncher software plays a significant

[16]See the website of John Smith: <http://bombay.indology.info/>.

role. CD-ROMs distributed by TITUS still contain the texts in the TITUS Indological 8-bit Encoding.

The TITUS Indological encoding departs significantly from CP 437; with the exception of the basic alphanumeric characters and basic punctuation, all symbols have been redefined. (Even CP 437 is not a superset of ASCII, as it redefines the ASCII control characters (0x00–0x19) as dingbats, and other symbols.) The TITUS encoding in addition overrides other characters in the ASCII range: 0x23 = # → ^{h} (indicates aspiration of the preceding segment); 0x24 = $ → r̥̄ (syllabic long *r*); 0x25 = % → ʿ (Semitic ʿ *ayin*); 0x26 = & → ʾ (Semitic *hamza*); 0x7f = BEL → *ṁ* (anusvāra). The upper half of the TITUS encoding contains modified Roman characters used in the transcription of Sanskrit, as well as other Indic and Dravidian languages, and such related languages as Avestan. Some characters frequently used in the orthography of Western European languages are retained as well.[17]

2.8 Unicode: Indic transliteration

Unicode contains the characters and diacritics needed for encoding transliterated Sanskrit. Characters for basic Sanskrit transliteration, as well as relevant diacritics, are found in the following blocks:

- Basic Latin (U+0020–U+007E)
- Latin-1 Supplement (U+0080–U+00FF)
- Latin Extended-A (U+0100–U+017F)
- Latin Extended Additional (U+1E00–U+1EFF)
- Combining Diacritical Marks (U+0300–U+036D)
- Devanagari (U+0900–U+097F).

Unicode lacks codepoints for characters with under-rings and for characters with the combination of an accent and another diacritic; these may

[17] Details of the encoding were kindly supplied by Jost Gippert (personal communication). A TrueType font for displaying texts in the TITUS Indological encoding is available from TITUS (<http://titus.uni-frankfurt.de/>).

be formed with a two-character sequence, using the combining diacritics. For example: r̥ = U+0071 (LATIN SMALL LETTER R) + U+0325 (COMBINING RING BELOW); ā́ = U+0101 (LATIN SMALL LETTER A WITH MACRON) + U+0301 (COMBINING ACUTE ACCENT). For Sanskrit, three stacked diacritics will sometimes be needed. Diacritic stacking for rendering takes place at the OS/font level or the application level.[18] Up to three diacritics may need to be stacked above a Roman character (length + nasalization + accent), in addition to one below (e g. ring below indicating syllabicity of a liquid).

2.9 7-bit meta-transliterations

7-bit meta-transliterations are designed to be pure ASCII transliterations that may be mapped unambiguously onto an encoding that assigns a unique codepoint to each character in an underlying Romanization (Lagally, 1999).[19] Reversibility is guaranteed by ensuring that the meta-transliteration satisfies the *Fano condition:* no code word is a prefix of any other code word (Fano, 1966, 67). If the meta-transliteration is based on a conventional Romanization, it should be human-readable to some degree.

To represent diacritics, meta-characters are chosen; thus ⟨.⟩ (ASCII PERIOD) may represent an underdot. Such a meta-transliteration for Romanized Sanskrit would use `.n` to encode *ṇ,* the retroflex nasal spelled in Devanāgarī with the character ण्. If it is desired to encode the period, this may be indicated uniquely as PERIOD + SPACE. A meta-transliteration inherits defects in the corresponding Romanization. Thus, if we Romanize the voiceless aspirate dental (in Devanāgarī, थ्) as *th,* the meta-transliteration `th` satisfies the Fano condition for the Romanization, but not for Devanāgarī — as will be exemplified in the next section.

[18] At the 12th World Sanskrit Conference in Helsinki, 13–18 July, 2003, a proposal was circulated, under the name "The Vāmana Project", to add to Unicode all characters needed for implementing ISO 15919 in precomposed format. It is, however, the policy of the Unicode consortium to add no new precomposed characters, where characters can be composed from presently-encoded characters.

[19] Such input schemes are used, for instance, in Lagally's excellent ArabTEX package (Lagally, 2004).

The meta-transliterations have the advantages of being round-trippable (e. g. to CSX) and easily manipulable in virtually any software environment, since they are pure ASCII and can be read by humans with only a minimum of effort. A tabular overview of a modified form of the Velthuis scheme, the Kyoto-Harvard scheme, the "wx" (or Hyderabad-Tirupati) scheme, as well as SLP1, is given by Huet (2009, 196).

2.10 Velthuis transliteration and ITRANS

The Velthuis transliteration is named for the Dutch scholar Frans Velthuis (Wujastyk, 1996).[20] It does not satisfy the Fano condition for representing Sanskrit phonemic strings, since (for example) the voiceless aspirate dental may be coded `th`, which is potentially ambiguous with respect to a sequence representing a voiceless dental /t/ followed by a voiced glottal fricative /ɦ/. Since Sanskrit phonotactics forbids such a sequence, Velthuis applications can assume that the sequence `th` uniquely represents the voiceless aspirate dental. Problems will still arise elsewhere, as in the case where digraphs for diphthongs are spelled identically with sequences of distinct vowels. For instance, additional means will be required to disambiguate between the diphthong *au* and sequence of simple vowels *a* + *u*.

Velthuis also offers alternative ways of transliterating certain speech sounds, e. g. `O` for the diphthong *au*, `T` for the voiceless aspirate dental *th*, and `.T` for the voiceless aspirate retroflex dental *ṭh*. If only these alternatives are used, the meta-transliteration satisfies the Fano condition.

Charles Wikner's package "Sanskrit for LaTeX 2ε" (Wikner, 2002) employs a modified version of the Velthuis scheme. The ITRANS (Indian languages TRANSliteration) scheme, used by a popular software package (developed by Avinash Chopde) for transliteration and recoding, also significantly resembles the Velthuis scheme (Pandey, 1998).[21] An ITRANS package is available for TeX, which allows for typesetting Devanāgarī, Tamil, Bengali, Telugu, Gujarati, Kannada, Panjabi, and Romanized Sanskrit using the ITRANS software and transliteration conventions (Syropoulos et al., 2003, 351–355).

[20] Cf. Bakker, Barkhuis & Velthuis (1990).

[21] <http://www.aczoom.com/itrans/>

2.11 wx

The authors of the textbook *Natural Language Processing: A Paninian Perspective* present a scheme for "[i]nternal representation in the computer" that shares many design principles with our SLP1 (Bharati, Chaitanya & Sangal, 1996, 193). In the wx scheme (so dubbed after the characters used to encode the dental stops *t* and *d*), a single character represents a single speech sound. Equivalences are more or less straight-forward. Lower-case ASCII letters represent short vowels or close diphthongs, while upper-case letters represent long vowels and open diphthongs. The symbol `q` represents *r̥*, and `L`, *l̥* (Huet, 2009, 196); while no provision is made at all for *r̥̄* or *l̥̄*. The graphic opposition lowercase–uppercase consistently represents the phonological opposition unaspirated–aspirated. Some characters have a peculiar representation: e. g. the velar nasal *ṅ* (`f`) and the palatal nasal *ñ* (`F`). The dental oral stops *t, th, d, dh* are represented as `w, W, x, X,` whereas the retroflex *ṭ, ṭh, ḍ, ḍh* are represented as `t, T, d, D`. This convention is no doubt motivated by the fact that speakers of Modern Indic and Dravidian languages regularly perceive English alveolar stops as retroflex.[22] The retroflex sibilant *ṣ* is represented as `R`. This scheme, despite its considerable virtues, seems not to be widely used, although Indian students in NLP study it, and it plays a role in the Anusaaraka suite of NLP software,[23] including the Sanskrit morphological analyzer of Amba Kulkarni and V. Sheeba. The scheme is, however, fundamentally limited, since it does not allow for the full set of vocalic liquids described by the Sanskrit grammarians, the unaspirated and aspirated retroflex lateral flaps *ḷ* and *ḷh*, any system of accents, or other sounds peculiar to Vedic traditions.

2.12 Kyoto-Harvard

The Kyoto-Harvard transliteration is not a meta-transliteration as defined above. It instead chooses one or two symbols for each Sanskrit speech sound, with the addition of some special-use symbols (Wujastyk, 1996).

---

[22] Thus in Hindi, for example, both instances of alveolar [t] in *tractor* become [ʈ]: ट्रैक्टर. The retroflex series of stops in Hindi contrasts (as in Sanskrit) with pure dentals: [t̪], [t̪ʰ], [d̪], [d̪ʰ] (not alveolars). Cf. Harley (1955, xix).

[23] <http://ltrc.iiit.net/~anusaaraka/>

Where the conventional Romanization for a Devanāgarī character can be represented in ASCII, Kyoto-Harvard uses that representation. Otherwise: r̥ → `R`, l̥ → `L`; long vowels are represented by their upper-case equivalents, except r̥̄ → `q`, l̥̄ → `E`; ṅ → `G`; ñ → `J`; retroflex consonants are uppercased (and followed by `h` if they are aspirated); ś → `z`; ṁ → `M`; ḥ → `H`. Special symbols exist also for anunāsika (`&`), jihvāmūlīya and upadhmānīya (`x` and `f`), the udātta and svarita accents (`;` and `:`), external sandhi (`^`), and compound junction (`.`). A variant form of the Kyoto-Harvard scheme is sometimes used, in which long vowels are indicated by doubling the symbol for the short vowel.

A significant number of Sanskrit texts have been entered in this format. Unfortunately, it is not ideal, since it allows ambiguity such as that between the diphthong *au* and the sequence of simple vowels *a* + *u*.

2.13 Varṇamālā

Joshi, Dharmadhikari & Bedekar (2007) have proposed a scheme for Sanskrit text encoding which they term *varṇamālā* 'garland of speech sounds'. Whereas ISCII and Unicode take as their starting point for the encoding of Indian-language texts the orthographic syllable (*akṣara*), Joshi et al. propose a phonemic approach in which the fundamental unit is the individual speech sound (*varṇa*). The proposed *varṇamālā* includes the fourteen vowels of Sanskrit; six additional vowels (short *e*, candra *e*, long candra *e*, short *o*, candra *o*, long candra *o*); anusvāra, nasalization (candrabindu), and visarga; and thirty-four consonants (including the retroflex lateral flap *ḷ*).

The *varṇamālā* scheme has been implemented in the context of the IndiX project developed by C-DAC Mumbai. IndiX is a set of libraries and applications based on the GNU/Linux operating system that provide support for Indic scripts.[24]

The *varṇamālā* scheme is indeed based on phonetic principles, many of which are in accord with principles that we develop below. The status of this encoding, however, remains unclear. Joshi et al. (2007) do not assign codepoints or provide an ordering of the sounds in the repetoire. Earlier work by Joshi (2006) presents the *varṇamālā* as a "Vedic San-

[24] <http://www.cdacmumbai.in/projects/indix/>.

skrit Coding Scheme". Codes are envisioned as being assigned in the (currently unused) Unicode block beginning `U+0800`. In Joshi's draft, the basic Sanskrit sounds, together with numerals, some special symbols (such as the danda), and a few control characters are allocated to `U+0800–U+087F`. In `U+0880–U+08FF` are signs used in various Vedic manuscript traditions, including diacritics that indicate accents. Here the consonants and vowels of Sanskrit are treated phonetically (although not all the sounds Joshi includes have *phonemic* status in Sanskrit), but the remainder of the coded items are not phonetic but rather visual (or script-based)! Marks for accents could be interpreted phonetically, although they are presented merely as uninterpreted symbols; but the *svastika* (`U+08E6`) represents nothing phonetic, and numerals (`U+0800–U+0809`) are properly non-glottographic (Hyman, 2006). This scheme is unsuitable for encoding in Unicode, since it is phonetically organized and duplicates material already encoded. At the same time, it cannot properly be called a sound-based encoding, since it includes a substantial number of characters that do not represent sounds.

Joshi et al. (2007) present a number of arguments in support of the *varṇamālā* that are specious. They assert, "Through the Varnamala approach the IPA equivalence for Sanskrit text (as well as other Indian language text) can be established as one to one correspondence" Yet many sounds will have to be represented with digraphs in IPA. They assert, "Through the Varnamala-Phonemic approach lexical order and sorting operations in the areas of dictionary etc. can be done in the logical and more efficient way". But collation is fundamentally independent of encoding (Wissink, 2001). Collating order varies for different languages written in the same script. And sometimes multiple collating orders are used even within a single language. Thus in the case of Sanskrit, anusvāra and visarga collate between the vowels and the consonants in dictionaries such as Monier Williams', while in Bloomfield's *Vedic Concordance*, anusvāra collates after visarga, jihvāmūlīya, and upadhmānīya. In addition the authors assert, "Under the phonemic scheme the keyboard in put [sic] procedure will be simplified by reducing keys for vowel matras". Yet input methods are independent of underlying encodings; an input method in which independent vowels and vowel mātras are entered in the same way could equally be used with the existing Unicode Devanāgarī encoding. As we shall see, there are more reliable justifications for a sound-based encoding than these.

Chapter 3

Critique of encoding systems seen so far

Most of the encoding systems surveyed above are based primarily either upon Devanāgarī script or upon the standard Romanization of Sanskrit. The difficulties with these systems are due in part to problems in the modes of graphic representation of Sanskrit sounds adopted in Devanāgarī and the standard Romanization themselves. Current encoding persists in being script-based; it allows display conventions to govern uses of encoding that transcend appearance. While free-hand drawing and typeface, upon which contemporary encoding systems are based, historically served only display purposes, contemporary character encoding serves linguistic and archiving purposes that transcend mere display. Hence, while it is understandable that initially character encoding was motivated by display issues in imitation of typeface or manuscript hand, recent exigencies require an explicit system for encoding complete linguistic information. It is therefore timely to consider the principles governing the design of character-encoding systems.

The difficulties with the Devanāgarī standards and the Roman standards surveyed above become evident by observing the discrepancies between the encoding of Sanskrit embodied in the Devanāgarī script and in standard Romanization. Consider especially the following three points:

1. In the Devanāgarī standards, there are separate characters for vowels when they appear post-consonantally versus when they appear phrase-initially or post-vocalically. In the Roman standards, a single character is used in all contexts.

2. In the Devanāgarī standards, post-consonantal /a/ is implicitly indicated by the graph of the preceding consonant, while its absence is explicitly represented by a sign indicating the cessation of speech (*virāma*). In the Roman standards, the distribution of ⟨a⟩ corresponds exactly to the distribution of the vowel /a/.

3. In the Roman standards, certain single sounds are represented by digraphs: the aspirate stops (*kh, gh, ch, jh, ṭh, ḍh, th, dh, ph, bh*) and the open diphthongs (*ai, au*). In the Devanāgarī standards, single characters represent each of these segments.

The common feature of these discrepancies is a departure from the principle of representing a single Sanskrit sound by a single character. Both the Devanāgarī and the Roman standards concur in departing from this principle in one additional case:

4. In both the Devanāgarī and Roman standards the aspirate retroflex lateral flap /ɭʰ/ is represented by a digraph: ळ्ह *ḷh*.

5. An additional discrepancy exists between the encoding of accent in Devanāgarī script and the encoding in standard Romanization. The Romanization encodes lexical or post-prosodic high pitch and independent circumflex, or deep accent. Devanāgarī encodes manifest pitch or surface accent. The failure of scholars to recognize the difference has led to confused explanations of Devanāgarī accentual systems and the obfuscation of genuinely different recitational traditions and dialects.

3.1 Ambiguity and redundancy

The deficiencies that current encoding systems inherit from the Devanāgarī and Roman orthographies raise questions regarding general principles. In particular, we will consider the principles of avoiding ambiguity and redundancy. To avoid ambiguity and redundancy requires that an encoding system be characterized by a one-to-one correspondence between characters and items to be encoded,[1] and that all encoded items be of the same kind (e. g., phonemes or written characters). In items (1), (3), and (4), above, a single sound is represented by more than one character, and in (2), a sound is inversely represented: that is, the presence of the sound is represented by the absence of a character, and the absence of the sound by the presence of a character. The departure from the principle of a one-to-one correspondence between what is to be represented and the representation signals confusion concerning the principles of encoding.

Although the adoption of digraphs to transcribe aspirate stops and the aspirate retroflex lateral flap /ḷ^h/ in the Roman transcription of Sanskrit departs from a one-to-one correspondence between what is to be represented and the representation, the character ⟨h⟩ was chosen because it represents aspiration, which is the common feature of all the aspirate stops and also of the voiced fricative /ɦ/. Similarly, although *ai* and *au* are digraphs representing single diphthongs, the individual components of the digraphs were chosen as representations of the subsegments of those diphthongs. Insofar as the individual characters in these digraphs represent individual features and subsegments in the sounds they represent, the Roman transcription of Sanskrit does observe a one-to-one correspondence. Yet it *still* garners the fault of inconsistency in the principles of representation: some characters represent sound segments, while others represent features; and others, subsegments.

It is not absolutely necessary that an encoding scheme adhere to the principle of one-to-one correspondence and a consistent basis for its encoding. Yet, if it does not, it runs the risk of ambiguity, which is a fault in itself. Freedom from ambiguity is the minimal requirement for the adequacy of an encoding scheme.

The standard Roman encoding is encumbered with the fault of ambiguity in either case, whether it adheres to a consistent basis of encoding sound segments while it departs from the principle of one-to-one representation, or else conforms to the principle of one-to-one representation while it adopts an inconsistent basis of encoding. If it consistently represents sound segments, it uses the characters ⟨h⟩, ⟨a⟩, ⟨i⟩, and ⟨u⟩ in ambiguous ways. Each serves the dual functions of (1) representing a

[1] Compare Whitney (1861, 301): "each single sign was originally meant to have a single sound, and each single sound a separate and invariable sign".

segment by itself as well aş (2) constituting a member of one or more digraphs that represent another segment. Sometimes the character ⟨h⟩ represents the voiced fricative /ɦ/; but when preceded by ⟨k⟩, ⟨g⟩, etc. it represents an aspirate stop /kʰ/, /gʰ/ etc.; and in conjunction with ⟨ḷ⟩ it represents the aspirate retroflex lateral flap /ɭʰ/. Moreover, the characters ⟨k⟩, ⟨g⟩, etc. also serve dual functions: each by itself represents an unaspirated stop (/k/, /g/); in addition, these characters serve as the first member of digraphs ⟨kh⟩, ⟨gh⟩ that represent aspirated stops (/kʰ/, /gʰ/). Similarly, sometimes the character ⟨a⟩ represents the short vowel /a/; sometimes, in conjunction with the characters ⟨i⟩ or ⟨u⟩, it represents the first portion of an open diphthong /ai/ or /au/. Conversely, sometimes the characters ⟨i⟩ and ⟨u⟩ represent short vowels; sometimes they represent the second portion of open diphthongs.

Although it is possible to disambiguate ⟨k⟩, ⟨g⟩, etc. and ⟨h⟩ by phonetic context, it is not always possible to do so for the characters ⟨a⟩, ⟨i⟩, and ⟨u⟩. Although the former characters are ambiguous individually, it is possible to disambiguate them contextually, because the voiced fricative /ɦ/ can never occur post-consonantally. Therefore, ambiguity can be avoided by interpreting the characters ⟨k⟩, ⟨g⟩, etc. **always** as part of the digraphic representation of a voiced aspirate stop or retroflex lateral flap /ɭʰ/ whenever they occur before ⟨h⟩ (and we can similarly disambiguate ⟨h⟩). It is not, however, possible to avoid ambiguity in the case of ⟨a⟩, ⟨i⟩, and ⟨u⟩. The sequence of characters ⟨au⟩ represents the sequence of two simple vowels in *prauga* but represents a diphthong in *prauḍha*. Similarly, the sequence of characters ⟨ai⟩ represents two simple vowels in *manaicchā* but represents a diphthong in *taiḥ*.

It would be an improvement to trade ambiguity for redundancy. One can at least free the Roman system from contextual ambiguity if one introduces the diaeresis over the second character in a sequence to show that both characters are simple vowels: thus *praüga, manaïcchā*. But in so doing one introduces redundancy, itself a fault. In some cases /i/ will be represented as ⟨i⟩, whereas in others it will have to be represented as ⟨ï⟩. Such inelegant means to avoid ambiguity reveal deeper structural problems.

The Devanāgarī standards depart from the principle of one-to-one correspondence in (1), (2), and (4), and from the principle of a consistent basis for encoding in (2). Yet they do not introduce the degree of ambiguity seen in the Roman standards. The Devanāgarī standards suffer from the same context-free ambiguity regarding the dual use of the characters ळ and ह् as the Roman standards do in their use of ⟨ḷ⟩ and ⟨h⟩. These characters represent the voiced unaspirated retroflex lateral flap /ɺ/ and the voiced fricative /ɦ/, respectively, when they are parsed as separate tokens; taken together, they indicate the aspirate retroflex lateral flap /ɺ^h/. Although these characters are ambiguous in isolation, it is possible to disambiguate them contextually, since the sequence of retroflex lateral flap /ɺ/ + /ɦ/ is not possible in Sanskrit.

In (1), the Devanāgarī standards suffer from redundancy in representing Sanskrit and in (2) from an inconsistent basis for encoding. While in general the Devanāgarī standards encode sound segments, the virāma does not. Even if it is accepted that the virāma encodes a zero segment (like the Arabic *sukūn*), the segment /a/ remains unencoded when it occurs after a consonant.

If the Roman standards conform to the principle of one-to-one representation while they adopt an inconsistent basis of encoding, they are still marred by the fault of ambiguity. If the character ⟨h⟩ represents the feature of aspiration common to the aspirate stops, the aspirated retroflex lateral flap /ɺ^h/, and the voiced fricative /ɦ/, then in the last case, the other features of the fricative (voicing, etc.) remain unencoded. It would remain ambiguous, when the character ⟨h⟩ is used in isolation, whether these other features were to be assumed or not. Context can resolve this ambiguity. Yet even if the other features of the voiced aspirate fricative are assumed by default when the character ⟨h⟩ occurs in contexts not preceded by one of the characters ⟨k⟩, ⟨g⟩, etc., the encoding scheme would be inconsistent as to the segment to which the feature of aspiration belongs: although it usually indicates aspiration of the preceding segment, in the case of the voiced aspirate fricative it indicates its *own* aspiration.

3.2 Ambiguity in the encoding of accentuation

Typically, explanations of the most common Ṛgvedic accentual system state that a high-pitched syllable is unmarked, the last low-pitched syllable before a high-pitched syllable is marked with a horizontal line below, and a circumflexed syllable is marked with a vertical line above. All low-pitched syllables preceding the first high-pitched or circumflexed syllable in a sentence are marked with a horizontal line below. Low-pitched syllables following a circumflexed syllable, yet preceding the last low-pitched syllable before a high-pitched syllable, are unmarked. An independent circumflexed syllable followed by a high-pitched syllable or another independently circumflexed syllable is marked by putting the digit १ or ३ to the right of the vowel, depending upon whether it is short or long respectively, and placing both a vertical line above and a horizontal line below the digit. If the vowel is long, it too is marked with a horizontal line below (Whitney, 1889, 28–31).[2]

Such a system, if indeed it marked what it has been claimed to mark, would be unnecessarily complex, because it would depart from a one-to-one correspondence between accents to be represented and graphs used to represent them. First, it would suffer from redundancy in the marking of low pitch. It would mark low-pitched syllables in some contexts with a horizontal line below and in others with the absence of any mark. Second, it would suffer from ambiguity in its use of the absence of marking, which in some contexts would represent high pitch and in others, low pitch. Third, it would violate the Fano condition, since the vertical bar above, which usually marks any circumflexed syllable, would, used over a digit with a horizontal line below, mark an independently circumflexed syllable followed by a high-pitched or circumflexed syllable. Finally, the vertical line above would cause further ambiguity since it would mark only the dependent circumflexed syllable in the *Vājasaneyisaṁhitā* and all circumflexed syllables in the *Taittirīyasaṁhitā,* but it would mark high-pitched syllables in the the Kashmiri recension of the *R̥gveda,* the *Kāṭhakasaṁhitā* and *Maitrāyaṇīsaṁhitā* of the *Yajurveda,* and in the *Paippalādasaṁhitā* of the *Atharvaveda.* Indeed, Böhtlingk and Roth, in their *Sanskrit-wörterbuch,* and Whitney, in his *Sanskrit Grammar,* abandon the system and instead adapt to Devanāgarī the system used to mark accent in Roman script. They indicate only what they consider to be the "really accented syllables": high pitch by means of an उ above and an independent circumflex by a vertical line above (Whitney, 1889, 31).

[2]Cf. Macdonell 1910, 77-78; Renou 1952, 68–69 (both cited critically by Cardona 1997, lvi–lxi).

Chapter 4

The basis for encoding: a reanalysis

In the preceding chapter we described how encoding standards for Sanskrit that are based on Devanāgarī or Romanization inherit the deficiencies inherent in the underlying scripts. They suffer from ambiguity and redundancy by departing from a one-to-one correspondence and by inconsistency in the basis for encoding. In the current chapter we examine the principles that underlie encoding. First we examine the motivations behind our principles. Why is it a minimum requirement for an encoding scheme to avoid ambiguity? Why should it avoid redundancy? Why should it conform to the principle of one-to-one correspondence? Why should it adopt a consistent basis? To begin to answer these questions, we must outline the dimensions of a **possibility space for encoding.**

The possibility space for text encodings is defined by three dimensions:

1. **Axis I: Graphic–phonetic:** Is the basic unit of the encoding a written *character* or a speech *sound?*
2. **Axis II: Synthetic–analytic:** Are units encoded as a single *Gestalt?* Or are they decomposed into distinctively encoded features?
3. **Axis III: Contrastive–non-contrastive:** Are codepoints selected only for units that contrast minimally (*graphemes* or *phonemes*)?

Or are non-contrastive units that exit in complementary distribution also encoded?

4.1 Axis I: Spoken communication is prior to written

Knowledge may be communicated by three types of expressive media: (1) speech, (2) static visual art, (3) movement. While drawing and dance exemplify the latter two, natural language takes the form of speech. Any knowledge expressed in one of these media may be secondarily represented in any of the others. Thus the visual and performing arts may be described in speech (as in art historical texts and in performance reviews), and speech may be represented in visual form (in scripts), or reenacted in movement (as in the game of charades). Written language is ordinarily a secondary representation of spoken language, although there is often also use of ideographs (such as the Indo-Arabic numerals) (Edgerton, 1941) and icons (arrows and so forth).

The possibility of information degradation arises at each stage of presentation. Some knowledge may be lost because the medium is not purely transparent. For example, at the first stage of expression, a skillful dancer and a klutz will enjoy varying degrees of success in communication through the movement of their bodies. At the second stage, even the best performance review will not adequately capture the experience of the reviewer who attended the performance. Similarly: at the first stage of expression, spoken language does not succeed in communicating ideational and affective content perfectly; at the second stage, a manuscript that transcribes speech loses even more content. In face-to-face interaction, humans possess diverse channels for communicating, ranging from spoken language through paralinguistic hand gestures (McNeill 1992; Goldin-Meadow 2003), physical deixis (Kita, 2003), head and body movements, and facial expression (Bruce & Young, 1998, 187–216). In an audio recording of speech, the informational content of these non-vocal channels is simply lost (Laver, 1994, 16). Yet the audio recording still succeeds in capturing something of the speaker's affective state through such variables as rate of speech, amplitude, tone, and global pitch and emphasis (cf. Wennerstrom 2001, 206–208). A phonemic or phonetic transcription loses all or much of this information. Trigger (1998, 43) observes that no orthography "records all the linguistic structure of speech. Few have developed means for systematically noting the tone, stress, pitch, speed, or loudness of specific utterances". Moreover, a transcription necessarily reduces the speech continuum to a succession of discrete units (cf. Aronoff 1992). The transition from manuscript to print may impose further information loss: for instance, Indian manuscripts of Vedic recitation often include strokes in colored ink that indicate pitch accents and word boundaries. Similarly, at one point in Arabic orthography, black ink was used for letters and the diacritic dots used to differentiate otherwise identical letters, red for the diacritics indicating short vowels (*naqṭ*), yellow for a dot used to mark the *hamza* (glottal stop), and green for the elided *hamza* (Mahmoud, 1979, 9).[1] Printed editions, restricted in their typographic range and limited for financial reasons to a single ink color, usually sacrifice some or all of this information.[2]

The primacy of phonology over graphic representation of a language is relevant to *phonographic* writing systems — i. e. those that represent spoken language by means of *symbols* for *sounds* (Sampson, 1985, 32–4). Most of the examples we discuss in this book, and in general the representation of the Sanskrit language in Devanagari and Romanization, are clear cases of phonography. Phonographic writing systems are distinguished from so-called *logographic* or *ideographic* systems. The latter encode concepts in written form directly, unmediated by phonology. Goodglass (1993, 168) aptly writes that

> human speakers are equipped to acquire a variety of techniques for encoding the sound units of speech and the meaning of concepts in the form of written characters, and correspondingly equipped to decode these characters into strings of sounds and meaningful concepts. Within the scope of this cognitive-linguistic endowment, various cultures have developed markedly different writing systems that call on different cognitive processes.

Human cognitive processes do interact directly with graphic representation in reading and drawing. Children's drawings have been analyzed

---

[1] For illustrations, see the color plates reproducing pages from Maghreb Korans in Erduman (2004, 104–109).

[2] Cf. Waller (1988, 45–46, 239) on the loss of color in the transition from manuscript to print in Europe.

into a small number of *graphemes* organized around a system of distinctive features (Olivier 1974; Krampen 1986), and psychological research confirms that in reading the *grapheme* has a salient status independent of phonetics. This status can be confirmed by disorders such as *pure global alexia,* in which patients cannot read written text, although they may be capable of writing with considerable fluency; at the same time, the patient may have no difficulty copying or naming *non-grapheme* shapes (Cohen & Dehaene 2004, 471–473; Caramazza 2000, 204).[3] Moreover, research suggests that the consonant/vowel distinction in orthography "reflects a psychological reality" that is not entirely parasitic on the same distinction at the phonological level (Cubelli, 1991, 260). Another confirming phenomenon is *grapheme-color synesthesia,* in which an involuntary color percept accompanies the visual presentation of a grapheme; this is the most commonly presented form of synesthesia (Esterman, Verstynen, Ivry & Robertson 2006; Simner, Ward, Lanz, Hansari, Noonan, Glover & Oakley 2005; Ward, Simner & Auyeung 2005; Smilek, Dixon & Merikle 2005; Rich & Mattingley 2005; Wollen & Ruggiero 1983). That the concomitant color is genuinely perceived is demonstrated by a number of experiments (Ramachandran, Hubbard & Butcher, 2004, 869–870).[4]

To the extent that current encoding systems are based primarily on the underlying script, their capacity to represent knowledge can be no bet-

---

[3]A complementary variety of agraphia occurs, in which a subject is incapable of following the phonetic–graphic route in writing (and thus is entirely incapable of writing nonsense words) but has well-preserved ability to write known words via the whole-word route (Shallice, 1981).

[4]There are two kinds of grapheme-color synesthetes: for *projectors,* the color percept is bound to the visually-presented grapheme, whereas for *associators* the color percept is "seen" before the "mind's eye" (Smilek et al., 2005). The most compelling current explanation of grapheme-color synesthesia is based on proximity of the V4 or V8 areas implicated in color vision to the so-called "visual number grapheme" area. These areas are all located within the fusiform gyrus. Additional connections between these areas could explain the synesthetic percepts (Ramachandran & Hubbard 2001; Ramachandran et al. 2004). Subsequent research has identified the "visual number grapheme" area as belonging to the *visual word form area* (VWFA), with the approximate location (–43, –54, –12) in Talairach space (Cohen & Dehaene, 2004). Although it is unlikely that the VWFA is entirely devoted to reading, it is hypothesized that the VWFA contains detectors tuned to recognize graphemes, as opposed to pseudo-graphemes. It is further hypothesized that "neurons in the fusiform region are tuned to progressively larger and more invariant units of words, from visual features in extrastriate cortex to broader units such as graphemes, syllables, morphemes, or even entire words as one moves anteriorily [sic: anteriorly] in the fusiform gyrus" (Cohen & Dehaene, 2004, 471).

ter than the orthography associated with that script. The complexity of the mapping between the orthographic and the phonetic levels is known as *orthographic depth* and can be precisely quantified (Frost 1992; van den Bosch, Content, Daelemans & de Gelder 1994; Treiman 2006, 595). To take two contrasting cases, Finnish orthography is very shallow (or *transparent*), while English is quite deep (Lyỳtinen, Aro, Holopainen, Leiwo, Lyttinen & Tolvanen, 2006, 40). Since orthographies are never entirely shallow or transparent (Weir, 1967), character encoding by its very nature represents knowledge that has already passed through several stages at which information loss is possible. The goal of encoding should be to minimize the loss of information. Since degradation can occur at each stage of expression and transition, one ought to capture the informational content at the earliest stage possible. Given that script is inherently a secondary phenomenon vis-à-vis spoken language, encoding should be based directly on spoken language.

As noted above (§1.3), Devanāgarī script itself was not specifically designed to represent Sanskrit phonology but rather was adapted to this use subsequently. Devanāgarī derives from Brāhmī script, which was in turn influenced by Kharoṣṭhī, which was itself adapted from Aramaic. Brāhmī was placed in service in India originally to represent the phonology of Prākrit, rather than Sanskrit; the former lacks a number of the latter's phonemes, including vocalic *r̥, r̥̄,* and *l̥,* and the open diphthongs *ai* and *au* (Oberlies, 2003, 168). Moreover, some phonological features of Sanskrit for which Devanāgarī incorporates an encoding mechanism, such as the glottal stop, are not explicitly recognized in the phonologies of Indian linguists. Since Devanāgarī was never systematically designed to represent the phonological systems of Indian linguists in the first place, it would be surprising indeed if it should serve as a more appropriate basis for encoding Sanskrit than Sanskrit phonology. In fact, very few of the world's writing systems were designed for the languages that they represent in extant texts and manuscripts. Borrowing is the norm in the history of writing, and adaptations almost always fail to capture the structure of the spoken language adequately.

Therefore, where one has access to the phonology of the language, where the orthography is fairly shallow, and where the orthography departs from an ideal coding of spoken language structure, the basis for text encoding should be phonetic rather than graphic. Sanskrit meets these conditions, and so it is better to encode Sanskrit speech sounds directly than to encode the secondary representations of those sounds in Devanāgarī script, Roman script, or any other script. Directly coding Sanskrit speech sounds will solve the problems of ambiguity and redundancy that we have noted in our survey of current encoding systems.

4.2 Axis II: General remarks on the units of spoken and written language

4.2.1 Segments

The continuum of knowledge is made discrete in expression (Pulgram, 1976). Since speech occurs over the temporal dimension, the expression of knowledge in language occurs in units serially over time. The size of these units is limited by natural human and environmental factors that result in cessation or significant alteration in the continuum of speech. In the European Middle Ages, law professors taught the *Corpus Juris* divided into sections called *puncta,* which could be read aloud within the time periods set by the academic calendar. The length of a day is a factor in the length of chapters of certain texts. Chapters of Patañjali's grammatical treatise, *Mahābhāṣya* (2nd C. B.C.E.), for example, are called *āhnika,* literally 'to be studied in a day'.[5] The attention span of speaker and listener and the conventions of dialogue establish limits on the lengths of utterances. Breath limits the length of a foot (*pāda*) or line of verse.[6] Working memory is a factor that may limit sentence length (Baddeley & Wilson 1988; Shapiro, McNamara, Zurif, Lanzoni, & Cermak 1992; Goodglass 1993, 122). Finally, mechanisms involved in articulation and auditory perception constrain the duration of speech sounds. The minimal independent unit in the chain of speech is the *phonetic segment* or *phone.*

Scripts that represent spoken language have a linear dimension that corresponds to the temporal dimension of spoken language. The length and form of literary productions are constrained by limitations of technology and human vision. In the ancient Mediterranean world, the length

[5] For further examples of this type, see Waller (1988, 228).

[6] Cf. Hixon (1987, 28–43); Watson & Hixon (1987).

of a papyrus roll fixed a limit on the extent of a book (or single section of a complete work).[7] In India, binding techniques and materials constrained the number of pages in a manuscript, and the size of palm leaves constrained the size of a page. Writing implements, the resolution of human vision, and manual motor limitations governed the size of characters. The minimal independent unit in script is the *graphic segment* or *graph*.

4.2.2 Features

Speech is not one-dimensional. Phonetic units may be decomposed into a number of acoustic or articulatory features that are realized simultaneously. Early work on phonetic features conceived features as constituents of phonetic segments; or, from a different perspective, segments were bundles of features (Jakobson, Fant & Halle, 1963, 3).[8] Yet more recently, linguists have come to see that features overlap segments; for instance, the feature of *voice* [+ voice] is realized across all six segments of the Sanskrit word form *babhūva* 'he was'.[9] Ancient Indian phonetic treatises recognized that pitch either spread from a vowel to neighboring consonants in its syllable (*TPr.* 1.43), or properly belonged to the syllable itself (cf. *R̥Pr.* 3.9; *VPr.* 3.130 (Rastogi); *APr.* 3.67) (Whitney, 1868, 314). In Sanskrit, the prosody of retroflexion extends rightward from *r̥*, *r̥̄*, *r*, or *ṣ*, causing non-final *n* to be realized as *ṇ* despite intervening vowels, semivowels, gutturals, labials, or anusvāra (*A.* 8.4.1–2; cf. Allen 1951, 940; Zwicky 1965, 61–63; Hock 1979, 52–53; Anderson 1985, 191–192; Dixon & Aikhenvald 2002, 17; Hamann 2003, 122). Thus a feature may be associated with a string of one or more segments; and a segment is associated with a set of features. It was J. R. Firth's insight that "some phonological properties are not uniquely 'placed' with respect to particular segments within a larger unit" (Anderson, 1985, 185); Firth refers to such properties as *prosodies.*[10]

[7] For details, see Kenyon (1951).

[8] We bypass here the question of whether the mental lexicon contains featural specifications (Feature-Segment Hypothesis) or just segments (Indivisible-Segment Hypothesis) (Stemberger, 1982).

[9] Cf. Zellig Harris' notion of *long components* (Anderson, 1985, 191).

[10] It is the norm that features overlap segments. Contemporary research on articulatory phonetics emphasizes the importance of *coarticulation,* which "can be detected in almost

Speech may be analyzed into acoustic parameters (frequency, phase, and amplitude of waveforms)[11] as well as articulatory parameters (manipulation of the vocal tract, including larynx, tongue, lips, etc.). Feature analysis seeks to characterize perceptible features by associating them with regular patterns of concurrent acoustic and articulatory parameters (Laver, 1994, 101–110).

Nor is writing one-dimensional. Just as speech is analyzable into phonetic features, so writing may be analyzed into graphic features. Analogous to articulatory and acoustic features in phonetics are stroke analysis and block adjacency graph (BAG) analysis in optical character recognition (OCR) (Sonka, Hlavac & Boyle, 1999; Kompalli, 2007). Just as articulatory features are correlated with the production of speech sounds, stroke sequence is correlated with the production of written characters, and just as acoustic features are correlated with auditory parameters of speech sounds, BAG analysis is correlated with the shape of the complete character.[12] Marked alterations in phonetic and graphic features occur at the boundaries between phonetic and graphic segments.

The analysis of graphic features is more obviously applicable to some writing systems than to others; it is of particular interest where graphic features are correlated with phonetic features. Perhaps the most obvious application is to Korean han'gŭl, "in which graphic shapes are de-

every phoneme sequence in normal speech" (Goodglass, 1993, 62). Cf. Oudeyer 2006, 24. Some researchers have moved in the direction of developing a *nonsegmental* phonology (Griffen, 1976).

[11]Sine waves (or sinusoids) may be uniquely characterized in terms of these parameters. Mathematically speaking, they correspond to equations of the form $y = a \sin b(x+c)$, where a determines the amplitude, b determines the frequency, and c determines the phase. In a linear oscillating system the output (a periodic time waveform) corresponds to the sum of a set of sinusoids. *Fourier analysis* allows us to find the complex coefficients C_n that represent the phases and amplitudes of the harmonic sinusoid components of the periodic time waveform $v(t)$ using the following equation:

$$C_n = \frac{1}{T} \int_{-T/2}^{T/2} v(t) e^{j2\pi nt/T} dt,$$

where T is the period of the waveform (Pierce, 1999). In speech, vowels are approximately harmonic, whereas consonants correspond generally to noise.

[12]Analysis of characters as mathematical graphs is not merely a recent development. Already Bondy (1972) presents a graph theoretical analysis of the Greek alphabet, together with some interesting remarks on palaeographic developments, some hints of prospective algorithms, and a good measure of humor.

signed in such a way that subsegmental phonetic features are systematically correlated" (Kim, 1997, 145).[13] Several modern artificial alphabets also include extensive featural components. Pitman's Shorthand (Pitman, 1837) uses segment thickness to represent the voiced/non-voiced contrast for non-nasal consonants (Sampson 1985, 41–42; Kelly 1981). Alexander Melville Bell's *visible speech* is a universal phonetic alphabet based entirely on the visual representation of phonetically distinctive features (Bell, 1870).[14] The phonetic variant of Henry Sweet's "Current" system of shorthand (Sweet, 1892) iconically represents place features by "projection" and manner features by shape (MacMahon, 1981, 269).[15] Graphic/phonetic features also play a significant role in the Shavian alphabet posthumously funded by George Bernard Shaw (1856–1950) (Shaw 1962; MacCarthy 1969).[16]

While the systems discussed above are remarkable in their correlation of phonetic and graphic features, it seems to us that research on the application of a purely graphic featural analysis to a multiplicity of writing systems is likely to produce interesting results (cf. Smith; Lott & Cronnell 1969; Gibson 1972, 5; Klima 1972, 63). Graphic units may be analyzed along at least three dimensions, from the perspective of production: horizontal and vertical stroke direction, and stroke thickness.[17] In

[13]Cf. Sampson (1985, 120–144). We may recall Sir William Jones' enjoinment: "a *natural character* for all articulate sounds might easily be agreed on, if nations would agree on anything generally beneficial, by delineating the several organs of speech in the act of articulation, selecting from each a distinct and elegant outline" (qtd. by Firth 1946, 122).

[14]Bell's system is indeed remarkable, and it is to be lamented that such a system was never developed further. On the other hand, from our perspective as twenty-first century linguists, there are many insufficiencies in *visible speech:* how, for example, to represent the retroflex series of Sanskrit, or the emphatic (pharyngealized) series of Arabic, or the ingressive sounds of certain African languages? Bell's system allows for 120 unique sounds, which is approximately equal to the maximum phonemic inventory of any known language; yet it is by no means adapted for transcribing a language such as !Xũ/!Kung, which has, on one count, 141 phonemes (Maddieson 1984, 421–422; cf. Ladefoged 2005, 9). (48 of these are "click" consonants. The phonemics of this language are somewhat controversial. The classic study is Snyman (1970).) On languages with a large phonemic inventory cf. Szemerényi (1967, 86), who characterizes the 84 phonemes of Ubykh as "a world record".

[15]"Yet Sweet differs from Bell by relating place to the passive, not the active, articulator" (MacMahon, 1981, 269).

[16]Shavian is now encoded in the SMP of Unicode (`U+10450–U+1047F`).

[17]For an early computational approach to online stroke-based analysis of handwriting, see Mermelstein & Eden (1964).

the same way that phonetic features may spread over multiple phonetic segments, graphic features may spread over multiple graphic segments. An example is the horizontal headstroke that runs across a sequence of Devanāgarī characters.

4.3 Axis III: What is relevant for encoding?

It may be demonstrated empirically that certain design principles lead to undesired effects. In the realm of communication, design mistakes lead to information loss. Information is lost when meaning-bearing distinctions fail to be copied, transmitted, or perceived. The design of a system for the purpose of transmitting or storing information requires first a consideration of what information is needed or desired. It is neither possible nor practical to transmit or store *all* information. Thus in videorecording and videoconferencing no provision is made for touch, taste, or smell. All modes of information storage and transmission presuppose a selection of *relevant* information. Decisions concerning text encoding depend on the set of distinctions present in the texts to be encoded and the uses to which an encoder anticipates the encoded texts will be put. A designer must reflect with care on the character of both the corpus of texts and the potential user base.

In coding phonetic and graphic segments and features, it is necessary that each be coded uniquely. Here we encounter the well-known problem of how a human recognizes sameness amidst difference and determines that individual instances which vary in their details belong to the same class. Phoneticians recognize that speech sounds vary in numerous ways from one speaker to the next and even from one utterance (of the same speaker) to the next. Speech sounds are like snowflakes: no two are ever identical. Yet humans (and even machines) learn to class certain sounds together. Certain speech sounds share distinctive acoustic patterns that allow them to be considered phonetically equivalent — that is, to be considered as instances of a particular phone (Laver, 1994, 29). Other information in the speech signal may be useful (inter alia) for gauging speaker affect or emotional state (Williams & Stevens 1981; Alpert 1981; Wennerstrom 2001, 221) or for performing the task of speaker recognition (Nolan, 1997). Such information is hardly ever transcribed, because it is not linguistically relevant; that is, it does not help to convey a *linguistic* message. Similarly, the stains, smudges, spills, and creases on the page of a manuscript, as well as the wiggles, trailers, absolute (as opposed to relative) stroke dimensions are irrelevant to the scholar who is deciphering the *linguistic* content of a manuscript (cf. Kropač 1991, 118). Yet to a palaeographer or codicologist, these same idiosyncratic marks may provide valuable information about the manuscript's date, its copyist, and the conditions under which it has been stored.

Speakers of a particular language normally do not distinguish phones that occur only in complementary distribution in their language. Thus Arabic does not distinguish between [b] and [p], which constitute distinct phonemes in English. English does not distinguish between [p] and [p^h], which are distinct phonemes in Sanskrit. For an English speaker [p] and [p^h] are the *same* phoneme, just as for the Arabic speaker [b] and [p] are the *same* (cf. Jakobson et al. 1963, 9).

The structure of an encoding should closely follow the structure of the linguistic units themselves. A character-encoding scheme ideally encodes only the minimally distinctive graphs of the language. A sound encoding scheme ideally encodes only the minimally distinctive phones of the language. In either case, codepoints are assigned only to contrastive units. The ancient Indian linguists understood a similar principle regarding the relationship between speech and meaning in the first stage of the expression of knowledge. They desired a one-to-one correspondence between the speech form and the object to be conveyed. The principle of the avoidance of redundancy is embodied in Patañjali's oft-repeated phrase, "one does not employ a speech form for what has already been stated" (*uktārthānām aprayogaḥ*).[18] Similarly, in Mīmāṁsāsūtra 1.3.26 *anyāyaś cānekaśabdatvam*, Jaimini states that it is improper for a single meaning to be donoted by multiple speech forms.

4.4 Encoding Sanskrit language vs. Devanāgarī script

It may at first seem natural to encode language in terms of written *characters*. We argue, however, that in certain cases it makes more sense to

[18] Kielhorn I 105.3, I 227.3, I 238.11, etc.

encode directly the sounds of the spoken language, rather than the characters that symbolize them. In making such decisions, one must consider whether the cultural heritage is received primarily in written or in oral form and, if written, how closely the written form represents the phonology of the language.

For English, the Roman script, rather than the oral language, is the predominant vehicle of the received cultural heritage. Scholarship is primarily written. Although regional pronunciation varies, spelling is highly standardized and needs to be taught even to native speakers up through secondary school. The Roman script, designed to model the Latin sound system, was never systematically remodeled to accord with English phonology.[19] Moreover, the phonology of English has changed significantly since the adoption of the Roman alphabet, widening further the gap between script and sound. Character encoding evolved first to capture the system of contemporary written English (Birnbaum, 1989), and ASCII (as well as supersets such as ISO 8859-1[20] and Unicode) provides a reasonable basis for archiving and processing English language text. A phonetic encoding of English would not be desirable for many applications, since it would necessarily impose arbitrary dialectal features on written texts. Furthermore, writers and readers of English are used to an orthography that often privileges morphological representation over phonological representation (consider for instance the different vowels in *potent* ['powtn̩t] and *impotent* ['ɪmpətn̩t]) (Weir 1967; Klima 1972; French 1976, 124; Sampson 1985, 204–205; Tolchinsky 2003, 92, 193–194; Snowling 2005; Lyytinen et al. 2006, 49). English spelling also possesses a lexical-semantic aspect, as shown by such homophonous but heterographic and heterosemantic sets as {*knew, new, gnu*} (Weir 1967,

[19]The earliest inscriptions in Old English are in the Runic *futhorc* alphabet, which derives from the Germanic *futhark* and is first attested (in the Caistor-by-Norwich runes) for the fourth or early fifth century (Page, 1999, 21). The adoption of the Roman alphabet was a response to the spread of Christianity. Originally, several added letters represented phonemes specific to English: ⟨æ, ð, þ, ƿ⟩ (the latter two directly borrowed from futhorc: þ = *þorn* 'thorn'; ƿ = *ƿynn* 'joy') (Page, 1999, 186, 212–213). With the rise of printing in the 15th century, the added characters fell into disuse, since they did not exist in the fonts of continental printers (McArthur, 1992, 31–32). Once again we see the limitations imposed by a shift in technology.

[20]See Gaylord 1995.

173–177; Miller 1994, xii).[21] Of course, in certain domains such as dialectology and child language research, phonetic encoding may be necessary.[22]

The case of Sanskrit is different. Here the standard Devanāgarī orthography is extremely faithful to the phonology. Even interword prosody is represented systematically in writing. The reasons are historical: after a millennium of oral transmission of texts, Sanskrit scholars had developed by the fifth century B.C.E. precise sciences of phonetics and grammar. Their systematization of Sanskrit phonology lay at the foundation of education in India and served as the basis for all written literature. Given the oral bias of Indian culture and the highly phonetic aspect of the traditional orthography, we may well consider whether Sanskrit phonology is a more appropriate basis for encoding Sanskrit language texts than a secondary encoding derived from the Devanāgarī script.

---

[21]Similarly, French orthography involves a number of elements that are not phonographic; thus, for instance, homophones are sometimes distinguished heterographically (*sain* 'sane' vs. *saint* 'saint'), and a "silent" *-s* morphographically indicates [+plural] (Jaffré & Fayol, 2006).

[22]Unicode provides IPA (U+0250–U+02AF) and other phonetic symbols. Several earlier systems allowed for phonetic transcription using only ASCII symbols. CHILDES (Child Language Data Exchange System) (<http://childes.psy.cmu.edu/>) uses the PHONASCII transliteration format (based on IPA) in its CHAT database (Allen 1988; MacWhinney 1991, 71–82). ARPAbet (Shoup, 1980) is a widely-used pure ASCII system for the phonetic transcription of American English.

Chapter 5

Sanskrit phonology

Sanskrit phonology has been a topic of investigation since phoneticians analyzed interword sound alterations in Vedic hymns at the beginning of the first millennium B.C.E.[1] During the 6th through 4th centuries B.C.E., around the time that Pāṇini composed his grammar of Sanskrit, phoneticians systematically analyzed the phonetic features of sounds and categorized sounds according to these features in treatises termed *Prātiśākhya* that were proper to particular Vedic schools (Staal, 1972, xxiv).[2] Subsequent treatises called *Śikṣā* continued the tradition of phonological analysis. The phonetic and phonological analyses in these texts differ from each other and from that assumed for the operation of Pāṇinian grammatical rules. Modern historical and comparative linguists analyze the sound structure of various Sanskrit dialects at various historical periods; in so doing they rely on the data of Indian predecessors and adopt or adapt many of their analytic principles. Relevant also are the independently-motivated featural analyses proposed by modern phonologists. While it is neither practical nor desirable for us to present all the

---

[1] By *phonology* we mean the study of the sound system of a language, including the relationship of sounds to one another and the patterned alternation of sounds. *Phonetics* denotes a broader science that may also describe paralinguistic, extralinguistic, and nonsystematic aspects of a spoken language.

[2] Dating is a matter of some controversy. Scharfe (1977, 129–30) dates the *Vājasaneyiprātiśākhya* to 250 B.C.E.

details of such analyses, we aim to survey here those aspects of phonemic and featural analyses of Sanskrit that are relevant to its encoding.

We summarize the system of phonological features of Sanskrit in TABLE 1 and show the classification of phonetic segments of Sanskrit in accordance with these features in TABLE 5. The system presented in these tables is based upon our own analyses of the Indian phonetic treatises and on recent contributions to Sanskrit phonetics. Significant differences and variations both in the system of features and in the classification of segments will be discussed in due course.

5.1 Description of Sanskrit sounds

Phonetic segments are categorized in TABLE 5 in rows by their *place of articulation* within the mouth and in columns by their *manner features:* stricture, voicing, aspiration, nasalization, and duration.[3] Indian phoneticians categorize the duration of segments by recourse to the measure of the short vowel. A short vowel measures one mora;[4] long vowels, two morae; prolonged vowels (not shown), three morae; consonants, half a mora.[5] In terms of pitch, Indian phoneticians categorize vowels as high-pitched, low-pitched, circumflexed, or monotone. A circumflexed vowel is described as dropping from high to low, and a series of syllables is monotone if devoid of relative distinction in pitch.

The vowels represented in Devanāgarī by ए and ओ, although typically categorized as diphthongs, are phonetically monophthongal mid vowels and hence Romanized *e* and *o*. The true diphthongs (written ऐ and औ) have two places of articulation — one each from the subsegments of which they are composed: *ai*, composed of subsegments *a* and *i*, is glottal-palatal; whereas *au*, composed of subsegments *a* and *u*, is glottal-labial. In the table they are placed in the row that corresponds to their second property. The vowels and semivowels other than *r* (i. e. *y*, *l*, and *v*) include nasalized variants (not shown) as well as the clear (un-

[3] Allen (1953, 20) differs in leaving out *ḷ* as well as the more open and most open manners of articulation, and in not categorizing anusvāra and *h* as semivowels.

[4] The *mora* is a unit of relative duration that holds constant over differing rates of speech.

[5] For comparison, in English spoken in a connected style and at an ordinary rate, the median absolute duration of a stressed vowel is 130 msec; that of a consonant or unstressed vowel is about 70 msec (Klatt, 1976).

nasalized) varieties. व्, conventionally Romanized as *v*, was originally a labiovelar approximant [w]; in some dialects it is described by ancient phoneticians as a labiodental [ʋ] (*Pāṇinīyaśikṣā* 18).

Indian phoneticians describe a number of other phonetic segments not shown in TABLE 5. Nasals called *yama* occur as a transition between an oral stop and a subsequent nasal stop. Four yamas characterized by the voicing and aspiration of the preceding stop are Romanized *k̃ kh̃ g̃ gh̃* and are designated variously in Indian phonetic treatises as कुँ खुँ गुँ घुँ[6] or कं खं गं घं.[7] Another nasal segment called *nāsikya* (*h̃*) occurs as a transition between *h* /ɦ/ and a subsequent nasal stop *ṇ*, *n*, or *m*.[8] Unreleased stops occur before stops, and reduced semivowels corresponding to *y*, *l*, and *v* occur word-finally; both are termed *abhinidhāna* (Varma 1929, 137–147; Allen 1953, 71–73). Firmer approximants *y* and *v* occur word-initially, and lighter approximants *y* and *v* occur word-finally in several dialects (Varma 1929, 126–132; Allen 1953, 68–69; *A*. 8.3.18). Short simple vowels *ĕ* and *ŏ* occur in Vedic recitation and in phonetic treatises.[9] The *Keśavīśikṣā* and *Pratijñāsūtra* notice slightly lengthened short vowels in the *Vājasaneyisaṁhitā*. The former states that short vowels are slightly long (*kiṁcit dīrgham*) except when followed by a syllable containing a long *ā* preceded by a consonant, or a vowel preceded by a consonant and followed by a visarga. The latter states that slight length (*īṣaddīrghatā*) occurs in a word-initial syllable containing the vowel *a* preceded by a consonant (Varma, 1929, 179).[10] Vowel segments ($^{a\,i\,u\,ṛ\,ḷ\,e}$) called *svarabhakti* break up certain consonant clusters (Schmidt, 1875, 1–8). In particular, a svarabhakti appears in clusters consisting of *r* plus a fricative, and in broken clusters consist-

[6] *VPr*. 8.31 (Rastogi, 1967, 89).

[7] The *Caturādhyāyikābhāṣya* on *CA*. 1.1.26 (Deshpande, 1997*b*, 139).

[8] See Allen (1953, 75–78), Mishra (1972, 87–88), van Nooten (1973, 412), Cardona (1977), Cardona (1980, 253 n. 14).

[9] *chandogānāṁ sātyamugrirāṇāyanīyā ardham ekāraṃ ardham okāraṁ cādhīyate*, etc. *MBhK*., I 22.21–24. See Cardona 1987, 28–30; Cardona 1983.

[10] The statement of the *Pāriśikṣāṭīkā Yājuṣabhūṣaṇa* that one should pronounce a short vowel like a long one in an aggravated svarita seems to lengthen a short vowel to a long one rather than account for a length between that of a short vowel and a long one. Likewise, it is not clear that shortened long vowels termed *kṣipra* 'quick' are any different in length from short vowels. The only evidence Varma (1929, 178) cites for them describes their length as that of a short vowel, and he himself notes that their length "may be confused with that of a short vowel".

ing of a voiced abhinidhāna plus a stop or fricative (Schmidt 1875, 1–8; Varma 1929, 133–136; Allen 1953, 73–75; *R̥kprātiśākhya* 6.46-53, 14.58). *Caturādhyāyikā* 1.4.10–11 distinguishes two lengths of svarabhakti. Vedic phonetic treatises also describe (1) longer and shorter lengths of anusvāra, which regularly occur after short and long vowels respectively (*Vājasaneyiprātiśākhya* 4.148–149; *R̥kprātiśākhya* 13.32–33); (2) realizations of anusvāra as velar nasalized stops before *r* and fricatives (*gũ* and, before unvoiced fricatives, *ṅk*) (Cardona, 2003, 110); and (3) extra high or extra low pitches and special varieties of circumflex accent determined by sandhi and phonotactics (*R̥kprātiśākhya* 3.4; *Vājasaneyiprātiśākhya* 4.136, 138; *A.* 1.2.40). Patañjali asserts that there are prolonged vowels measuring four morae (*MBhK.* III 421.13–14). Certain *Śikṣā* texts distinguish in addition to short and long anusvāra (1) a two-mora (*dvimātra*) anusvāra before consonant + *r̥* (*Yājñavalkyaśikṣā* 139; *Pārāśarīśikṣā* 31) or (2) a heavy (*guru*) anusvāra before a consonant cluster (*Laghumādhyandinīyaśikṣā* 14–15; *Keśavīśikṣā* 5). Some *Śikṣās* describe nasalized vowels prolonged by up to six morae (*raṅga*) (*Mallaśarmakr̥taśikṣā* 43–46). Vocalic and consonantal subsegments comprise the vowels *r̥* and *l̥* (Allen, 1953, 61–62). Subsegments of diphthongs are of similar quality to independent vowels. Unaspirated and aspirated retroflex lateral flaps /ɭ/ and /ɭ^h/, written ळ *ḷ* and ळ्ह *ḷh*, occur intervocalically in R̥gvedic (as well as in the *Nirukta*) in place of *ḍ* and *ḍh* (Allen, 1953, 73).[11]

[11] After consultation with the colleagues mentioned in parentheses below, it remains unclear whether the Vedic ळ *ḷ* and ळ्ह *ḷh* were flaps, taps, or approximants. In Modern Indic (Gujarati, Marathi, Oriya, and the four Dravidian languages), ळ *ḷ* is a retroflex lateral approximant, not a flap (Aklujkar. Cardona, Deshpande, Bhaskararao), and it is reasonable to assume that retroflex lateral approximants developed from the intervocalic voiced retroflex stops ड *ḍ* and ढ *ḍh* (Cardona). In Tamil the retroflex lateral approximant ள் *ḷ* is not exclusively intervocalic but occurs in clusters, including geminates (Steever) and contrasts with a central retroflex approximant with lateral contact between the sides of the mid-tongue and the palate ழ் *ḻ*, as well as with a non-lateral post-alveolar ற் *ṟ* (which may be in the process of merging with alveolar ர் *r*) (Keane, 2004, 113) (with thanks also to Chevillard). Likewise, the Vedic retroflex laterals are distinguished from the modern Hindi retroflex flaps ड़ and ढ़. The development of weaker allophones in intervocalic position in Vedic is paralleled in Middle Indo-Aryan: *nn* > *ṇ*, and *ll* > *ḷ* (Hock).

5.2 Phonetic and phonological differences

Ancient and modern authorities disagree over the classification of particular phonetic segments as well as over the system of classification. When Indian phonetic treatises differ in their classification of phonetic segments, it is not immediately obvious whether the differences are phonetic or phonological. Different treatises may reflect actual differences in pronunciation due to historical or dialectal variation or may impose different classification of the same sounds to achieve elegance or utility in the system of classification itself or in the system's use in formulating linguistic rules.

5.2.1 Phonetic differences

Ancient Indian treatises themselves report genuine phonetic differences. For example, *R̥kprātiśākhya* 1.45 states that *s, r,* and *l* are produced at the base of the teeth, but 1.47 reports that some teachers hold *r* to be produced at the alveolar ridge (*barsvya*) (Shastri, 1937, 7). Differing from both, the *Pāṇinīyaśikṣā* classifies *r* as coronal (Varma, 1929, 6–7). Alveolar, coronal, and velar places of articulation are reported for vocalic *r̥* (Varma, 1929, 8–9, 53).[12] Ancient treatises report differences concerning the relative duration of subsegments that compose diphthongs (see commentaries on *A.* 8.2.106, *MBhK.* III 421.3–14 and Varma 1929, 180–181) and about types and durations of anusvāra (Varma, 1929, 151). Varma (1929, 53–54) demonstrates that such differences reflect dialectal variation by showing that the reflexes of Sanskrit words in regional languages originate in differences found in Indian phonetic treatises. He (8–9) shows, for instance, that dental and coronal pronunciations of vocalic *r̥* correlate to reflexes in regional Ashokan inscriptions and modern languages that developed subsequent dental versus retroflex geminate consonants respectively.

In a few cases, ancient phoneticians disagree with each other even about the existence of certain sounds. For example, is there a long *l̥̄* corresponding to *r̥̄*? *Taittirīyaprātiśākhya* 1.2 omits *l̥̄*, and *Āpiśaliśikṣā* 6.4 and the *Kāśikā* on *A.* 6.1.101 deny its existence, while *R̥kprātiśākhya*

[12] Whitney (1868, 431) lists the differences of opinion mentioned in the *Taittirīyaprātiśākhya*.

Intro. 9, and Kātyāyana and Patañjali on *A.* 6.1.101 (*MBhK.* III 77.18–19) accept its existence. Are there prolonged (i. e. trimoraic) versions of *r̥* and *l̥* (Mishra, 1972, 62–4)? *Taittirīyaprātiśākhya* 1.2 omits not only *l̥̄*, but also *r̥3*, *l̥3* (Whitney 1868, 10; Varma 1929, 25). Do jihvāmūlīya, upadhmānīya, and intervocalic *ḷ* and *ḷh* occur? Some sources do not include them (Whitney 1868, 282; Varma 1929, 54).

In several cases, ambiguity concerning the phonetic character of segments has continued into the modern literature. Allen, citing evidence of Westermann and Ward, refutes Müller's and Whitney's denial that ह ⟨h⟩ and the series of voiced aspirate stops could be produced with both voicing and aspiration simultaneously (Allen, 1953, 34–6). In fact, contra Whitney (1868, 52), standard modern treatments of phonetics do recognize a voiced glottal fricative or approximant [ɦ] (Pullum & Ladusaw, 1986, 67). The situation with the voiced aspirated stops is rather more complex. Ladefoged (1971, 13) argues that voicing and aspiration are incompatible states of the glottis: "Phonemically it may be very convenient to symbolize these sounds as /b bh p ph/, and so on; but when one uses a term such as voiced aspirated, one is using neither the term voiced nor the term aspirated in the same way as in the descriptions of the other stops". What we call "voiced aspirated stops", Ladefoged calls "murmured stops" and Ohala (1983, 2) calls "breathy-voiced stops". Chomsky & Halle (1968) allow the term "voiced aspirated stops", for which they require the feature *heightened subglottal pressure.* Ladefoged (1971, 96) is skeptical of this analysis. Experimental data are presented by Ohala (1983, 155-160) that the "voiced aspirated stops" of Hindi speakers are not necessarily accompanied by increased subglottal pressure. Allen also reviews the evidence for and against the ancient view that semivowels were produced with greater closure than their corresponding vowels, defending this view at least for initial semivowels in later times (Allen 1953, 27–9; Varma 1929, 126–32).

Ancient Indian treatises differ in their description of the pitches that result from phonotactics. The *R̥kprātiśākhya*, with which the *Taittirīyaprātiśākhya* primarily agrees,[13] describes a set of three pitches — extra-high, high, and low — in contrast to the set of three pitches — high, low,

[13] *TPr.* 1.41–42, 14.29–31, 21.10–11. Yet it also reports several disparate views including those that correspond to the views of Pāṇini and the *Vājasaneyiprātiśākhya,* which are not always clearly indicated as the views of others.

and extra-low — described by Pāṇini and the *Vājasaneyiprātiśākhya*. According to the *Ṛkprātiśākhya*, the first part of a circumflex is higher-pitched than a high-pitched syllable (*ṚPr.* 3.4); the latter part is high-pitched (3.5) unless the following syllable is high-pitched or circumflexed, in which case the remainder is low-pitched (3.5–6). It particularly prohibits making a circumflexed syllable too low (3.32). Low-pitched syllables that follow a high-pitched syllable become circumflexed (3.17), whereas those that follow a circumflexed syllable become high-pitched (3.19); but followed by a high-pitched or circumflexed syllable, a low-pitched syllable remains low-pitched (3.21). According to Pāṇini, on the other hand, the first part of a circumflexed vowel is high-pitched and the latter part is low-pitched (*A.* 1.2.32). A low-pitched vowel followed by a high-pitched or circumflexed vowel is replaced by a lower-pitched vowel (1.2.40). Similarly, according to the *Vājasaneyiprātiśākhya*, a low-pitched vowel and the last part of an independently circumflexed vowel followed by a high-pitched or circumflexed vowel both become lower-pitched (*VPr.* 4.136, 138 according to Rastogi). Otherwise, low-pitched vowels that follow a circumflexed vowel remain low-pitched (4.141–142 according to Sharma, Tripāṭhī; = 4.139–140 Rastogi).[14]

In sum, in the system of pitches that result from phonotactics described in the *Ṛkprātiśākhya*, the initial portion of the circumflex assumes a higher pitch than the underlying high pitch, while in the system of Pāṇini and the *Vājasaneyiprātiśākhya*, it doesn't. According to the latter, instead, low pitches followed by high pitches and circumflexes become lower than the low pitch. These descriptions clearly reflect phonetic differences in the accentuation of the saṁhitā texts recited in different Vedic schools and may in addition reflect dialectal differences. Cardona (1993) demonstrates even greater phonetic differences in the accentuation of the *Śatapathabrāhmaṇa* and argues that they represent dialectal variation.

[14] According to the text in Sharma's edition 4.141 reads *svaritāt param anudāttam anudāttamayam*, but commentators and Rastogi's edition 4.139 read *udāttamayam* instead of *anudāttamayam*. If Sharma's edition is simply mistaken, the accentual system prescribed is more complex than here described, but it is possible that commentators and Rastogi have revised the text to conform to the *Ṛkprātiśākhya* description without recognizing that the *Vājasaneyiprātiśākhya* described a different accentual system.

TABLE 5.1: The systems of accentuation of the *Ṛkprātiśākhya* versus *Vājasaneyiprātiśākhya*

tone	*Ṛkprātiśākhya*	*Vājasaneyiprātiśākhya*
extra high	beginning of svarita	
high	udātta, pracaya, end of svarita	udātta, beginning of svarita
low	anudātta, end of svarita before udātta or svarita	anudātta, pracaya, end of svarita
extra low		anudātta and end of svarita before udātta or svarita

5.2.2 Sounds of problematic characterization

The differences in the description of certain sounds by Indian phoneticians is due to genuine challenges in characterizing sounds whose principal articulators are extra-buccal. Ancient descriptions of anusvāra (*ṁ*) reflect phonetic differences in its production (Allen 1953, 40–6; Bhaskararao & Mathur 1991; Cardona 2003, 110). Yet most of these differing descriptions concur in attributing to it no specific oral place of articulation. Some regard its place as the nose alone, others as the nose and throat, and others still as dependent upon the place of articulation of a neighboring sound.[15] Such descriptions, understood as phonological classifications that partially capture the phonetic realizations of the sound, are consistent with other ancient and modern evidence. Ancient phonetic treatises and grammars generally distinguish anusvāra not only from the nasal stops (*ṅ, ñ ṇ, n, m*), but also from nasal semivowels (*ỹ, l̃, ṽ*) (*A.* 8.4.59), and nasalized vowels (*ã, ĩ*, etc.) (*A.* 8.3.4; Cardona 1983*a*).[16] *Āpiśaliśikṣā* 4.5 describes it as aspirated; and *Ṛkprātiśākhya* 1.10, as a fricative. Modern

[15]Other differences include that *Āpiśaliśikṣā* 4.4 describes it as voiced; *Ṛkprātiśākhya* 1.11, as unvoiced.

[16]Whitney 1868, 66–9, 318–9. Varma (1929, 148–55) wrongly denigrates the distinction between anusvāra and anunāsika across the board.

phoneticists describe anusvāra as a nasal glide whose designated articulator is the soft palate. The velum is lowered. Debuccalization of a nasal consonant eliminates its buccal place feature and designated articulator, and its secondary articulator takes over (Halle 1995, 13, 16; Trigo 1988). The distinction between anusvāra (*ṁ*) and the velar nasal stop (*ṅ*) is accounted for by the fact that there is no dorsal movement (of the tongue body) for the former, while there is for the latter.[17] Elimination of the buccal place feature and designated articulator explains why the Indian phonetic treatises usually avoid ascribing a particular intrabuccal place of articulation to the anusvāra, even if they do differ in other aspects of its character. Consistent with these descriptions is a nasal (rhinal) glide minimally characterized by lowering of the velum and nasality, while it adopts other features from its environment. Yet there is no evidence for the realization of anusvāra without additional buccal features. In the dialect represented by the *Ṛkprātiśākhya*, it is realized as a nasalized fricative by adopting the aspiration and voicing of the following *r* or fricative. In the dialect represented by the *Pāṇinīyaśikṣā* for instance, it is realized as the nasalized vowel offglide of a clear vowel by adopting the articulator, place of articulation, stricture, and voicing of the preceding vowel (Cardona, n.d., 42).[18] In some dialects, it does have a definite buccal place of articulation: it is realized as a velar stop accompanied by nasality (*gũ; ṅk* / ___ [– voiced]) in White Yajurvedic traditions (Cardona,

[17] Bhaskararao & Mathur (1991) conclude that anusvāra is phonetically identical to a velar nasal by arguing that if anusvāra is phonetically a pure nasal, as some ancient treatises describe it, its production would require dorsovelar closure. This identity cannot be accepted, however, because Indian phonetic treatises consistently distinguish anusvāra from the nasal stops, including the velar nasal. A uvular place of articulation would account for the distinction of the anusvāra from the velar nasal stop (Laver, 1994, 209–14). It might also account for the diverse descriptions of its place of articulation: the uniqueness of the uvula as a place of articulation would account for its escaping the notice of the ancients, or if it were recognized, the systematic inelegance of creating a sixth buccal place of articulation solely for this sound would have discouraged ancient phoneticians from so categorizing it. Yet a voiced uvular nasal stop is rare in the phonetic inventories of the world's languages and is not recognized by any Indian phonetic treatises.

[18] Busetto (2003, 193 n. 3, 205 n. 18) combines the voicing of the *Pāṇinīyaśikṣā* and related traditions with the aspiration of the *Ṛkprātiśākhya* tradition. He characterizes anusvāra as originally being a voiced fricative homorganic with the subsequent segment. While ancient phonetic treatises generally characterize anusvāra as voiced, the *Ṛkprātiśākhya*, which characterizes it as unvoiced, represents the earliest phonetic description in the Indian tradition.

n.d., 36–7), and other evidence supports its articulation as a palatal or dental in connection with the epenthesis of homorganic palatal or dental stops. Reflexes in Panjabi and Sindhi show palatal stops (Varma, 1929, 153); the metrical version of the *Pāṇinīyaśikṣā* and its *Pañjikā* commentary report its production at the base of the teeth; and there is inscriptional evidence for dental as well as velar retroflexes (Cardona, n.d., 48–9).

The situation with *h* and visarga (*ḥ*) is similar to that of anusvāra. The voiced approximant *h* /ɦ/ contrasts with voiced aspirated stops (*gh, jh, ḍh, dh, bh*). Ancient treatises generally distinguish the voiceless visarga from voiceless fricatives produced at buccal places of articulation (*ẖ* [x], *ś* [ç], *ṣ* [ʂ], *s* [s], *ḫ* [ɸ]). Moreover, they concur in attributing to *h* and *ḥ* no specific oral place of articulation. Debuccalization of stops and fricatives eliminates their buccal place features and designated articulators, and secondary articulators take over. Some ancient treatises regard the place of articulation of *h* as that of the following vowel and of *ḥ* as that of the preceding vowel. Others regard their place of articulation as the glottis or chest.[19] These distinctions could reflect either phonetic differences or a difference in phonological classification. If phonetic, in some dialects, the *h* and *ḥ* adopt the buccal place of articulation of the following and preceding vowels (respectively), just as in the dialect represented by the *Pāṇinīyaśikṣā* anusvāra adopts the place of articulation of the clear vowel that precedes it. In other dialects, it could be the case that feature spreading is resisted and an extrabuccal secondary articulator takes over as the designated articulator. Debuccalized stops and fricatives would result in fricatives whose only articulator is the glottis, just as the debuccalized nasal results in the anusvāra whose only designated articulator is the velum. Yet just as there is no evidence for the realization of anusvāra without additional buccal features, there is no evidence for the realization of visarga and *h* with no additional features. Visarga, for instance, regularly adopts features of the preceding vowel. Modern pronunciations echo the preceding vowel after visarga in pausa, and Yajurvedic traditions mark the visarga differently depending upon the pitch of the preceding vowel, thus demonstrating that the pitch feature spreads

[19] *Ṛkprātiśākhya* 1.39-40; *Taittirīyaprātiśākhya* 2.46-48; Allen 1953, 48–9; Mishra 1972, 90.

to the syllabified visarga.[20] Differences in the designation of the place of articulation of *h* and visarga are therefore probably due to phonological considerations.

5.2.3 Differences in phonological classification of segments

It is not necessarily the case that different classifications reflect differences in phonetics. Phonologists make different decisions concerning how to classify complex phonetic data as they balance fidelity to phonetic detail against elegance in the phonological system.[21] Hence it is probably due to the consideration of secondary articulations that some treatises place the vowels *r̥* and *l̥* at the base of the tongue.[22] A similar consideration accounts for the disagreement over whether the place of articulation of *h* and *ḥ* is that of a neighboring vowel, the glottis, or the chest. Those who consider the place of articulation as that of the neighboring vowel regard spread buccal place features as more primary than extrabuccal place features; those who consider the place of articulation as the glottis regard glottal stricture as primary; and those who consider the place of articulation as the chest regard the regulation of pulmonic airflow as primary. Similarly, although nasalization might be regarded as a resonance feature, a number of treatises make the nose a second place of articulation for nasal vowels, semivowels, and stops (Allen 1953, 39; Bare 1976, 75).

In several other cases there is reason to believe that ostensibly phonetic descriptions are colored by phonological considerations. Some Indian treatises classify *e* and *o* as monophthongs with single places of articulation (as we do) (*R̥kprātiśākhya* 13.40; Shastri 1937, 98); others classify them as diphthongs with dual places of articulation (Deshpande, 1997*a*, 76). They are phonetically realized as monophthongs; but historically and underlyingly, in terms of phonology, they are diphthongs (Allen 1953, 62–4; Cardona 1983, 13–32). Similar is the case of *v*, which some

[20] Likewise the pitch feature spreads to syllabified anusvāra in the White Yajurvedic *gū̃* pronunciation, as demonstrated by a horizontal line beneath the sign for *gū̃* after extra-low-pitched vowels.

[21] Cardona (1983) considers the interplay of phonetics and phonology in Indian treatises.

[22] *R̥kprātiśākhya* 1.41; Allen 1953, 55; Mishra 1972, 80; Varma 1929, 7.

classify as labiodental; others as purely labial (as we have) (Deshpande 1997*a*, 76; Allen 1953, 57). Pāṇinian prosodic rules operate as though *v* were a labial semivowel, even though commentators recognize that it is realized as a labiodental fricative. For like reasons, while Pāṇinians recognize the phonetic occurrence of diphthongs measuring three or four morae, they classify them all as *prolonged* (i.e. trimoraic) in order to preserve a strict tripartite division of vocalic length.[23]

While *ṚPr.* 6.29 describes yamas as non-nasal stops that have developed a nasal offset before a nasal,[24] the *TPr.* 21.12, *APr.* 1.99, and *CA.* 1.4.8 describe them as epenthetic nasals inserted between a non-nasal stop and a following nasal. Uvaṭa, in his comment on *ṚPr.* 6.29 (Shastri, 1931, 206), *VPr.* 8.31 (Rastogi, 1967, 89), the *Tribhāṣyaratna*, in its initial enumeration of sounds (Whitney, 1862, 10) and its comment on *TPr.* 21.12 (Whitney, 1862, 389), and the *Caturādhyāyikābhāṣya* on *APr.* 1.1.14–15 (Deshpande, 1997*b*, 117–119) and 26 (Deshpande, 1997*b*, 139) all count four yamas. Yet Whitney (1862, 393–395) and Deshpande (1997*b*, 251–254) are of the opinion that the *CA.* held there to be twenty yamas. Whitney and Deshpande's insistence that there were twenty must be accepted as a phonetic evaluation on the grounds that the yama inherits properties of the preceding sounds, of which there are twenty, in addition to the nasality of the following sound. Conversely, the ancient texts enumerated four yamas on the grounds of phonological abstraction based upon the features of voicing and aspiration of the preceding sound. The *ṚPr.* and *VPr.* 1.103 syllabify yamas with the preceding vowel while the *TPr.* 21.8 syllabifies them with the following. Varma (1929, 79–80) attributes different reflexes in different dialects to dialectal differences in the syllabification of yamas described by the two *Prātiśākhyas.*[25]

[23]Nageśa writes that the term *trimātra* is indicatory (*upalakṣaṇa*) of anything longer than two morae (*ūkāla eveti. tatra trimātragrahaṇam ekadvimātrabhinnopalakṣaṇam iti bhāvaḥ. MBh. Uddyota* on Patañjali's comment *iṣyate eva caturmātraḥ plutaḥ* under *A.* 8.2.106. *MBhK.* III 421.14, Rohatak ed. V.427, Guru Prasad Shastri, vol. VIII, p. 149.

[24]Whitney (1862, 393–394) interprets the passage as doubling and therefore as epenthesis in the manner of the other *Prātiśākhyas.*

[25]See the additional note of Shastri (1937, 192) on *ṚPr.* 6.29.

5.2.4 Differences in the system of feature classification

Apart from differences concerning the classification of specific segments, ancient authorities differ over the system of feature classification.[26] Phonetic treatises vary in the number of places of articulation enumerated, generally distinguishing the place of articulation of velar stops and jihvāmūlīya from that of *a, h,* and *ḥ.* They place the jihvāmūlīya at the base of the tongue (*jihvāmūla*) and the velar stops either there or at the base of the jaw (*hanumūla*); *a, h,* and *ḥ* they place in the throat (*kaṇṭha*) (Allen 1953, 51–2; Deshpande 1997*a*, 76; Bare 1976, 74; Mishra 1972, 77, 80). In contrast, Pāṇinian grammarians operate with five places of articulation rather than six; they combine the glottal and velar places under the term *guttural* (*kaṇṭhya*) (Allen 1953, 52; Mishra 1972, 77,119).[27] They avoid having to posit different places of articulation for distinguishing between *a* and *h* (on the one hand) and the velar stops (on the other) by employing efficient techniques of reference to the segments instead. Pāṇinian grammarians consider the nose (nasality) as a means, rather than a place, of articulation. Thereby they avoid complications that would result from considering all nasals (their distinct oral places of articulation notwithstanding) as homorganic.[28]

5.2.5 Indian treatises on phonological features

Significantly, certain Indian phoneticians give particular prominence to features. A few explicitly state that features are entities distinct from both articulatory processes and phonetic segments and serve as the elements of which the latter are composed. Such analyses directly inspired feature analysis in modern linguistics. Beyond classifying sounds according to their common features, the *Āpiśaliśikṣā* operates with the features associated with those sound classes (Cardona, 1965, 248). After classifying sounds according to their place of articulation in section 1, the second section explicitly associates these sound classes, designated

[26]These differences have been studied by Bare (1976) and summarized by Deshpande (1997*a*).

[27]Bhaṭṭojidīkṣita preserves for etymological reasons the base of the tongue as a separate place of pronunciation only for the jihvāmūlīya: *Siddhāntakaumudī* 10 (Cardona, 1965, 227).

[28]Deshpande (1997*a*, 84). *Kāśikā* on *A.* 1.1.8.

by terms that refer to their common place of articulation, with articulators (van Nooten, 1973, 425). Thus 2.4 states that velars are produced with the base of the tongue; 2.5, that palatals are produced with the mid-tongue; 2.6, that coronals are produced with the tongue blade; 2.7, that the coronals are alternatively produced with the back of the tongue blade (retroflex); and 2.8, that the dentals are produced with the tongue-tip. While the sounds associated with these places of articulation all have some part of the tongue as their independent articulator, 2.9 states that the rest of the sounds have their respective places of articulation as their articulator. The third section describes the degree of contact of the articulator at the buccal place of articulation for stops, semivowels, fricatives, and vowels. This method of description gives an operative role to features beyond noting shared characteristics of segments. It also describes articulation in terms that directly associate features with articulatory components and only make indirect reference to speech segments. (See TABLE 2.)

In the eighth section it becomes clear that the *Āpiśaliśikṣā* establishes articulatory features intermediate between the articulatory processes themselves, and sets of sounds with shared properties. The fourth section already categorized sounds according to their common extrabuccal articulatory processes and resultant characteristics: certain sounds are open-glottis, breath-reverberant (*śvāsānupradāna*), unvoiced; others by contrast are closed-glottis, sound-reverberant (*nādānupradāna*), voiced. Certain sounds are unaspirated in contrast to others that are aspirated. Section 8 establishes that articulatory processes produce features that in turn produce other features. For example, 8.7 states that closure arises from the glottis being closed, while openness arises from the glottis being open. 8.8 concludes that these are closure and openness. Clearly the author intends to establish the existence of features as entities in their own right. To interpret the statements otherwise would be to accuse him of serious redundancy (Cardona, 1980, especially p. 248).

Other Indian phonetic treatises establish different systems of features. Some features are identified with articulatory constituents; some are restricted to a domain in which they are contrastive. The *Ṛk-* and *Taittirīyaprātiśākhyas* concur with the *Āpiśaliśikṣā* in restricting the features of voicing (*ghoṣa*) and non-voicing (*aghoṣa*) to consonants, while the former allow the features breath (*śvāsa*) and sound (*nāda*) for all sounds.

According to *Ṛkprātiśākhya* 13.3–6, breath and sound are the materials from which all speech segments are produced: breath is the material of voiceless segments; both breath and sound are the material of voiced aspirates and *h*; and sound is the material of the rest.

Rkprātiśākhya 13.1–21 forms a treatise on the features of segments. In 13.14, the author, presumed to be Śaunaka, distances himself from the view that segments are fundamental, immutable entities. Yet he also distances himself from the view — in the case of a number of sounds but not all of them — that certain segments are the constituents of others. 13.15 reports the view of others that the segments *a* and anusvāra constitute the voicing in non-nasalized voiced stops and nasal stops. 13.6–17 attributes to others a view expressed in the *Āpiśaliśikṣā*. *Āpiśaliśikṣā* 4.9–10 states that the unvoiced aspirates contain the fricative produced at the same place of articulation (i. e. *kh, ch, ṭh, th, ph* contain *ẖ, ś, ṣ, s, ḫ*, respectively) and that the voiced aspirates contain *h*.

The commentary on *Atharvavedaprātiśākhya* 1.10 reports that some consider there to be only five stops (the first in each series). These become differentiated by the addition of certain features. United with the unvoiced fricatives, they become the unvoiced aspirates; united with voicing, they become the voiced unaspirates; united with their corresponding fricative in addition, they become the voiced aspirates; and united with voicing and nasalization, they become nasal stops.[29] These statements name both features and segments as the constituents of other segments. Still, they demonstrate a penetrating phonological analysis in terms of constituents that are more fundamental than segments.

5.2.6 Modern feature analysis

Modern feature analysis is concerned with discovering the internal organization of phonological features in human language.[30] The fact that features have internal organization was, of course, already known to the ancient Indian phoneticians. Indian phoneticians typically organized their feature systems in such a way that the binary voicing and aspiration features were constrained by buccal stricture. Voicing and aspiration apply only to consonants in Sanskrit; vowels are inherently voiced

[29] Whitney 1862, 346, 591; cf. Shastri 1937, 221–2, n. on 13.15–20.

[30] A seminal work in this area is Bell (1870), on which see p. 55.

and aspiration-neutral. Indian phoneticians also typically organized their feature systems in such a way that the length feature was constrained by stricture. They reserved lengths greater than half a mora to vowels. Āpiśali already understood that the binary nasalization feature was constrained to buccal places of articulation. He does not assign the extrabuccal nasalization feature to sounds to which he gives exclusively a nasal place of articulation. Still, the modern discovery that features have internal organization has inspired exciting progress in modeling the relations between features.

Modern linguists make essentially three advances in feature analysis. First, they apply analysis of changes in a language's feature system to the understanding of historical language change. Second, they extend feature analysis to virtually all of the world's languages and investigate feature universals. Third, they understand that features can endure and spread in time independently of each other and of fixed temporal units. Halle (1988) draws attention to Jakobson's insightful recognition of the importance the system of features and its evolution holds for historical linguistics (Jakobson, [1929] 1971).[31] According to Halle, Jakobson realized that phonemes were not the ultimate constituents of language; rather, they are composed of distinctive features, and the change of distinctive features is the principal vehicle of sound change. Hence, sound change ordinarily affects entire classes of sounds and not just individual phonemes. Language change involves reorganization of the system of distinctive features known to the speakers, rather than an arbitrary classification of features. And the phonotactic rules that constrain the form of words are part of the realization of the phonological system.

Zwicky (1965) employed a set of twelve binary features, based on the system of Jakobson, Fant, and Halle, for Sanskrit.[32] An analysis by Ivanov & Toporov (1968, 35–41) makes use of ten binary features.[33]

---

[31] For the history of Jakobson's thinking on these matters, see Joseph (2000, 170–183).

[32] To wit: (1) consonantality, (2) vocalicity, (3) obstruence, (4) continuance, (5) gravity, (6) compactness, (7) diffuseness, (8) nasality, (9) voicing, (10) tenseness, (11) flatness, (12) stridency. Zwicky does not make reference to the analysis of Ivanov and Toporov, originally published in Russian in 1960.

[33] (1) aspirate–non-aspirate, (2) voiced–voiceless, (3) nasal–oral, (4) cerebral–non-cerebral, (5) palatal–non-palatal, (6) grave–acute, (7) compact–diffuse, (8) continuant–discontinuous, (9) consonantal–non-consonantal, (10) vocalic–non-vocalic. Features (2), (3), (6), (7), (8), (9), and (10) correspond to features used by Zwicky. Ivanov and Toporov observe that opposition (1) might be interpreted in terms of *checked–unchecked* or in terms

Early work in generative phonology primarily treated features as vectors without internal organization.[34] Chomsky & Halle (1968), in their influential sketch of a system of universal phonetic features, presented a hierarchical system, which they characterized, however, as primarily expository in purpose (300). At the same time, they noted the desirability of research into the organization of features. More recently, exciting progress has been made in modeling the relations between features. Halle (1983) demonstrated that articulatory mechanisms, acoustic data, and phonological rules all provide constraints on the organization of features. Clements (1985) suggested that features follow a hierarchical organization governed by limits regarding both their sequential ordering and their simultaneous grouping. On this view, features are regarded not as properties of sound segments but as independent units in their own right. Associated with each point in the speech signal is a *feature geometry* that is orthogonal to the temporal dimension of the signal. Perhaps the most significant aspect of Clements' account is a "constrained theory of assimilation processes, according to which all assimilation rules involve the spreading of a single node: the root node, a class node, or a feature node" (Clements, 1985, 247). In feature spreading, multiple segments, which were previously linked to separate features, are relinked to a single feature.[35] Since feature groupings recur across the world's languages, the aim of phonologists is to discover an adequate universal feature organization (Clements & Hume, 1995).

Halle (1995) and Halle, Vaux & Wolfe (2000) arrange features under their articulators instead of grouping them according to constriction, which was the organizing principle of feature geometry in Clements' model. Halle also considers that acoustic aspects of features play a secondary role. He believes "that there is a direct connection only between features in memory and the articulatory actions to which they give rise" (2002, 7). He therefore groups features under the only moveable parts of the vocal tract, namely: lips, tongue blade, tongue body, tongue root, soft palate, and larynx, and provides each with a unary designated artic-

---

of *tenseness*; (4) might be interpreted in terms of *flatness*; and (5) might be interpreted in terms of *stridency*.

[34] Ivanov & Toporov (1968, 40), however, present a feature tree, with (10) as the root node and with higher nodes branching on the basis of features with decreasing indices in their (inversely) ranked list (see n. 33 above).

[35] See e. g. Halle (1995); Calabrese (1998, 9).

ulator feature (Halle et al. 2000, 388–389; cf. TABLE 12). The fact that articulators are controlled by paired sets of agonistic and antagonistic muscles is directly reflected in the binary character of their subordinate features. Further, he requires that features constitute only terminal nodes and that only these spread; he thereby abandons Clements' (1985) provision that higher nodes spread. If this proposal proves correct, then a network model might better represent feature organization than a tree model does. Halle's recent research validates the articulatory feature analysis employed by the ancient Indian phoneticians, especially that of Āpiśali, who gives prominence to articulators (see above §5.2.5).

Since the feature organization of Halle et al. represents the most advanced feature analysis in the field of phonology and since it shares the articulatory approach to feature analysis of ancient Indian treatises, it may be a fruitful basis for analyzing the feature systems and sound catalogs of the Indian treatises. Certain features and articulators Halle employs are not distinctive in Sanskrit, such as the articulator *tongue root* and its subordinate features, and the articulator-free feature *suction*. Halle reduces the number of articulators considered separate by Āpiśali (TABLE 2, II); he accounts for the required distinctions instead by introducing disposition features subordinate to the remaining articulators (*back, low, high, anterior, distributed*) and the articulator-free feature *lateral.* His laryngeal features capture well the observations of Āpiśali and Śaunaka concerning the effect of the larynx on pitch (TABLE 2; TABLE 3 IV, VI[E]) and revise the effect Śaunaka describes of glottal aperture on voicing (TABLE 3 III, V). Halle converts the feature *nasal* from a place-of-articulation (TABLE 2, [II]D; TABLE 3, [I]G) or an extra-buccal feature (TABLE 2 [III]B5; TABLE 3 [VI]C) to an articulator. He captures stricture features, used conservatively by Śaunaka (TABLE 3, II) and liberally by Āpiśali (TABLE 2, III) by the articulator-free features *continuant, consonantal,* and *sonorant.* The direction of Halle's research would seem to lead to an articulatory account of the latter two. TABLE 4 summarizes the articulatory features of Sanskrit sounds per Halle et al. (2000).

Chapter 6

Sound-based encoding

6.1 Criteria for selecting distinctive elements to encode

In a comprehensive linguistic encoding scheme, whether based on speech segments or on phonological features, it is not necessary to encode all the elements that may be observed; one need only encode *distinctive elements.* For an encoding scheme based on segments, we select a set of Sanskrit sounds that are minimally distinctive in the sense described above (§4.3). For a scheme based on features, we select a set of minimally distinctive features to describe the set of distinctive segments. The set of minimally distinctive features we select is shown in TABLE 1. It is not possible to eliminate (as did Pāṇini) the distinction between the guttural and velar places of articulation, if we wish the feature system uniquely to distinguish the visarga from the velar fricative jihvāmūlīya. Pāṇini did not need this feature distinction, since he was able to refer to segments directly (not just through the feature system). Further reductions to the feature systems of the Indian phoneticians are not possible. We preserve the stricture distinctions of Āpiśali between open, more open, and most open in order to distinguish vowels that Pāṇini distinguishes by explicitly classifying certain vowels as guṇa and vr̥ddhi. We abandon, however, the purely phonetically motivated stricture feature *close* (*saṁvr̥tta*) of a number of phonetic and grammatical treatises including Āpiśali's; the category is associated only with the vowel *a*, which is already uniquely characterized by place and length features.

We select our set of minimally distinctive Sanskrit sounds to encode from those discussed in section 5.1. In order to clarify our criteria for determining which sounds are distinctive, we discuss next the concept of a *phoneme,* its limiting parameters, its relation to Pāṇini's concept of a *sound class,* and the relevance of some of the limiting parameters to generative grammar and to historical and comparative linguistics. At each stage in this discussion we specify the set of sounds that our developing concept of a distinctive segment would include. Finally, having arrived at a satisfactory concept of a distinctive segment, we specify the set of sounds we wish to encode and justify the inclusion of various segments with reference to the limiting parameters already discussed.

6.1.1 Phoneme

Kemp (1994) summarizes the major elements and history of the concept of a phoneme. Early definitions of the phoneme limited features that could distinguish phonemes to those qualifying timbre, but since the 1950s the concept has been extended to include duration, stress, and pitch.

Phonemes are the minimally contrastive segments of sound in a language, on the basis of the contrast between which lexical and grammatical distinctions can be made. Sounds that are lexically or grammatically contrastive in parallel distribution are independent phonemes. Conversely, where phonetically similar sounds differ only post-lexically, they are not independent phonemes; rather they are either allophones or free phonetic variants. Phonetically similar sounds that occur in complementary distribution are allophones; phonetically similar sounds that are non-contrastive in parallel distribution are free phonetic variants. A middle category concerns sounds that are barely contrastive (Goldsmith, 1995*a*, 10–12). Two sounds, both of which are common, may be contrastive in just a small set of environments; one of two contrastive sounds may occur only in limited contexts; or there may be some other asymmetry between contrastive sounds. The contrast here possesses a *low functional yield.*

The concept of a phoneme is yoked with two parameters that limit its utility as the sole basis for encoding. The first is that the sounds belong to the same language in the strictest sense, namely, "the speech of one individual pronouncing in a definite and consistent style" (Jones, 1962, 9). Differences in style, rate, or dialect are not included in the same phonemic system. The second limiting parameter of the concept of a phoneme is that for sounds to be considered contrastive they are required to differentiate semantic content in a narrow sense.

A number of the phonetic segments described in section 5.1 are not phonemes. These include inseparable phonetic segments described as subsegments. The status of subsegments within the vowels *ṛ* and *ḷ* and within *e, o, ai,* and *au* cannot be considered independently of those vowels. Although Old Indo-Aryan *e, o, ai,* and *au* are historically derived from Proto-Indo-Iranian sequences of separate vowels **aï, *aü, *āï,* and **āü,* they cannot be eliminated as independent phonemes in a synchronic description of Sanskrit. The rest of the subsegments described in section 5.1 are overlapping phases, that is, they are simultaneously the offset phase of the first of two segments and the onset phase of the second. As such, they form parts of allophones. These include the nasals yama and nāsikya in the phonological description of the *Ṛkprātiśākhya,* where they are the overlapping phases of a stop or *h* and the following nasal stop. While Indian phoneticians make a great contribution to the science of phonetics by providing descriptions of these sounds, the subsegments are not phonemic. They occur in very limited environments as parts of sounds that occur in complementary distribution with other allophones of their respective phonemes.

Several other marginal phonetic segments are not phonemes in the strict and narrow sense. They occur only in complementary distribution with other sounds in parallel contexts and hence are allophones. The short vowels *ĕ* and *ŏ* occur word-initially in hiatus after *e* and *o* in complementary distribution with *a* in certain Vedic dialects. They also occur in *Sāmaveda* as free phonetic variants in a specific recitational repetition called *nyuṅkha.* Slightly lengthened short vowels in *Vājasaneyisaṁhitā* occur in complementary distribution with short vowels.[1] The retroflex ळ् *ḷ* and ळ्ह् *ḷh* occur intervocalically in complementary distribution with *ḍ*

[1] Long vowels shortened in specific contexts and termed *kṣipra* likewise would not be phonemes, even if they did differ in length from short vowels.

and *ḍh* in R̥gvedic dialect. In several dialects, in complementary distribution with normal *y* and *v*, firmer palatal and labial approximants occur word-initially, and lighter palatal and labial approximants occur word-finally. The epenthetic vocalic segments svarabhakti are automatically inserted in predictable environments and thus are not phonemic. For the same reason, the nasals yama and nāsikya, which in the phonological description of most ancient Indian phonetic treatises are epenthetic nasals automatically inserted in predictable environments, are not phonemic.

Certain members of two subgroups of phonetic segments, sibilants and nasals, occur only non-contrastively either in complementary distribution in specific dialects or as free phonetic variants. In the sibilant subgroup, jihvāmūlīya and upadhmānīya are allophones of *s* and *r* word-finally before unvoiced velar and labial stops. Visarga generally occurs in pausa (*dahati agniḥ*) in complementary distribution with *r* and voiceless fricatives *ẖ, ś, ṣ, s* and *ḫ* (*agnir dahati, agniẖ karoti, agniś carati, agnis tiṣṭhati, agniḫ pūjyate*), and as a dialectal or free phonetic variant of jihvāmūlīya (*ẖ*) and upadhmānīya (*ḫ*) before unvoiced velar and labial stops (*agniḥ karoti, agniḥ pūjyate*),[2] and of sibilants before sibilants (*agniś śr̥ṇoti : agniḥ śr̥ṇoti*). It also occurs as a phonetic variant before palatal and labial stops in certain dialects (*yajuḥ karoti : yajuṣ karoti*). A parallel situation is found with certain sounds in the nasal subgroup. Nasalized semivowels are allophones of word-final[3] *m* before their corresponding clear semivowels (*cakame purūravasam : saỹ-yama*). Anusvāra generally occurs in complementary distribution with *m* before a fricative (*saṁ-śaya*) and as a dialectal or free phonetic variant of nasal stops before oral stops (*śaṅ-kara : śaṁ-kara*), and of nasalized semivowels before semivowels (*saỹ-yama : saṁ-yama*). Different lengths of anusvāra are allophones additionally determined by the length of the preceding vowel and by following consonant clusters or consonant + *r̆*. Among the nasal stops the palatal nasal is not a phoneme. It is an allophone of *m* before a palatal stop (*sañ-caya*) and is a phonetic variant

---

[2]Labial and velar sounds, such as [ɸ] and [x], are acoustically similar and share the feature **gravity**. Historically, the voiceless velar fricative symbolized by ⟨gh⟩ in English words like *cough* is in Present Day English a voiceless labio-dental fricative [f] (Ladefoged, 1971, 44).

[3]We use *word-final* as a translation of *padānta*, that is, occurring at the end of a *pada* (independent word, preverb, or compound element).

of anusvāra in the same context (*saṁ-caya*). It is likewise an allophone of *n* before a voiced palatal stop (*jalaṁ piban, pibañ jalam*).

Visarga and anusvāra are marginally contrastive with sibilants and nasals respectively. Visarga occurs in contrastive distribution with *s* and *ṣ* in limited environments: before *k* and *p*. For example, *paspaśa : antaḥ-pura; paras-para : saraḥ-padma; antaḥ-karaṇa : uras-kā; vācas-pati : vācaḥ pati.* Anusvāra occurs in contrastive distribution with *m* in limited environments: *sam-rāṭ : saṁ-rāddha; samyak : saṁ-yata; amla, a-mlāna : saṁ-lāpa;* and *ā-mreḍita : saṁ-rihāṇa.* By virtue of this contrastive occurrence, they retain phonemic status. Yet the narrow range of this contrastive occurrence raises questions. Fry (1941) denies that visarga is phonemic, while Emeneau (1946) concludes that anusvāra is. Arguments to show that phonetic segments in such cases are not phonemes depend on showing that the particular examples of contrastive distribution do not properly belong to the same language. Hence Fry argues that sibilants before velar and labial stops are holdovers from an earlier historical dialect to which they properly belong. Vacek (1976) argues on similar grounds that the retroflex sibilant *ṣ* is not phonemic but is an allophone of the palatal and dental *ś* and *s*. Similar reasoning would deny that retroflex stops have phonemic status in Sanskrit.[4]

Prolonged vowels similarly have marginal phonemic status; they are barely contrastive. Such vowels occur in contrastive distribution with shorter durations of their corresponding vowels in fairly narrowly circumscribed contexts and conditions. The contrastive semantic content is always of a paralinguistic nature (cf. Wennerstrom 2001, 60–4). In *A.* 8.2.82–107, Pāṇini prescribes prolonged vowels in such pragmatic contexts as return salutation of an upper casteman, calling from afar, specific ritual situations, and answering a question (the last optionally in the word *hi* 'certainly'). For example, the sentence-final vowel is prolonged, as indicated by the numeral 3, in एहि देवदत्त३ *ehi devadattá3* "Come, Devadatta!" used in calling from afar but not in *ehi devadatta* used otherwise. Because such paralinguistic content is not regarded as semantically contrastive, prolonged vowels are not considered to be separate phonemes.

---

[4] Hock 1975, Hock 1979, and Hock 1993 examine the issue of retroflexion in Sanskrit in detail.

Pitch in Sanskrit is contrastive. Patañjali, the author of the great commentary on Pāṇinian grammar (*Mahābhāṣya,* Kielhorn's ed., I 2.10–11, second century B.C.E.), provides the famous example of the word *índra-śatru,* which, accented with initial high pitch as shown (preserving the original accent of the first compound element *índra* 'Indra'), is a bahuvrīhi compound (*A.* 6.2.1) meaning 'having Indra as his slayer'. When accented with high pitch on the final syllable, however, *indra-śatrú* is a tatpuruṣa compound (*A.* 6.1.223) meaning 'slayer of Indra'. *Śatapathabrāhmaṇa* 1.6.3.8–10 tells of Tvaṣṭṛ, who utters the word with the improper accent in a rite to secure the birth of Vṛtra to slay Indra and fulfills the import of his erroneous utterance, thus getting Vṛtra slain by Indra. Although lexical pitch is contrastive in Sanskrit, the differences in the surface pitch that result from different phonotactic rules in the *Prātiśākhyas* proper to various Vedic schools (see §5.2.1) are not contrastive. They are variants proper to different speech communities — the reciters of various Vedic schools — and arguably to different dialects. Hence distinctions in surface pitch are not phonemic distinctions, because phonemic distinctions belong to the same language *stricto sensu.* Differences in style and dialect are not included in the same phonemic system.

Eliminating just allophones and phonetic variants but still affording phonemic status to the marginal phonemes, the set of phonemes of Sanskrit would consist of the sounds shown in TABLE 5 plus prolonged vowels, minus jihvāmūlīya, upadhmānīya, and the palatal nasal. If marginal phonemes also are eliminated, the set also subtracts the prolonged vowels, anusvāra, visarga, and retroflex ṣ (see TABLE 8). By comparison, the Pāṇinian sound catalog differs from TABLE 5 in that it lists only one length for each simple vowel, the short one, and does not include anusvāra, visarga, jihvāmūlīya, or upadhmānīya.

6.1.2 Generative grammar

Certain formal synchronic descriptions of language capture phonological information that is not captured in an unordered set of phonemes of the language. The Pāṇinian derivational system, for example, not only captures the alternation of anusvāra, visarga, jihvāmūlīya, upadhmānīya and the palatal nasal with their respective allophones but in addition obviates the need to posit the velar nasal as an original speech sound.

Historical and comparative linguists recognize the velar nasal *ṅ* as an independent phoneme in the set of phonemes of Sanskrit because it occurs word finally in forms such as *prāṅ, pratyaṅ, udaṅ, yuṅ,* and *kruṅ* in contrastive distribution with *n* and *m,* for example in *balavān, rājan,* and *vipram.* In Pāṇini's derivational system, however, the velar nasal is consistently generated by rules from *n.* The forms in question are masculine and feminine nominative singulars of nominal derivates of the roots √*anc* 'bend' (*DhP.* 1.118, 1.595), √*yuj* 'yoke' (*DhP.* 7.7), and √*krunc* 'shrink' (*DhP.* 1.116) accounted for by *A.* 3.2.59. After its original penultimate *n* is deleted by *A.* 6.4.24, the root √*anc*, followed by nominal terminations termed *sarvanāmasthāna*, is again supplied with penultimate *n* by *A.* 7.1.70.[5] Uncompounded, the root √*yuj* is similarly supplied with penultimate *n* by *A.* 7.1.71. The palatal stop in all three roots is replaced by a velar stop in specified contexts, including word-final context (*A.* 8.2.30). The *n* is replaced by anusvāra (*A.* 8.3.24) which is in turn replaced by the featurally closest sound homorganic with the following non-nasal stop (*A.* 8.4.58). Deletion of the final stop (*A.* 8.2.23) then leaves the velar nasal in the contrastive position (e.g. *anc* > *ank* > *aṁk* > *aṅk* > *aṅ*). By systematically accounting for the palatal/velar stop alternation and replacing the preceding nasal by the featurally closest sound homorganic with the following stop, Pāṇini accounts for the alternation of both palatal and velar nasals with *n* and *m.* The Pāṇinian account of final *ṅ,* like Jakobson's (1929) account of Russian soft consonants, recognizes that Sanskrit sounds form a system related to each other by a system of features.

6.1.3 Historical linguistics

Analogous to the fact that generative descriptions of language capture phonological information not available on the surface level, the historical and comparative method captures phonological information not available through synchronic analysis by using diachronic analysis. The phonemic inventory of a language changes through time. In a few rules strikingly reminiscent of the rules of Pāṇini discussed in the previous section,

---

[5]Original penultimate *n* in √*krunc* is excepted from deletion according to the *Kāśikā* on *A.* 3.2.59

Jakobson's (1929) historical explanation of the loss of final vowels after soft consonants allowed him to explain the alternation of hard and soft consonants in Russian systematically by a rule of palatalization before front vowels prior to the loss of the final vowel.

Although diachronic analysis may provide insight into the phonological system of a language, a phonological system is a system which belongs to a particular language, in the narrow sense, that is, to a particular speech community at a particular time. Such a system varies diachronically and geographically. Hence one must distinguish the synchronic phonemic analysis of Sanskrit from the diachronic analysis which attempts to reconstruct the phonemics of Proto-Indic, Proto-Indo-Iranian, or Proto-Indo-European (PIE). The phonemic inventory of these earlier languages differs from that of Sanskrit in a number of respects. In Szemerényi's (1967) reconstruction of PIE (see Table 11), for instance, retroflex sounds are absent, semivowels and vowels occur in complementary distribution, diphthongs are reducible to clusters of simple vowels, which include vowels *e* and *o*, and the consonant inventory includes a laryngeal stop.

In the case of the two marginal phonemes anusvāra and visarga, diachronic analysis interferes with the synchronic analysis of the phonological system of Sanskrit. We noted in §6.1.1 that, in order to show that these phonetic segments are not phonemes, linguists argue that the few examples demonstrating contrastive distribution do not properly belong to Sanskrit *stricto sensu.* Hence, concerning the examples in which *ṣ* occurs in contrast to *ś* and *s,* Vacek (1976, 409) argues, "All these words must be considered as phonological foreignisms which exist in the periphery of the Sanskrit system. In all probability these words were borrowed either from the Prākrits or (via Prākrits or a different OIA dialect) from a non-IA source". He concludes that *ṣ* is not a "genuine Sanskrit phoneme"; "Therefore, the present state of Sanskrit sibilants has to be defined by referring *ṣ* to a foreign subsystem in the language" (1976, 412). Similarly, in order to demonstrate that visarga is not a Sanskrit phoneme, linguists argue that *paspaša, paras-para, uras-ka,* and *vācas-pati* are borrowings from earlier stages of the language, and to demonstrate that anusvāra is not a Sanskrit phoneme, linguists argue that *sam-rāṭ, samyak* (unsuccessfully in these cases), and *amla* are borrowings from lifferent speech communities.

In describing his method of analysis, Vacek (1976, 407) notes, "every language is likely to be composed of two or more [coexistent phonemic] subsystems — some of the subsystems may be foreign, some may be traditionalisms and some may also be dialectal features from a different local or social dialect". He explains that it is typical for written or standard languages to be "composed of more than one phonological layer" resulting from "the leveling of several ... layers".

Now, the methodology of segregating foreign loanwords and detecting the influence of foreign phonological subsystems in a language is sound for attempting to reconstruct the historical predecessors of the language; yet one is completely misled if one understands the results synchronically, in which case it can only be compared to ethnic cleansing. Words with unusual phonological structure are vestiges of other speech communities, just as idioms are vestiges of syntactic structures of an historically prior dialect. Nevertheless, they are present in the language and must be accounted for in the synchronic description of the language. In isolation, segments in loanwords may present one system of contrasts reminiscent of the language from which they were borrowed. Yet to evaluate synchronically the phonological structure of the language which has adopted them, the sounds of the loanword must be compared with that of words in the adopting language. Contrastive and complementary distribution is always with respect to a specific context. The provision in the definition of the phoneme that the sounds belong to the same language in the strictest sense and that differences in style and dialect are not included in the same phonemic system implies the necessity of specifying the boundaries of the language clearly. If the loanwords are included in the language, they must be explained in the same phonological system. If they are considered part of some other language, they must be bracketed. The same clarity of scope is required in framing a phonetic encoding scheme.

6.1.4 Paralinguistic semantics

Another methodolical consideration concerning the scope of phonological contrasts arises in the case of the other marginal phonemes. Prolonged vowels were not considered to be separate phonemes because paralinguistic content was not regarded as semantically contrastive. One of the provisions in the definition of a phoneme was that for sounds in parallel distribution to be contrastive they serve to differentiate semantic content in a narrow sense. Such a segregation of semantic content is somewhat arbitrary. Decisions to exclude paralinguistic information were based on the conventions of the Roman alphabet to represent Northwest European languages. Similar decisions had earlier excluded duration, stress, and pitch from the concept of the phoneme, but these were incorporated when phonologists realized the necessity of extending the idea of contrastive distribution to these linguistic attributes in order to accurately represent the minimally contrastive segments of languages such as tonal languages. A comprehensive phonological system of the language should be able to convey whatever information speech conveys.

It is precisely the purpose of semiotic theory to recognize that communication transcends the arbitrary boundaries of such categorizations. If paralinguistic information had to be separately categorized, a separate phonological system would have to be adopted in order to explain how such information was communicated. It would more likely be simpler to segregate sytems of communicative analysis according to the means of communication, namely, speech, static visual art, or movement — and to include the paralinguistic information conveyed through speech in the criteria for determining the phonological system — than it would be to segregate systems of communicative analysis according to terrains of informational content.

In view of the methodological points discussed in this and the previous section, it is necessary to broaden the conception of a phoneme to tolerate linguistic variation, borrowing, and paralinguistic semantics. A phoneme in such a comprehensive phonological system remains the minimally contrastive phonetic segment in a language on the basis of which one word could be distinguished from another. However, it differs from the strict definition by relaxing its limiting parameters. By a language is meant a specified range of dialects including borrowings, and for sounds in parallel distribution to be contrastive they serve to differentiate a specified range of semantic content. Conventionally in Sanskrit linguistics and critical theory, this semantic content includes paralinguistic content.[6]

[6]For a survey of semantic content included in Pāṇini's *Aṣṭādhyāyī*, including paralinguistic content, see Scharf (2009).

6.1.5 Contrastive segments

Employing the broader concept of a phoneme just described, we reexamine the phonemic status of Sanskrit phonetic segments. A number of sounds which were not phonemic in the narrow sense, are phonemic in the broader sense. Since the semantic content of Sanskrit includes paralinguistic content, trimoraic duration, which conveys some distinction in paralinguistic content, is contrastive and so phonemic. Since contrasts can extend to lexical borrowings, the sounds anusvāra and visarga, which are in contrastive distribution over pairs with borrowings like *samrāṭ* and *vācaspati,* are contrastive and so phonemic. So are the retroflex sounds. Since the language in question ranges over various dialects of Vedic and classical Sanskrit, these dialects merge within that range. Hence the retroflex ळ *ḷ* and ळ्ह *ḷh,* short simple vowels *ĕ* and *ŏ,* slightly lengthened short vowels in the *Vājasaneyisaṁhitā,* the firmer and lighter *y* and *v*, and unreleased stops and semivowels (*abhinidhāna*), which are in complementary distribution only insofar as such dialects are distinguished, are now in contrastive distribution as indices of the paralinguistic semantic information that the utterances in which they occur belong to those different dialects. Likewise, surface accentuation, which is non-contrastive within a particular recitational tradition, is contrastive when set side by side with differently accented text from another recitational tradition within a single language that encompasses both traditions. Similarly, different lengths and syllabifications of anusvāra and nasalized vowels prolonged more than three morae (*raṅga*), which are allophonic within a particular recitational tradition, are contrastive across the single language that encompasses the various traditions. Since the language in question ranges over various genres, including linguistics where dialectal and free phonetic variants are compared side by side, allophones, which are contrastive in that genre (just as allophones in narrow transcription are) become phonemic. Hence jihvāmūlīya, upadhmānīya, and nasal semivowels are phonemic in the comprehensive phonological system. And since the palatal nasal *ñ* in technical terms in linguistic treatises (e. g. *añ, ñit*) occurs in contrastive distribution with *n* and *m,* it is phonemic in the broader sense. Finally, epenthetic nasals (*yama*) and vowels (*svarabhakti*), which are entirely predictable in particular Vedic dialects by rules stated in treatises concerned with those particular dialects, are unpredictable in the broader range of the Sanskrit language, in which the various dialects merge.

On the other hand, a few phonetic segments discussed in the preceding chapter that were not phonemic in the narrow sense of the term are neither phonemic in the broader sense of the term, because they are not contrastive. It is not necessary to distinguish two or three lengths of contrasting svarabhakti vowels, even though the *Caturādhyāyikā* notices a distinction in length and reports an authority that notices a distinction between two different lengths. *Caturādhyāyikā* 1.4.10 describes svarabhakti after an *r* before a spirant followed by a vowel equivalent to half an *a*, or a quarter according to some authorities. *Caturādhyāyikā* 1.4.11 describes a shorter svarabhakti after *r* before another consonant besides a spirant equal to a quarter *a* or an eighth according to the authorities by which the longer svarabhakti is a quarter. Deshpande (1997*b*, 258) argues that the term *sphoṭana* refers to the shorter svarabhakti. The svarabhakti termed *sphoṭana* carries the accent of the previous vowel and does not dismember the consonant cluster according to *Caturādhyāyikā* 1.4.13. There are two issues to address. First, must one distinguish a svarabhakti of length $\frac{1}{8}$ to accomodate the short svarabhakti noticed by the reported authority in addition to two lengths of svarabhakti $\frac{1}{4}$, and $\frac{1}{2}$ noticed by the authors of the *Caturādhyāyikā* itself? Second, are the two lengths distinguished by each authority contrastive? Both questions must be answered in the negative. First, it is not clear that the two authorities offer anything more than two scientific estimates regarding the length of the same epenthetic segments in the same text in the same tradition. There is no independent evidence of two different traditions of recitation that contrast with each other, each of which recites two lengths of svarabhakti. Should such evidence be found, it would serve as grounds to contrast the two traditions, and the svarabhaktis in each tradition would contrast with the svarabhaktis in the other tradition as indices of the broader semantic content that the texts in which they occur belong to distinct traditions. Second, the two distinct lengths of svarabhakti reported by each authority are allophonic, not phonemic. The contexts in which the long svarabhakti occurs (before spirants) are different from the contexts in which the short svarabhakti occurs (i. e. before other consonants), so long svarabhakti does not contrast with short svarabhakti in either tradition. Moreover, it is not clear that the distinction as to whether svarabhakti inherits the accent of the preceding vowel is associated with the length of the svarabhakti as argued by Deshpande. There is no independent evidence that long svarabhakti vowels do not inherit the high or low pitch of the preceding vowel, nor that short svarabhakti vowels are not recited with accumulated (*pracaya*) pitch after a svarita vowel. There is therefore no independent evidence that the term *sphoṭana* applies only to the short svarabhakti as Deshpande argues. It is doubtful that it does and doubtful that the text itself asserts a different behavior regarding accent inheritance. Therefore there is insufficient evidence to establish any contrast between short and long svarabhakti. Should evidence be found to establish such a contrast, of course, it would serve as grounds to recognize short and long svarabhakti as distinct phonemes.

6.1.6 Phoneme in the broader sense

It is clear that the limiting parameters placed on the concept of a phoneme, in the strict and narrow sense, diminish its utility as the sole basis for a single character-encoding scheme for Sanskrit texts. If an encoding scheme is to convey the same information that the language conveys, it should provide the means to distinguish all minimally contrastive segments, insofar as any contrastive information is conveyed by the difference between those segments. And it must include differences in style, dialect, and genre, insofar as these are significant contrasts within the scope of the collection encoded. The corpus of Sanskrit texts includes various dialects of Vedic and classical as well as more varied speech communities such as Buddhist Hybrid Sanskrit (Edgerton, 1970). It includes borrowings from early dialects, Prākrits, substrate languages (cf. Witzel 1999, Hock 1975), and foreign languages. In many cases, the only evidence for such loan words is in the Sanskrit itself. And extant documents indicate paralinguistic semantic content through such devices as prolonged vowels, at least in the Vedic texts. The extended parameters in the concept of a phoneme discussed in sections 6.1.3–6.1.5 are adequate to convey the desired contrasts. Hence the phoneme in the broad sense is suitable to serve as the basis for a single character-encoding scheme for all Sanskrit dialects, borrowings, and linguistic uses.

6.1.7 Contrastive phonologies

Incompatible phonological schemes have been proposed for the description of Sanskrit (see above §5.2). The form in which Sanskrit and Vedic texts have been received in oral recitation as well as in manuscripts and the various scripts and encodings used to transmit Sanskrit texts all adopt — at least implicitly — *some* phonological scheme. The various encodings used to transmit Sanskrit texts are not entirely compatible with one another. Information contained in one phonological scheme cannot necessarily be captured in another. Although we have attempted to devise an encoding that captures all the distinctions made by all the phonological schemes used to describe and transmit Sanskrit, most existing texts do not represent all these distinctions. Most Sanskrit texts do not represent epenthetic nasals (*yamas* and *nāsikya*), unreleased stops and semivowels (*abhinidhāna*), epenthetic vowels (*svarabhakti*), accent, distinctions in the weight of semivowels, and distinctions in types of anusvāra. Where accent is represented, it is often not represented in such a way that one can determine how it is to be mapped onto the range of tones needed to describe the various traditions of Vedic accentuation completely. When information is not provided about epenthetic nasals (*yamas* and *nāsikya*), unreleased stops and semivowels (*abhinidhāna*), epenthetic vowels (*svarabhakti*), accent, semivowel weight, and length of anusvāra, these features should simply be ignored. Since sufficient information is not always available to encode a text with the full repertoire of phonological distinctions required for a completely contrastive description, an encoding scheme must provide defaults to allow the information that *is* provided to be represented, even if that information is less than complete.

In the case of epenthetic sounds (*yamas*, *nāsikya*, and *svarabhakti*), the default is simple: leave them out. In the case of the unusual weight of semivowels, unreleased varieties of stops and semivowels, and accented vowels, in the absence of special information, the normal, clear, unmodified sound will be the default. If a semivowel is not specified as heavy, light, or unreleased, the default semivowel, without specification of special weight will be used. If accent is not specified, the monotone vowel will be used. In such cases the default does not necessarily indicate the lack of the special feature; it merely indicates the absence of information concerning the feature. Only when the text does specify a particular contrastive feature can the default be construed as indicating the lack of that feature.

In the case of anusvāra, it is necessary to encode a unit to represent a default anusvāra unspecified as regards length — in addition to a short, long, heavy, and two-mora anusvāra. Although the *Vājasaneyi-prātiśākhya* (4.149) assigns a length of $\frac{1}{2}$ mora to the short anusvāra it describes as contrasting with a long anusvāra, and the *Ṛkprātiśākhya* (1.34) assigns the same weight of $\frac{1}{2}$ mora to the only anusvāra it approves, it would not be suitable to use the short anusvāra as a default anusvāra, since the *Ṛkprātiśākhya* (13.32–33) reports that other authorities specify the short and long anusvāra as measuring $\frac{1}{4}$ mora and $\frac{3}{4}$ mora respectively. The *Ṛkprātiśākhya* anusvāra is thereby distinguished from both short and long anusvāra. Similarly, it is necessary to encode a system of three accents in addition to the system of four tones and monotone, because many texts indicate three accents without providing any information about which of the four tones are represented. Ancient Indian linguists provide rules of accent sandhi that transform isolated accent into contextual tone. To allow encoding of accent both before and after the application of these rules, it is necessary to adopt both a system of three underlying accents (to capture the pitch distribution before accent sandhi) as well as four surface tones (to capture the pitch distribution after accent sandhi). While the surface tone scheme is required to capture the contrasts of different traditions of pitch distribution after accent sandhi, European scholars have established a tradition of representing Vedic accent utilizing the system of three contrasting pitches belonging to the derivational level at which accent sandhi has not yet applied.

6.2 Higher-order protocols

There are alternatives to creating a single character-encoding scheme for all Sanskrit dialects, borrowings, and linguistic uses. One could use higher-order text-encoding devices to bracket off stretches of text for which the character-encoding scheme was inadequate to distinguish the informational content. Thus one could bracket off different dialects, loanwords, and paralinguistic uses of language by Extensible Markup Language (XML) tags and employ a separate character-encoding scheme for such sequences that was adequate to distinguish the contrasts within it. For example, the unaspirated and aspirated retroflex lateral flaps /ɺ/ and /ɺ^h/ do not occur in Classical Sanskrit; the phonemes /ɖ/ and /ɖ^h/ do. In certain R̥gvedic dialects, unaspirated and aspirated retroflex lateral flaps occur in complementary distribution with [ɖ], [ɖ^h] and hence are allophones of [ɖ], [ɖ^h]. In separate encoding schemes for Classical Sanskrit and for the R̥gvedic dialects, encodings are necessary only for the two phonemes /ɖ/, /ɖ^h/.

In a database that includes passages both in the R̥gvedic dialect and in the Classical Sanskrit dialect, one could tag the passages in one or both of the dialects and apply phonetic rules to produce the contextually appropriate allophones proper to each dialect. For instance, Yāska's *Nirukta*, which is predominantly in the Classical Sanskrit dialect, cites passages in the R̥gvedic dialect. *Nirukta* 3.11 cites *R̥V.* 2.23.9, which contains the word *taḷito* with an intervocalic retroflex lateral flap, Romanized *ḷ*. *Nirukta* 3.11 then cites the linguist Śākapūṇi explaining that *taḷit* refers to lightning in the passage *vidyut taḷid bhavatīti śākapūṇiḥ*. Rather than including both the retroflex lateral flap [ɺ] and [ɖ] in the character encoding, one might tag the text in R̥gvedic dialect and allow special rules to realize /ɖ/ as the retroflex lateral flap [ɺ] in text so tagged. Such a tagging in the latter passage could be achieved as follows:

```
<embed dialect="rv">vidyut taqid bhavati</embed>
iti SAkapURiH
```

Within the tagged dialect portion, intervocalic /ɖ/ will always be realized as the retroflex lateral flap [ɺ]; outside such tags, it will always be realized as [ɖ].

It is not likely that such a system would be practical at the present stage, however, since this encoding would have to be fairly fine-grained, and since we possess insufficient information about dialectal differences and loanwords. We are uncertain, for instance, whether Śākapūṇi writes consistently in R̥gvedic dialect or just cites the single word *taḷit* in R̥gvedic dialect. If the latter, the above demonstration includes too much of the passage within the `<embed>` tag. Moreover the *Nirukta* itself uses the retroflex *ḷ, ḷh* even when not directly citing. Immediately after referring to Śākapūṇi, the *Nirukta* continues, *sā hy avatāḷayati,* using *ḷ* outside R̥gvedic dialect. The text as received makes no mention/use distinction. With the lack of reliable information about the author's dialect, one is forced to accept that [ɖ], [ɖ^{h}] and unaspirated/aspirated retroflex lateral flaps [ɭ], [ɭ^{h}] occur in contrastive distribution. Sequences V*ḷ*V occur in the *Nirukta* external to Ṛgvedic citations and alongside V*ḍ*V, setting [ɖ] and the retroflex lateral flap [ɭ] in contrast; for example, *avatāḷayati* 'strikes down' (3.11) : *lambacūḍaka* 'one having long locks (of hair)' (1.14). Therefore, the unaspirated and aspirated retroflex lateral flaps [ɭ], [ɭ^{h}] occur in contrastive distribution with [ɖ], [ɖ^{h}] not only within the collection comprising all the dialects of Sanskrit, but even in the classical Sanskrit dialect that excludes the Ṛgvedic dialect. Hence all four must be encoded separately at the character level.

Similarly, an encoding of surface accent at the character level must embrace the range of pitches utilized across Vedic schools and dialects because it is not always practical to use higher-order text-encoding devices to bracket off excerpts from the texts of various Vedic schools and dialects. Many texts, especially ritual texts, cite passages from more than one Vedic saṁhitā. One could bracket passages of the *Śākalasaṁhitā* of the *Ṛgveda* and passages of the *Vājasaneyisaṁhitā* of the *Yajurveda* separately in XML tags and employ separate encoding schemes adequate to capture the surface pitch contrasts within each.[7] Yet many ritual texts include passages, which, though accented in accordance with either the system described in the *Ṛkprātiśākhya* or that described in the *Vājasaneyiprātiśākhya*, are untraced to known collections. To be sure higher level text bracketing may be preferrable in instances in which the significance of accentual marks is only known by identifying the text and knowing the accentual system described by a particular phonetic treatise. There are, however, instances in which the accentual system is known, yet the text is unidentified. Such texts lack clear criteria for higher-order tagging. While a character-level surface pitch encoding does require choice of pitch level, it does not commit one to textual identifications for which there is no evidence.

Separately each system described in section 5.2.1 requires the distinction of only three pitches. The system of the *Ṛkprātiśākhya* distin-

---

[7]Neither the *Mādhyandina* nor the *Kāṇva* recension of the *Vājasaneyisaṁhitā* employs the system described in the *Vājasaneyiprātiśākhya* according to which one would expect the vertical line above the high-pitched syllable rather than above the circumflexed syllable, if graphic marks correspond with pitch contours as suggested by Witzel 1974. But several saṁhitās (cf. §3.2) do employ a vertical line above the high-pitched syllable (Mīmāṁsaka, 1964, 12, 21, 25, 42).

guishes between extra-high, high, and low, while the system of Pāṇini and the *Vājasaneyiprātiśākhya* distinguishes between high, low, and extra-low. Although each of the systems of surface accentuation distinguishes only three pitches, a system of surface accentuation that will accommodate contrasts across these systems must distinguish four pitches. A system that captures distinction in pitch across Vedic dialects must therefore distinguish between extra-high, high, low, and extra-low. Consequently, it is necessary to devise a character-encoding scheme adequate to capture phonemic distinctions in the broad sense across all Sanskrit dialects.

Higher-level bracketing does not seem suitable to capture distinctions in various Sanskrit dialects and loan words since there may be insufficient evidence to identify the various dialects and source languages for loan words. There exist, however, phonetic distinctions that are more suitably captured by using higher-level bracketing than by incorporating them in a character encoding based on the phoneme in the broad sense. Higher-level bracketing is appropriate where the phonetic distinction is made only with explicit reference to units at a higher level than the phoneme. For instance, higher-level bracketing is appropriate where the phonetic distinction is made only with reference to lexical items. For example, *Mallaśarmakr̥taśikṣā* 45–46 describes nasalized vowels prolonged to five and six morae. While there is no reason to doubt the phonetic accuracy of the description, there is no need to include the distinction of five- and six-mora lengths in the featural scheme of Sanskrit nor to include nasalized vowels having a length of five or six morae in the broadly phonemic character inventory. Such lengths need not be included because their only occurrence is in the final vowels of particular lexical items. The length of five morae occurs only in the word *mahā,* and the length of six morae occurs only in the word *ati* (*Mallaśarmakr̥taśikṣā* 46). Because the occurrence is lexically specific, the phenomenon is best described lexically, as it was described by the Śikṣā itself. The Śikṣā calls the occurrence of these extra-long nasalized vowels *mahāraṅga* and *atiraṅga,* i.e. the raṅga of *mahā* and the raṅga of *ati.* The defining character of the distinguishing feature seems to be the lexical item rather than the length of the sound. Therefore, we consider it a lexical feature rather than a phonetic one.

It is difficult to capture suprasegmental features such as accent in a segmental encoding; hence, one might choose to utilize higher-order units — in particular syllabic units — to encode accent. One could thus tag syllables and assign accentual features to them. Indian phonetic treatises themselves recognized the syllabic nature of accent. As mentioned in §4.2.2, ancient Indian linguistic treatises recognized that vocalic accent spread to adjacent consonants. Other Indian treatises limited accent to vowels and ignored consonants in accentual rules (*Vyā. Pa.* 33). Yet difficulties would arise in attempting to encode the accent of syllabified visarga and anusvāra. In these cases the techniques of marking accent in Vedic texts are more easily correlated with individual characters. Certain Vedic traditions mark accent of the non-vocalic elements anusvāra and visarga. Such marking, and the oral recitation of the texts, demonstrate that anusvāra and visarga are syllabified. Visarga is syllabified by echoing the preceding vowel or final subsegment of an open diphthong, and anusvāra is syllabified in White Yajurvedic recitation as *gũ*. Yet no vowel belongs in the underlying text and no vowel is written. Since the syllabification is clearly indicated by the marking of accent on the anusvāra and visarga characters and the syllabification can be most reliably inferred from the accent marking, it seems preferable, given the lack of other explicit information about the syllabification of these elements, to include accent in a character encoding.[8] In the purely segmental encoding SLP2, we include characters for high-pitched visarga, low-pitched visarga, and svarita visarga, and for low-pitched anusvāra. We do not, however, include characters for high-pitched and svarita anusvāra. Although the vertical stroke above, used in Devanāgarī script to indicate a svarita in the *Vājasaneyisaṁhitā*, is found above the sign for an anusvāra, it is found there instead of above the sign for the preceding syllable onset and core, unlike the signs for visarga accent, which appear in addition to the vertical stroke above the preceding syllable onset and core, and unlike the horizontal stroke that indicates low pitch, which appears below the sign for anusvāra in addition to below the sign for the syllable onset and core. The vertical stroke above the sign for anusvāra is therefore a graphic transposition that still indicates the accent of the entire syllable,

[8]Phonetic treatises disagree as to whether anusvāra is syllabified. *Varṇaratnapradīpikāśikṣā* 50-51 states that anusvāra is among the group of sounds called *yogavāha* that are devoid of their own accent. Several Śikṣās (e.g. *Keśavīśikṣā* 5, *Taikrtā padyātmikā Śikṣā* 15, *Svarabhaktilakṣaṇapariśiṣṭaśikṣā* 19), in contrast, state that anusvāra is replaced by nasalized *a* when a spirant or *r* follows.

not a distinct accent of the anusvāra. Since the svarita accent of the syllable is encoded by the vowel accent, it would be redundant to encode it again for the anusvāra.

6.2.1 The phonetic encoding schemes

In view of the discussion of criteria in section 6.1 "Criteria for selecting distinctive elements to encode", we have decided not to limit our phonetic encoding scheme to a strictly phonemic one. Rather, by using the concept of a phoneme in the broad sense, we have designed a single scheme capable of showing all the contrastive information in the corpus of Sanskrit texts. The phonetic encoding scheme encodes the segments shown in TABLE 5, described in the notes appended thereunto, and discussed in section 6.1.5 "Contrastive segments". The scheme has three forms called Sanskrit Library Phonetic Basic (SLP1) (see Appendix B), Sanskrit Library Phonetic Segmental (SLP2) (see Appendix C), and Sanskrit Library Phonetic Featural (SLP3) (see Appendix D). In the first, we associate each sound in TABLE 5 with an upper- or lower-case alphabetic Roman character, with the additional use of several other characters from the ASCII set for the aspirated retroflex lateral flap and for modifiers. Modifiers signify alterations of stricture, length, accent, and nasalization. In SLP2 we associate a single codepoint with each sound, including all varieties of stricture, length, accent, and nasalization. In SLP3 we propose a featural encoding of Sanskrit based on Halle's (2000) set of articulatory features described in Table 4.

In view of the discussion of higher-level bracketing in section 6.2 "Higher-order protocols", we include within the scope of the single language encoded all the various dialects of Sanskrit and Vedic as well as loanwords regardless of their source. On the other hand, we limit our encoding to items that contrast by distinctions identified in phonetic terms and exclude items that contrast only in terms of higher-order units such as lexemes. Yet we do maintain the encoding of accent at the character level in spite of its suprasegmental status. By utilizing modifiers to capture the accentual features of Sanskrit sounds, SLP1 encodes the four pitch distinctions necessary for cross-dialect encoding of surface pitch by a numeral ranging from 6 to 9. Pitch contours that combine more than one pitch within a single character are coded by combinations of numerals. For example, the vowel *a* with a dependent circumflex which falls from extra-high to high according to the description in the *Rkprātiśākhya* is coded `a^98`; with the independent circumflex before a high-pitched or circumflexed syllable, `a^97`. As described in the *Vājasaneyiprātiśākhya*, these are coded `a^87` and `a^86` respectively. Contours that include three pitches within a single vowel can be similarly accommodated.

Chapter 7

Script-based encoding

Although discussion so far has focused on sound-based encoding, we note that there are many applications for script-based encoding. Much of the human cultural heritage has been transmitted primarily in written form. Some forms of writing are independent of spoken language (Hyman, 2006), and written and spoken language manifest parallel structures that are partly independent (Weir 1967; Vachek 1973). The typographic form — meaning the visual aspects of written and printed language (Waller, 1988, 5) — conveys information that may need to be encoded in machine-readable documents. Researchers concerned with historical manuscripts, for instance, attend to characteristics such as scribal hands, ink color, abbreviations, letterforms, ductus,[1] margins, and spacing (Kropač, 1991).

A focus on the primacy of spoken language in particular contexts need not, and should not, lead to a denigration of writing. In the 1920s the Soviet psychologist L. S. Vygotsky recognized that writing is both the product of human cognition and an environmental factor that contributes to cognitive development. More adventurously, he argued that the invention of writing led historically to new complexity in human cognition (Vygotskii 2005, 417; Cole, Levitin & Luria 2006, 44–45).[2] The fact

[1]Cf. Skelton 2008, 161.

[2]On the sociogenesis of such complex cultural products as writing see also (Tomasello, 1999, 41–48) and (Damerow, 1996, 316–321).

that human psychology shapes writing, and writing in turn shapes human psychology, he argued, produces a feedback loop that allowed for rapid evolution. Writing is associated with the rise of complex forms of social and cultural organization, the accrual of specific historical knowledge, and the abstract thought that led to the sciences and technologies. The written document allows for increasing distance from the primary act of communication; it "speaks" to an imagined reader, or a generally literate audience. Writing abstracts distinctive features from the *chaine de la parôle,* levels the differences between spoken language dialects (and a fortiori idiolects) (Weir, 1967, 172), and removes many of the context-dependent features of face-to-face interaction.

There is no question that writing contributes to certain elements of cognitive development, and that it has historically been associated with the development of complex social organization and the accrual of specific knowledge. The accrual of specific knowledge itself allows for progress in science and technology. However, the contention that writing is directly responsible for the development of abstract thought in human evolution is speculative at best. Indeed, the opposite may be the case. The reliance on writing may contribute to the deterioration of cognitive ability. In the Phaedrus, Socrates denigrates writing by relating the words of king Thamus of the Egyptian Thebes to the god Theuth when Theuth revealed the art of writing to him. When Theuth promised that it would make the people wiser and improve their memories, king Thamus retorts that it would have the very opposite effect. He says, "it will implant forgetfulness in their souls; they will cease to exercise memory because they rely on that which is written". (Phaedrus 275a.) Specific knowledge inherited through the oral tradition could produce the development of abstract thought just as well as specific knowledge inherited through written means. The development of linguistic sciences in India are evidence against the claim that writing is responsible for the development of the abstract thought that led to the sciences. These sciences developed in oral medium. Pāṇini composed the *Aṣṭādhyāyī* using phonetic, not visual, markers. The oral transmission of Vedic texts spawned the development of mnemonic techniques that led to prodigous feats of memory. To this day students trained in traditional methods know thousands of verses or sūtras by heart. The composition of poetry in early cultures attests to the ability to speak to an imagined reader in the abstract, in the absence of writing.

Although writing cannot claim sole responsibility for producing abstract thought in the history of human cognitive development, nevertheless writing has been the dominant medium for knowledge transmission in the past couple of millenia. Attention to the structure of written language is important to historians, psychologists (Ellis, 1979), and educators. Moreover the study of written language has technological application in optical character recognition (OCR), handwriting recognition, and the design of new media (Rosenberger, 1998). The investigation of written-language structure begins with segmentation. Writing systems give different cues to segmentation at different levels, for instance by punctuation and regularity of spacing, which may be present or absent to varying degrees. Words are delimited in most present-day Western writing, whereas in East Asian writing they are not (nor are they in many premodern Western manuscripts) (Saenger, 1991); printed Sanskrit texts in Devanāgarī lie somewhere in-between, with word separation only where sandhi and the graphotactic structure of the script permit it. Analysis of written language into abstract units called *characters* that are repeated with variable visual features is the basis for most computer processing of language as it is known today. Characters may be discretely realized, as in contemporary English texts, or unsegmented, as in a printed or handwritten Arabic text (Abu-Rabia & Taha, 2006). Handwriting (as well as printing, insofar as its glyphs are imitative of handwritten ones) can be analyzed into units smaller than the character, in particular, "a set of upstrokes and downstrokes ordered in time" (Mermelstein & Eden, 1964, 257). Such a level of analysis takes into account the physical mechanism involved in writing and is capable of identifying units that are invariant, while characters may be realized with infinite variation.

7.1 Featural analysis

Type designers have long recognized that characters can be decomposed into primitive graphic elements (Mohanty, 1998). Albrecht Dürer (1471–1528) designed an alphabet using only ruler and compass construction (Hoenig, 1990). The designers of the Romain du Roi, commissioned by Louis XIV and completed in 1745, "drew up the design of each letter on a strictly analytical and mathematical basis, using as their norm a rectangle subdivided into 2,304 (i.e. 64 times 36) squares" (Steinberg, 1961, 169).[3] These approaches anticipate a rigorous featural analysis of graphemes.

Notwithstanding the pessimism of Vachek (1973, 48)[4] with respect to such efforts, psychologists of visual perception and pattern recognition in the 1960s and 1970s developed schemes for classifying characters of the Latin alphabet by means of distinctive features, akin to those that had become popular in phonology (Gibson 1969, 86–91; Geyer 1970; Laughery 1971; Geyer & DeWald 1973; Massaro 1973; Naus & Shillman 1976; Estes 1978, 171–177; Reed 1978).[5] In addition, the quest for visual features was inspired by the description of processing in the primary visual cortex by Hubel & Wiesel (1968).[6] Gibson (1969, 86–88) gives criteria for establishing a set of distinctive features for an alphabet:

> 1) the features had to be critical ones, present in some members of the set but not in others, so as to present a contrast; 2) they should be relational so as to be invariant under brightness, size, and perspective transformations; 3) they should yield a unique pattern for each grapheme; and 4) the list should be reasonably economical.

Gibson (1969, 88) proposes a set of distinctive features, divided into five classes, for capital letters of the Roman alphabet:

1. *straight:* [± horizontal], [± vertical], [± diagonal /], [± diagonal \]
2. *curve:* [± closed], [± open V], [± open H]
3. *intersection:* [± intersection]
4. *redundancy:* [± cyclic change], [± symmetry]
5. *discontinuity:* [± vertical], [± horizontal]

---

[3] Cf. Morison (1972, 316–317).

[4] Cf. Badecker 1996, 72.

[5] An extension of featural theories is visual grammar theories (Reed, 1978, 145–146, 150–151). A set of attributes used in a visual grammar of the upper-case Roman letters includes {*shaft, leg, arm, bay, closure, weld, inlet, notch, hook, crossing, symmetry, marker*} (Reed, 1978, 146). Cf. Narasimhan & Reddy (1967).

Featural analysis has also been applied to graphic systems other than written language, e. g. children's drawings (Krampen, 1986, 87–88).

[6] See Gibson (1969, 88–89).

Similar sets of features were proposed by Geyer (1970) and Laughery (1971), both of whom made use of computer simulation models; the latter author proposed features to distinguish not only capital letters but also Arabic numerals. The validity of such feature sets can be tested by empirical data for letter confusion errors derived from psychological experiments (Geyer & DeWald, 1973).

These schemes take the form of *feature lists*, that is, essentially unordered sets of features. It is possible also to organize features into trees, which have an inherent geometry, reflecting systemic relations between features (cf. p. 77, above). Tversky (1977, 346) presents a *feature tree* for the lower-case letters (save ⟨w⟩), using the binary features {*curved, arched, vertical, angular, circular, tailed, lŏng, dotted, twisted, forked*}.

In developing her Prosodic Font system, Rosenberger (1998, 41–42) identified five similarity groups for Latin characters: "[t]hose that are constructed as combinations of vertical strokes and circles, those formed of circles left open for some interval (e. g. like a horseshoe) and a vertical line, those constructed of slanted lines, the class of letters that combines elements from the other three, and the letter 's'".[7] Her original system used only four stroke primitives: line, circle, open circle, and *s*. Because of implementation difficulties, a second system added three stroke primitives (dot, curved tail, cross-bar) and recognized two basic principles of stroke positioning: *consecutiveness* vs. *simultaneity* and *dependence* vs. *independence* (Rosenberger, 1998, 43–47).

Analysis of characters in terms of graphic features is important in work on OCR and handwriting recognition (Bansal & Sinha, 2000). In the case of cursive handwriting, general features (both single-valued and multi-valued) may be tested for each column within the word rectangle, e. g.: *projection profile, partial projection profile, upper/lower word profile, background to ink transitions, grayscale invariance, Gaussian smoothing,* and *Gaussian derivatives* (Rath & Manmatha, 2003). "Word spotting" is an information retrieval technique that uses one or more images of a written or printed word as a prototype (or prototypes) to find other tokens of the same word in a set of document images. This approach treats the word as a holistic entity, rather than as a string of graphemes. Gradient, Structural, and Concavity (GSC) features are extracted from the entire word at multiple scales/resolutions. The gradient

[7]Cf. Estes (1978, 175).

features indicate changes in stroke orientation; the structural features indicate the presence of corners as well as diagonal, horizontal, and vertical lines; and the concavity features indicate "bowls" and open cavities (Srihari, Srinivasan, Huang & Shetty, 2006).[8]

In an OCR system for Devanāgarī, characters (together with frequent ligatures) are pre-classified into major categories depending on the position (or absence) of a vertical bar (termed *danda* by the authors) (Govindaraju et al., 2004). Gradients (i. e. the magnitude and direction of intensity changes around the pixels of a digitized image of a character) are thresholded and quantized for a 3 × 3 grid. The resulting feature vector of length 72 forms the input to a neural network with an input layer of 72 perceptrons. The network classifies characters from a blind test set at around 95% accuracy (Govindaraju et al., 2004).[9]

Chinese characters (hanzi/kanji) are traditionally classified (in dictionaries and reference works) on the basis of a number (most commonly 189 or 214) basic elements termed "radicals". In the Rosenberg Graphical System the characters are more conveniently classified according to 22 basic graphical elements, which can be subsumed under five categories of stroke direction: (1) horizontal, (2) vertical, (3) sloping downward to the left, (4) sloping downward to the right, (5) reverse curved down (Barlow, 1995). In OCR of Chinese characters, characters are modeled as a set of linear primitives (Suen, Mori, Kim & Leung, 2003). It is possible analytically to decompose Devanāgarī characters into primitives, but these primitives are non-linear, and no computational technique has been implemented to decompose characters in such a fashion (Kompalli, 2007). Chinese calligraphy recognizes seven or eight basic strokes. A computational implementation demands further distinctions. Thus the Hàn Zì software implemented by Douglas Hofstadter and David Leake in the 1980s required about 40 distinct basic strokes (Hofstadter, 1985, 294).

Donald Knuth's METAFONT system, begun in 1978 in collaboration with Charles Bigelow and Kris Holmes, implements a high-level

[8]Such a computational approach may not be wholly foreign to ways in which humans recognize words. Psychological evidence suggests that parallel to other word-identification processes is a holistic process that is sensitive to salient peripheral features of a word's shape (Beech & Mayall, 2007).

[9]For an elaboration of this model, including reports of word accuracy, see Kompalli (2007).

programming language that can be used to construct font glyphs mathematically. METAFONT allows for the creation of a *family* of fonts, by specifying a fairly large number (about 60) of parameters that determine the particular realization of glyphs. The best known fonts created with METAFONT are Knuth's own Computer Modern fonts, frequently used with TEX. In Indic typography METAFONT was first used to create a Devanāgarī font (NCSD) by Ghosh (1983). Subsequently, Frans Velthuis used METAFONT to create a font *Devanag* (Pandey, 1998) and Charles Wikner employed the software in creating his *Sanskrit* Devanāgarī font (Wikner, 2002).

Douglas Hofstadter in his ingenious 1982 reply to Knuth argues that semantic categories (such as the character ⟨A⟩) are *productive sets* (Hofstadter, 1985, 263). That is, no finite parameterization is capable of specifying all the ways in which a particular character may be graphically realized. Hofstadter understands characters as belonging to a structural system (such as the system of Latin letters) that employs a set of contrasts (thus ⟨p⟩ and ⟨b⟩ differ in the relative position of their "post" and "bowl") (Hofstadter, 1985, 280). Although Hofstadter rejects analysis of letterforms into geometric parts, he allows instead for *conceptual roles* (such as "crossbar", "bowl", "post", "tail") that may be variously realized by particular glyphs. Glyphs are accepted as characters to the degree that they are successful in fulfilling a set of roles. Hofstadter's approach resembles in certain respects prototype theories (Reed, 1978, 153–158).

One potential use of featural analysis is to investigate the history of writing systems. Coding a set of palaeographic characters by means of feature vectors might serve as a preliminary to studies employing the methods of phylogenetic systematics (cladistics) (Skelton, 2008). From the feature vectors, characters for producing a data matrix of the sort that is used in phylogenetic analysis might be extracted. Phylogenetic analysis uses algorithms or optimality criteria to compute an evolutionary tree that describes the relations between taxa. Such categories as scribal hands, documents, or find sites might be chosen as appropriate taxa.

Featural analysis also can model character confusion, as in palaeographic situations when a scribe mistakes one character for a visually similar one. Feature systems can be used to predict the likelihood of particular confusions. By combining a set of graphic features with an edit function such as stepped distance function (SDF), it is possible to compute the orthographic similarity between two strings (Singh, 2006). Because the orthographic syllable is such a salient unit in Indic scripts, analysis of this type has many potential applications in manuscript studies and textual criticism.

7.2 Analysis of Devanāgarī script

We have surveyed a number of attempts to analyze writing at the subgraphemic level. As we move from typographers to psychologists, new media designers, lexicographers, OCR implementors, and cognitive scientists, we see, with shifting goals, shifting levels of analysis. There is no real consensus on what meaningful distinctions to draw below the level of the grapheme. This situation is in contrast to that obtaining in phonology, where — although there is disagreement about particular features and about issues such as whether articulatory or acoustic features are more relevant; or whether *n*-ary, and not just binary, features should be adopted — there is a consensus that speech sounds can be understood in terms of sets of distinctive features (Jakobson et al., 1963; Chomsky & Halle, 1968; Ladefoged, 1971; Halle, 1983; Clements, 1985; Clements & Hume, 1995).

Although in most writing systems there is normally no correlation between graphic and phonetic features, we do occasionally find such a correlation. ⟨p⟩ and ⟨b⟩ differ in only one visual feature, while /p/ and /b/ differ only in the feature [± voice]. Similarly, ⟨b⟩ and ⟨d⟩ differ only in one visual feature, while /b/ and /d/ differ only in place of articulation. Such distinctions appear to emerge synchronically in a process of "re-signification". The parallelisms do not hold for letterforms such as {⟨B⟩, ⟨D⟩, ⟨P⟩} (from which the lower-case forms developed) or a fortiori {⟨𝔅⟩, ⟨𝔇⟩, ⟨𝔓⟩} or {⟨B⟩, ⟨Δ⟩, ⟨Π⟩}.

Historically, we know or suspect that certain characters were derived from others. Thus in Brāhmī, characters for aspirated stops are derived from characters for unaspirated stops (Dani, 1963). Sometimes the character for the aspirated stop is formed by completing part of the shape of the character for the homorganic unaspirated stop, as in 𑀙 ⟨cha⟩ < 𑀘 ⟨ca⟩ and 𑀞 ⟨ṭha⟩ < 𑀝 ⟨ṭa⟩. In other cases an extra "curlicue" is added, as in 𑀠 ⟨ḍha⟩ < 𑀟 ⟨ḍa⟩ and 𑀨 ⟨pha⟩ < 𑀧 ⟨pa⟩. The derivational relationship may still be evident in Devanāgarī, where ⟨प⟩ and ⟨फ⟩ represent /p/ and /pʰ/

respectively, which differ only in [± aspirated]; ⟨ब⟩ and ⟨व⟩ represent /b/ and /w/, which are both non-syllabic voiced segments with labial articulation;[10] and ⟨भ⟩ and ⟨म⟩ represent /bʰ/ and /m/, which differ only in the values of [± aspirated, ± nasal]. Moreover, the four retroflex non-nasal stop characters ⟨ट⟩, ⟨ठ⟩, ⟨ड⟩, and ⟨ढ⟩ all share the graphic feature of a round bottom. Graphic similarity, however, is by no means always correlated with phonetic similarity, and Devanāgarī has several close graphical pairs corresponding to sounds that are not especially similar, such as य ⟨ya⟩ and थ ⟨tha⟩, प ⟨pa⟩ and ष ⟨śa⟩, भ ⟨bha⟩ and झ ⟨jha⟩.

7.3 Component analyses of Devanāgarī script

In *A Grammar of the Sanskrīta Language* (1808) Charles Wilkins included an engraved plate entitled "The Elements of the Devanagari Character". The plate presents the strokes and combinations of strokes used to build up characters ordered according to the traditional *varṇamālā* sequence. Strokes or combinations that have been previously introduced are not repeated. In this scheme the Devanāgarī characters are reduced to 55 "elements", ranging in complexity from a vertical bar to the entire character ॠ (save the *śirorekhā*). The analysis is clearly based on calligraphic technique, and the aim is pedagogical. There is no attempt to reduce shared stroke combinations rigorously to a minimal set of component strokes.[11]

A more rigorous approach is adopted in the linguistic survey of Ivanov & Toporov (1968). A set of 21 binary distinctive features, each corresponding to a graphic component, is posited for the graphemes of Devanāgarī (see TABLE 13). The authors note that the scheme is provisional, and no empirical evaluation of the feature set is attempted. They observe moreover that certain features are always expressed, whereas

[10] In some ancient dialects /w/ was realized as labiodental /ʋ/ (*Pāṇinīyaśikṣā* 18), and in modern pronunciations it is sometimes realized as a bilabial fricative [β] (a sound that differs from [b] only in the feature [± continuant]).

[11] Hock (n.d.) presents an analysis along similar lines, also intended for pedagogical application. Character components fall into four groups: (a) straight lines (5), (b) circles and curlicues (7), (c) dots (2), (d) other shapes (24). Several components are given in variant forms. We thank Hans Hock for sharing these materials with us.

others are neutralized in the allograph demanded by a particular graphic context.

At the Indian National Centre for Software Technology (NCST) in the mid 1980s, R. K. Joshi identified a basic set of 55 graphic primitives that could be combined to create the skeletons of basic Devanāgarī characters. His analysis was used in the context of *Vinyas*, a digital type design system collaboratively created at NCST (Parida, 1993). Primitives include horizontal lines (2), vertical lines (2), diagonal lines (4), circles of different sizes (4), quarter circumferences (9), half circumferences (11), various additional curves (22), and a dot (FIGURE 7.1).[12] Joshi noted that the basic set of primitives could be considerably reduced by applying command tags to primitives when selecting them for character construction. Such command tags include *extend, extract, mirror x/y axis, repeat, condense, flip, and rotate.* Joshi also noted that his component analysis has a predecessor in the standard orthographic pedagogy introduced in primary education under British rule in the late nineteenth century. An attempt was made to provide a series of primitive elements of Devanāgarī script for students to copy and then combine following similar pedagogical techniques used for Roman script.

Also in the 1980s Pijush K. Ghosh, in designing his NCSD font (cf. p. 107, above), undertook a "Stroke Analysis and Synthesis" of Devanāgarī, in which primitives were identified and rules for composing complete characters from the primitives were specified. Ghosh suggested that such a method might lead in the future to "Syntactic Letter Form Generation", in which glyph shapes could be specified using a context-free grammar (Ghosh, 1983, 47).[13] Ghosh identified a Pattern Primitive Set (PPS) with 48 elements. His aims were to identify primitives that were simple enough to be concatenated algorithmically and to minimize the size of the PPS. Despite the systematic aspect of such an approach, Ghosh acknowledged that the selection of any such set must involve subjective factors.

---

[12] The late R. K. Joshi kindly granted us permission to reproduce this drawing.

[13] Cf. Narasimhan & Reddy (1967).

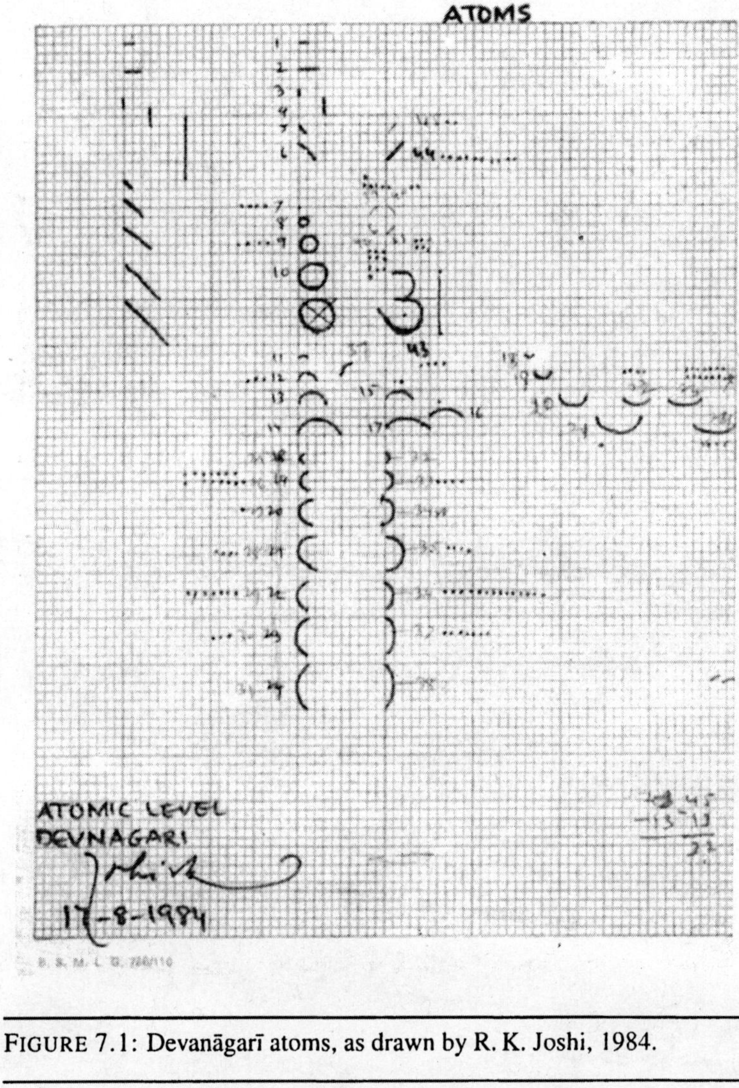

FIGURE 7.1: Devanāgarī atoms, as drawn by R. K. Joshi, 1984.

Chapter 8

Conclusions

Although computers manipulate linguistic and textual data in sophisticated ways, current encoding systems reflect orthographic design factors to the exclusion of more relevant information-processing principles. Even the most recent standardized encoding systems reproduce deficiencies inherent in the traditional orthographies themselves. These traditional orthographies have undergone a long history of adaptation in technologies for the visual representation of language. Beginning with styli, brushes, etc., and continuing with the invention of movable type, machine typesetting, the typewriter, remote transmission by means of teletype machines, the invention of standardized computer encodings from ASCII to Unicode, right up to the desktop publishing revolution, each stage in technological development represents language visually. Yet display is only one of numerous functions that computers now perform. Computers exchange textual data over space and time and perform linguistic processing, such as spell-checking, machine translation, content analysis and indexing, and morphological and syntactic analysis. Therefore display for a human reader should no longer be considered the primary determinant of an encoding scheme. Rather, language should be encoded in such a way as to facilitate automatic processing, to minimize extrinsic ambiguity and redundancy, and to ensure longevity. To avoid ambiguity and redundancy requires that an encoding system be characterized by a one-to-one correspondence between characters and items to be encoded, and that all encoded items be of the same kind.

Text-processing technology arose in the English-speaking world and assumed as a norm the use of the Roman alphabet with few or no diacritics. Adaptation to some non-European scripts required considerable effort and compromise. The adaptation of Roman script itself required the use of a number of diacritics to represent the phonology of non-European languages accurately. The greatest challenge remains the application of encoding principles to the representation of non-European languages. Sanskrit, the primary culture-bearing language of India, with its enormous body of literature, strong oral tradition, and highly developed linguistics presents a particularly appropriate case for study.

The encoding schemes used for Sanskrit are based primarily either upon Devanāgarī script or upon the standard Romanization of Sanskrit. The difficulties with these schemes are due in part to problems in the modes of graphic representation of Sanskrit sounds adopted in the scripts themselves. Both depart from one-to-one correspondence between characters and items to be encoded and from consistency in the type of encoded item. Devanāgarī employs redundancy in the representation of phrase-initial and post-vocalic vowels, and an inversion in the graphic representation of phonetic elements in its representation of /a/. Romanization employs digraphs for the representation of aspirate stops and open diphthongs. Both employ digraphs for the representation of the aspirated retroflex lateral flap /ḷ^{h}/. The duplicate use of a sign used to represent an aspirate segment additionally to represent the feature of aspiration, and the use in Romanization of *a, i,* and *u* to represent phonetic segments as well as subsegments of diphthongs, garners inconsistency in the type of item represented and therefore introduces ambiguity. Or, if it avoids ambiguity by using the diaeresis over the second of two vowels, Romanization still suffers from redundancy in the representation of the vowels *i* and *u*. Encoding standards for Sanskrit that are based on Devanāgarī or Romanization inherit the deficiencies inherent in the underlying scripts. They suffer from ambiguity and redundancy by departing from a one-to-one correspondence and by inconsistency in the basis for encoding.

Clear principles of encoding require determining the location of the encoding in the space defined by three axes: graphic–phonetic, synthetic–analytic, and contrastive–non-contrastive. One must determine whether to encode written characters or speech sounds, segments or features, and what criteria to use to contrast items. Since information degradation arises at each stage in representation of knowledge, it is felicitous to encode the primary medium of knowledge transmission. Given that script is inherently a secondary phenomenon vis-à-vis spoken language, encoding should be based directly on spoken language. Devanāgarī script itself was not specifically designed to represent Sanskrit phonology, but rather was adapted to this use subsequently; hence it is not surprising that it proves to be a less appropriate basis for encoding Sanskrit than Sanskrit phonology itself.

Few of the world's writing systems were designed for the languages that they represent in extant texts. Most were adapted, and adaptations almost always fail to capture the structure of the spoken language adequately. Therefore, in general, where one has access to the phonology of the language, where the orthography is fairly shallow, and where the standard orthography departs from an ideal coding of spoken language structure, the basis for text encoding should be phonetic rather than graphic. Sanskrit meets these conditions, and so it is better to encode Sanskrit speech sounds directly than to encode the secondary representations of those sounds in Devanāgarī, Roman, or any other script. Directly coding Sanskrit speech sounds will solve the problems of ambiguity and redundancy that we have noted in our survey of current encoding schemes.

Spoken language has a temporal dimension, and scripts that represent spoken language have a linear dimension that corresponds to the temporal dimension of spoken language. The minimal independent unit in the chain of speech is the phonetic segment or phone. The minimal independent unit in script is the graphic segment or graph. A segmental linguistic encoding is based upon minimal phonetic or graphic segments. Yet both phonetic and graphic units may be decomposed into systems of features orthogonal to this dimension of segmentation and not necessarily coterminous with the minimal units of segmentation. Phonetic units may be decomposed into a set of acoustic or articulatory features that are realized simultaneously. Similarly, writing may be analyzed into graphic features. Although the boundaries between phonetic and graphic segments are sites of marked alterations in phonetic and graphic features, each feature may independently be associated with a string of one or more phonetic or graphic segments. Encodings may be entirely segmental, at one pole of the synthetic–analytic axis, or entirely featural at the other. For Sanskrit, we have devised an entirely segmental phonetic encoding (SLP2) (see Appendix C), an encoding based entirely on articulatory features (SLP3) (see Appendix D), and a phonetic encoding that utilizes both segmental and featural units, while remaining clear about which is which (SLP1) (See Appendix B. The features in SLP1 are indicated by modifiers described in section B.3).

All modes of information storage and transmission presuppose a selection of relevant information. The selection of the set of distinctions to be encoded depends upon the nature of the textual corpus and the information of interest to its users. Encoding requires classifying items, identifying items within each class by ignoring irrelevant distinguishing information, and designating each class by unique identifiers. A linguistic transcription of speech ignores non-linguistic information such as absolute tempo and pitch; a linguistic copy of a manuscript ignores absolute line thickness and character height. An encoding assigns codepoints to units that have significant contrasts. Yet a segmental phonetic encoding of a corpus of Sanskrit texts for a general scholarly community cannot limit itself to the narrow concept of a phoneme as the distinctive segment to be encoded, even with its recent extension to include distinctions in duration, stress, and pitch. Typically, phonemes are the minimally contrastive segments of sound in a language, on the basis of the contrast between which lexical and grammatical distinctions can be made. But a comprehensive phonological system of the language should be able to convey whatever information speech conveys. Contrastive and complementary distribution is always with respect to a specific context. If one stretches two parameters in the typical definition of a phoneme, the modified concept may serve as a suitable basis for a phonetic encoding: (1) The language must collapse within its bounds diachronic differentiation, regional dialects, and stylistic strata. (2) The range of the semantic content that contrastive sounds are required to differentiate must include paralinguistic semantics.

It is necessary to broaden the concept of a phoneme to comprise linguistic variation, borrowing, and paralinguistic semantics. A phoneme in such a comprehensive phonological system remains the minimally contrastive phonetic segment in a language on the basis of which one word could be distinguished from another. It differs, however, from the strict definition by relaxing its limiting parameters. A language then refers to a specified range of dialects, including borrowings. And for sounds in parallel distribution to be contrastive, they serve to differentiate a specified range of semantic content, including paralinguistic content. We have employed the broader conception of a phoneme to classify Sanskrit sounds as distinctive in our phonetic encodings. We utilize the SLP1 encoding for the storage of a corpus of Sanskrit texts in our digital Sanskrit library and for linguistic processing. We transcode to a variety of Indic scripts and Romanization in Unicode for display purposes and employ various meta-transliterations, Indic Unicode, as well as clickable input keyboards for data input.

8.1 Dynamic transcoding

By storing text in a single underlying format that maximizes fidelity to the phonetic representation of the spoken language, we allow for extreme flexibility in display and input options. Text stored in a single underlying representation may easily be displayed in Devanāgarī, Roman transliteration, phonetic transcription (e. g., that of the IPA), or one of the regional scripts of India. Likewise, text entered and viewed in Roman transliteration or one of the Indic scripts may be transcoded and processed in the underlying phonetic format. Rules for translating the underlying format to one of the surface representations (typically encoded as Unicode) can be implemented with finite state transducers (Huet, 2005). We have developed a number of model transcoders using `lex` (Kernighan & Pike, 1984) and similar scanner generators (which generate deterministic finite automata). Philosophically, such an approach is satisfying, since it conceives of written Sanskrit as a rule-based transformation from an underlying level that corresponds in some sense to speech. Practically, it is very useful to be able to display the same stretch of Sanskrit text in multiple ways; this possibility allows one to reach multiple audiences, including beginning students (who cannot yet read an Indic script), and Indian scholars, whether pandits or amateurs, who are used to using an Indic script other than Devanāgarī.

The Sanskrit Library has deployed a full set of transcoding routines written in Java that allow Sanskrit text encoded in SLP1 to be displayed in most major Indic scripts (Bengali, Devanagari, Gujarati, Gurmukhi, Kannaḍa, Malayalam, Oriya, or Telugu), standard Romanization, or any of several popular encodings (Kyoto-Harvard, wx, ITRANS, etc.), depending upon user preference. Data-entry, and the display of entered text, is likewise available in numerous formats based upon user preference. Clickable input keyboards provide data-entry for those unfamiliar with any of the available encodings. A transcoding page also allows users to enter short passages or upload files for transcoding. Although pre-existing encodings generally capture less information than ours, the Sanskrit Library has developed automatic and machine-assisted facilities for conversion of prior and legacy data into the Sanskrit Library Phonetic encodings.

It would also be easy to develop additional input modes that can be used with the encoding schemes. These input modes could be customized for the needs of different users: e.g., Western scholars used to dealing with Sanskrit in Romanization, Indians accustomed to differing regional keyboard layouts, and scholars accustomed to legacy schemes.[1] Suitable input methods can also be developed for devices with alternative input hardware, such as pen computers, PDAs, and mobile phones (Shanbhag, Rao & Joshi 2002; Gupta 2006).[2] In cases where input methods are being developed for users who are not already accustomed to existing methods, attention should be paid to ergonomic factors such as finger travel, error rate, typing speed, cognitive load, and learning curve.

8.2 Text-to-speech and speech-recognition

The discussion of transcoding between data-input, linguistic processing, and display formats in the context of phonetics raises questions concerning text-to-speech software and phonetic input methods. Text-to-speech software and phonetic input methods are designed on the basis of the sound structure of language, rather than on the traditional visual presentation of language. The phonetic encodings described here, particularly the featural encoding (SLP3), may serve as a starting point for develope-

[1] QWERTY keyboards are not well-adapted to Indic script typing, especially for Indian users who are not familiar with English and English keyboard layouts. New hardware addresses these challenges (Joshi et al., 2004).

[2] As of March 2010, India had about 545 million mobile phone users. Source: <https://www.cia.gov/library/publications/the-world-factbook/geos/in.html>.

ment of a correlation between acoustic parameters and encoded units and thereby set the foundation for this promising area of research.

8.3 Higher-level encoding

The present book has focused on issues of character-encoding with particular reference to Sanskrit. Yet accurate and comprehensive character-encoding merely lays the foundation for digital linguistic and philological research. Once the machine-readable text is available in a consistent form, it is possible to encode linguistic and literary information of the language and the text. Linguistic encoding captures morphological, syntactic, and semantic information in the language. Literary encoding captures textual metadata and facets of artistic appreciation such a poetic figures and sentiments.

Formal and computational linguistics was dominated by English at its inception and developed in subsequent decades primarily in the environment of European languages. More recently there has been a concerted effort to undertake formal linguistic analysis of a wide variety of languages, with particular interest in those with dramatically different features, and to enrich linguistic theory to account for linguistic variety. In spite of this effort, analytic structures and procedures utilized in formal linguistics remain dominated by those invented for, and most suitable for, English and other European languages. Linguistic theory remains unduly weighted in favor of European languages even as their extension to the variety of the world's languages involves undue complication thereby revealing their inadequacy in representing language universally. It would prove particularly useful in developing universally adequate linguistic theory to investigate sophisticated linguistic theories, structures, and procedures developed to describe languages of a very different character from English.

India developed an extraordinarily rich linguistic tradition over more than three millennia that remains under-appreciated and under-investigated. A cursory glance at the long tradition of discussion and argumentation within and between Indian sciences of phonetics (*śikṣā*), grammar (*vyākaraṇa*), logic (*nyāya*), ritual exegesis (*karmamīmāṁsā*), and literary theory (*alaṅkāraśāstra*) reveals that Indian linguistic traditions have much to offer contemporary linguistic theory in the areas of phonetics, morphology, syntax, and semantics. The current book drew heavily from the first. The tradition of grammar (*vyākaraṇa*) offers interesting modes of morphological and syntactic analysis that may prove to be more suitable to highly-inflected free-word-order languages than methods employed in contemporary computational frameworks. The traditions of grammar, logic (*nyāya*), ritual exegesis (*karmamīmāṁsā*), and literary theory (*alaṅkāraśāstra*) offer various competing intricate theories of verbal comprehension. These Indian linguistic traditions might contribute useful insights to contemporary formal linguistics.

Indian linguistic theories can be formalized and implemented computationally. Research to work out the details of Indian semantic and syntactic theory could contribute to contemporary research at the semantics-syntax interface where computational linguistic work is flourishing. The authors' current work draws upon major semantic and syntactic treatises in the Indian grammatical tradition and contemporary techniques of formalization and computational implementation to bring ancient Indian theories face to face with contemporary computational linguistic work. On the one hand, we articulate Indian theories in contemporary terms and offer a critique and insights useful to contemporary linguists. On the other hand, we suggest ways of modeling ancient Indian theories computationally. The latter will allow computational modeling to clarify those ancient theories and assist in answering difficult questions regarding their principles and historicity. Implementing Indian theories of morphology, syntax, and semantics computationally requires working out methods to encode the categories and distinctions articulated in these theories. Research that compares the Indian theories with contemporary theories requires correlating the encodings of Indian linguistic categories with traditional European categories. We hope to develop these higher-level linguistic encoding schemes and to utilize them in the creation of tagged corpora for linguistic research.

XML has emerged as the standard method of implementing higher-level encoding in digital texts. The Text-Encoding Initiative (TEI) has developed standards for encoding metadata of digital texts in XML, and for encoding various literary aspects of texts. Investigation of the categories and distinctions of sentiments (*rasa*) and literary figures (*alaṅkāra*) in the Indian traditions of literary criticism and artistic appreciation (*alaṅkāraśāstra*, *nāṭyaśāstra*) remains a fruitful field for future research.

Appendices

Appendix A

Tables

A.1 Phonetic features

TABLE 1 shows the structure of phonetic features that serve to characterize and contrast the phonetic segments of Sanskrit. The authors selected the phonetic features shown after examining the sets of features described in ancient Indian phonetic treatises including those of Āpiśali, Śaunaka, and others. These features include both place of articulation and stricture features as well as length and pitch, which have often been excluded from the discussion of features. Place of articulation features do not include nasal, although both Āpiśali and Śaunaka include this feature. On the other hand, stricture features include some of the finer distinctions described by Āpiśali. Recent universal linguistic featural systems devised by Halle and Clements, utilize articulatory and stricture features as their primary elements respectively.

TABLE 1: Phonetic features

I. place of articulation
- A. guttural
- B. velar
- C. palatal
- D. retroflex
- E. dental
- F. labial

II. manner of articulation (stricture)
- A. contacted
- B. slightly contacted
- C. slightly open
- D. open
    - 1. simply open (*saṁprasāraṇa*)
    - 2. more open (*guṇa*)
    - 3. most open (*vṛddhi*)

III. voicing [±]

IV. aspiration [±]

V. nasalization [±]

VI. length
- A. half
- B. short
- C. slightly long
- D. long
- E. protracted 3
- F. protracted 4+

VII. underlying pitch
- A. none
- B. high
- C. low
- D. circumflex

VIII. surface tone
- A. extra low
- B. low
- C. high
- D. extra high

A.2 Sounds categorized by Āpiśali

TABLE 2 shows the structure of phonetic features described by the ancient Indian phonetician Āpiśali. Most conspicuously, Āpiśali explicitly describes the active articulators of sounds (II), anticipating the approach adopted by the contemporary phonologist Morris Halle. Āpiśali characterizes nasals by including a nasal place of articulation ([I]G) and includes a full set of stricture distinctions including five degrees of openness ([III]A4). The extrabuccal features that are associated with the glottis ([III]B1) imply particular features of the larynx ([III]B2), which in turn imply voice features ([III]B3). Implications are represented by right arrows (→). To the right of each feature in parentheses are shown the phonetic segments to which the feature belongs. Āpiśali attributes the feature *dorsolingual* only to the jihvāmūlīya ([I]B), while Śaunaka associates it with several sounds (TABLE 3 [I]B).

Notes:

1. *ṅñṇnm* have a secondary place of articulation in the nose.
2. *e ai* gutturo-palatal.
3. *o au* gutturo-labial.
4. *v* dento-labial.
5. *ĕŏ* in Sātyamugri and Rāṇāyanīya *Sāmaveda* (*ĀŚ*. 6.9).
6. *ḹ* in imitation of proper names (*ĀŚ*. 6.6).

TABLE 2: Sounds categorized according to phonetic features by Āpiśali

- I. place of articulation
  - A. guttural (*akkhgghṅ*[1] *hḥeai*[2] *ȯau*[3])
  - B. dorsolingual (*ẖ*)
  - C. palatal (*icchjjhñ*[1] *yśeai*[2])
  - D. coronal (*r̥ṭṭhḍḍhṇ*[1] *rṣ*)
  - E. dental (*l̥tthddhn*[1] *lsv*[4])
  - F. labial (*upphbbhm*[1] *ḫ v*[4] *oau*[3])
  - G. nasal (*ṁk̃k̃hg̃g̃hṅñṇnm*)
- II. articulator
  - A. tongue
    - 1. root (dorsolingual)
    - 2. middle (palatal)
    - 3. undertip (coronal)
    - 4. tip (dental)
  - B. throat (guttural)
  - C. lips (labial)
  - D. nose (nasal)
- III. manner of articulation
  - A. buccal: stricture
    - 1. contacted (stops, yamas)
    - 2. slightly contacted (*yrlv*)
    - 3. slightly open (*śṣsḥẖḫhṁ*)
    - 4. open (vowels)
      - a. simply open (*iur̥l̥*)
      - b. more open (*eo*)
      - c. even more open (*aiau*)
      - d. most open (*ā*)
      - e. close (*a*)
  - B. extrabuccal (1 → 2 → 3)
    - 1. glottis
      - a. spread (→ 2a, 8b) (low pitched vowels, *kcṭtp khchṭhthphśṣsḥẖḫk̃ k̃h*)
      - b. constricted (→ 2b, 8a) (high-pitched vowels, *gjḍdbghjhḍhdhbhyr lvhṁg̃g̃h*)
    - 2. larynx
      - a. breath (→ 3–) (= 1a)
      - b. sound (→ 3+) (= 1b)
    - 3. voice [+/–] (= 1b) / (= 1a)
    - 4. aspiration [+/–] (*khchṭh thphśṣsḥẖḫk̃hghjhḍhdh bhhṁg̃h*) / (*kcṭtpk̃gjḍd byrlvg̃ṅñṇnm*)
    - 5. nasalization [+/–] (*ṅñṇn mãĩũr̥̃l̥̃ẽaĩõaũỹl̃ṽ* / (others)
    - 6. breath impact
      - a. iron (stops, yamas)
      - b. wood (semivowels)
      - c. wool (spirants, vowels)
    - 7. length
      - a. short (*aiur̥l̥ĕŏ*[5])
      - b. long (*āīūr̥̄l̥̄*[6] *eaioau*)
      - c. protracted
    - 8. relative pitch (vowels)
      - a. high
      - b. low
      - c. circumflex (→ 8a, 8b)

A.3 Sounds categorized by Śaunaka

TABLE 3 Shows the structure of phonetic features described by Śaunaka. Most conspicuous is Śaunaka's inclusion of an intermediate feature of glottal aperture ([III]C), only recently recognized as accurate by modern phoneticians, and his discussion of the material of sounds (V), which the three dispositions of glottal aperture imply (as indicated by the arrow). Also significant is Śaunaka's recognition of the implication of vocal fold disposition (IV) on pitch ([VI]E). Like Āpiśali (see TABLE 2), Śaunaka utilizes a full set of places of articulation including a nasal place of articulation ([I]G). In contrast to Āpiśali's full set of stricture features ([III]A), he includes only three manners of articulation (II).

TABLE 3: Sounds categorized according to phonetic features by Śaunaka

- I. place of articulation
  - A. guttural (*ahḥ*)
  - B. dorso-lingual (*r̥l̥kkhgghṅẖ*)
  - C. palatal (*ieaicchjjhñyś*)
  - D. coronal (*ṭṭhḍḍhṇṣ*)
  - E. dental (*tthddhnrls*)
  - F. labial (*uoaupphbbhmvḫ*)
  - G. nasal (*ṁk̃k̃hg̃g̃hh̃*)
- II. manner of articulation
  - A. non-continuously contacted (stops, yamas)
  - B. slightly contacted (*yrlv*)
  - C. continuously open (vowels, *h śṣsḥẖḫṁ*)
- III. glottal aperture
  - A. open (→ V[A])
  - B. closed (→ V[B])
  - C. between (→ V[C])
- IV. disposition of vocal folds
  - A. stretching (→ VI[E1])
  - B. slack (→ VI[E2])
  - C. tossing (*ākśepa*) (→ VI[E3])
- V. material
  - A. breath (unvoiced segments: *kcṭtpkhchṭhthphk̃k̃hśṣsḥẖḫ ṁ*)
  - B. sound (voiced unaspirated segments: *gjḍdbg̃ṅñṇnmyr lv;* vowels)
  - C. both (voiced aspirates and spirant: *ghjhḍhdhbhg̃hh*)
- VI. other features
  - A. voice [+/−] (*gjḍdbg̃ṅñṇnm yrlvghjhḍhdhbhg̃hh*) / *kcṭt pkhchṭhthphk̃k̃hśṣsḥẖḫṁ*
  - B. aspiration [+/−] (*khchṭhthph k̃hśṣsḥẖḫṁghjhḍhdhbhgh h*) / (*kcṭtpk̃gjḍdbyrlvg̃ṅñṇ nm*)
  - C. nasalization [+/−] (*ṅñṇnmãĩ ũr̥̃l̥̃ẽaĩõaũỹṽl̃*) / (others)
  - D. length in moras
    - 1. $\frac{1}{4}$ (short *svarabhakti*)
    - 2. $\frac{1}{2}$ (consonants, *ṁ*, long *svarabhakti*)
    - 3. 1 (*aiur̥l̥'*)
    - 4. 2 (*āīūr̥̄l̥̄eaioau*)
    - 5. 3 (protracted vowels)
  - E. relative pitch (vowels)
    - 1. high
    - 2. low
    - 3. circumflex

A.4 Sounds categorized after Halle et al.

TABLE 4 shows the Sanskrit sounds categorized according to the articulatory feature geometry described recently by Halle et al. (2000). Articulators and features are reorganized in the order generally presented by Indian phonetic treatises: articulators from back to front followed by articulator-free features. The higher nodes Place and Guttural, and the root node are ignored.

TABLE 4: Sounds categorized using phonetic features of Ḥalle et al.

I. articulators
   A. Larynx (Glottis)
      1. [glottal] (*hḥ*)
      2. [constricted glottis] (**not used**)
      3. [spread glottis] (aspirates: *khghchjhṭhḍhthdhphbh*; spirants: *śṣ s h ḥ ẖ ḫ ṁ*)
      4. [stiff vocal folds] (high-pitched and circumflexed vowels; unvoiced consonants: *kkh cchṭṭhtthpphśṣsḥẖḫ*)
      5. [slack vocal folds] (low-pitched and circumflexed vowels; voiced consonants: *gghj jhḍḍhddhbbhṅñṇnmhṁ ḷḷhlĺryỹvṽ*)
   B. Tongue Root (**not used**)
      1. [radical]
      2. [retracted tongue root]
      3. [advanced tongue root]
   C. Soft Palate
      1. [rhinal] (anusvāra, yamas, nāsikya: *ṁk̃k̃hg̃g̃hh̃*)
      2. [nasal] (anusvāra, yamas, nāsikya: *ṁk̃k̃hg̃g̃hh̃*; nasal stop, vowels, semivowels: *ṅñṇnmãĩũr̥̃ l̥̃ẽaĩõaũỹṽl̃*)
   D. Tongue Body
      1. [dorsal] (*kkhgghṅẖ*; vowels: *aiueoaiau*)
      2. [back] (*auo*)
      3. [high] (*iu*)
      4. [low] (*a*)
   E. Tongue Blade
      1. [coronal] (*cchjjhñṭṭhḍḷ ḍhḷhṇtthddhnrlĺyỹśṣs*)
      2. [+ anterior] (*tthddhnlĺs*)
      3. [− anterior]
         a. [+ distributed] (*cchjjh ñyỹś*)
         b. [− distributed] (*ṭṭhḍḷ ḍhḷhṇrṣ*)
   F. Lips
      1. [labial] (*uoaupphbbhmv ṽḫ*)
      2. [rounded] (*uoauvṽ*)

II. articulator-free features
   A. [+ consonantal] (cavity)
      1. [+ sonorant] (no pressure)
         a. [+ lateral] (lateral resonants: *ḷḷhlĺ*)
         b. [− lateral] (nasal stops: *ṅñṇnm;* approximant: *r*)
      2. [− sonorant] (pressure)
         a. [+ continuant] (spirants: *ẖśṣsḫ*)
         b. [− continuant] (non-nasal stops)
      3. [suction] (**not used**)
      4. [strident] (**not used**)
   B. [− consonantal] (no cavity) (glides: *yỹvṽ;* vowels; *hḥṁ*)

A.5 Sanskrit phonetics

TABLE 5 shows Sanskrit phonetic segments categorized according to the features in TABLE 1. Place of articulation features appear in the leftmost column. Stricture appears in the third row of headings with subcategories of vowel stricture in the fourth row. The subcategories of vowel stricture serve to distinguish vowel grades termed *samprasāraṇa, guṇa,* and *vṛddhi* in Pāṇinian grammar. The fifth row of headings shows voicing; while the sixth row shows aspiration and nasalization of consonants, as well as length of vowels. Pitch is not shown. Less common segments are discussed in the notes.[2–3,6–8] Unusual is the placement of *h* with semivowels,[4] and the placement of anusvāra with the velars.[5]

Notes:

1. The diphthongs *ai* and *au* have, and the monophthongs *e* and *o* are considered to have, two places of pronunciation: (i) the glottis, (ii) the palate or lips.
2. Vowels include prolonged lengths called *pluta;* three pitches *udātta, anudātta, svarita;* and nasalized variants.
3. Semivowels *y, l, v* include nasal variants *ỹ, l̃, ṽ.*
4. Short vowels *ĕ* and *ŏ* occur in Vedic recitation and in phonetic treatises.
5. Slightly lengthened short vowels occur in certain traditions of the recitation of the *Vājasaneyisaṁhitā.*
6. With partial stricture and voicing, *h* shares features with buccal semivowels.
7. Anusvāra is a nasal glide with the velum as its primary articulator.
8. Unaspirated and aspirated retroflex lateral flaps written ळ *ḷ* and ळ्ह *ḷh* occur intervocalically in Ṛgvedic dialect (and in the *Nirukta*), instead of *ḍ* and *ḍh.*

TABLE 5: Sanskrit phonetics

	CONSONANTS							VOWELS[1,2]				
	stops					semivowels[3]	spirants					
	contacted					*slightly cont.*	*slightly open*	*open*				
								simply open		more open		most open
	UNVOICED		VOICED			VOICED	UNVOICED	VOICED		VOICED		VOICED
	unasp.	asp.	unasp.	asp.	nasal			short[4,5]	long	short	long	long
GUTTURAL						ह् *h*[5]	: *ḥ*			अ *a*		आ *ā*
VELAR	क् *k*	ख् *kh*	ग् *g*	घ् *gh*	ङ् *ṅ*	˙ *ṁ*[7]	≍ *ẖ*					
PALATAL	च् *c*	छ् *ch*	ज् *j*	झ् *jh*	ञ् *ñ*	य् *y*	श् *ś*	इ *i*	ई *ī*		ए *e*	ऐ *ai*
RETROFLEX[8]	ट् *ṭ*	ठ् *ṭh*	ड् *ḍ*	ढ् *ḍh*	ण् *ṇ*	र् *r*	ष् *ṣ*	ऋ *ṛ*	ॠ *ṝ*			
DENTAL	त् *t*	थ् *th*	द् *d*	ध् *dh*	न् *n*	ऌ् *l*	स् *s*	ऌ *ḷ*	ॡ *ḹ*			
LABIAL	प् *p*	फ् *ph*	ब् *b*	भ् *bh*	म् *m*	व् *v*	≍ *ḫ*	उ *u*	ऊ *ū*		ओ *o*	औ *au*

A.6 Sanskrit phonetics according to Āpiśali

TABLE 6 shows Sanskrit phonetic segments categorized according to the phonetic features described by the ancient Indian linguist Āpiśali and shown in TABLE 2. Place of articulation features appear in the leftmost column. Stricture appears in the third row of headings. The fourth row of headings shows voicing, and the fifth row shows aspiration and nasalization of consonants. Articulators — as well as the extrabuccal features glottis, larynx, breath impact, length, and pitch — are not shown. Less common segments are discussed in the notes.[1–3] Noteworthy is the placement of anusvāra (*ṁ*) with spirants.

Notes:

1. Vowels include prolonged lengths called *pluta;* three pitches *udātta, anudātta, svarita;* and nasalized variants.
2. Semivowels *y, l, v* include nasal variants *ỹ, l̃, ṽ*.
3. The long vowels **ई** *ī* **ॠ** *ṝ* **ॡ** *ḹ* **ऊ** *ū* are classified here, with the same place of articulation as the corresponding short vowels.
4. Four additional nasals *k̃, k̃h, g̃,* and *g̃h,* called *yama,* occur instead of non-nasal stops before nasals.
5. The more open diphthongs **ए** *e* **ओ** *o* also have a guttural place of articulation.
6. The even more open diphthongs **ऐ** *ai* **औ** *au* also have a guttural place of articulation.
7. The nasal stops **ङ्** *ṅ* **ञ्** *ñ* **ण्** *ṇ* **न्** *n* **म्** *m* have a secondary nasal place of articulation.

TABLE 6: Sanskrit phonetics according to Āpiśali

	CONSONANTS								VOWELS[1]				
	stops					semivowels[2]	spirants		simple	diphthongs		simple	
	incontinuously contacted					*slightly cont.*	*slightly open*		*open*[3]	>	>>	*most open*	*close*
	UNVOICED		VOICED			VOICED	UNVD.	VD.	VOICED				
	unasp.	asp.	unasp.	asp.	nasal[4]								
GUTTURAL	क् *k*	ख् *kh*	ग् *g*	घ् *gh*	ङ् *ṅ*		: *ḥ*	ह् *h*		⇓[5]	⇓[6]	आ *ā*	अ *a*
DORSOLINGUAL							≍ *ẖ*						
PALATAL	च् *c*	छ् *ch*	ज् *j*	झ् *jh*	ञ् *ñ*	य् *y*	श् *ś*		इ *i*	ए *e*	ऐ *ai*		
RETROFLEX	ट् *ṭ*	ठ् *ṭh*	ड् *ḍ*	ढ् *ḍh*	ण् *ṇ*	र् *r*	ष् *ṣ*		ऋ *ṛ*				
DENTAL	त् *t*	थ् *th*	द् *d*	ध् *dh*	न् *n*	ऌ् *l*	स् *s*		ऌ *ḷ*				
LABIAL	प् *p*	फ् *ph*	ब् *b*	भ् *bh*	म् *m*	व् *v*	≍ *ḫ*		उ *u*	ओ *o*	औ *au*		
NASAL					⇑[7]		*ṁ*						

A.7 Sanskrit phonetics according to Śaunaka

TABLE 7 shows Sanskrit phonetic segments categorized according to the phonetic features described by the ancient Indian linguist Śaunaka and shown in TABLE 3. Place of articulation features appear in the leftmost column. Stricture appears in the third row of headings. The fourth row of headings shows voicing, and the fifth row shows aspiration and nasalization of consonants, as well as length of vowels. Not noted in TABLE 3, Śaunaka distinguishes fused complex vowels from diphthongs, as shown in the sixth row of headings. Glottal aperture, vocal fold disposition, material, and pitch described in TABLE 3 are not shown. Less common segments are discussed in the notes.[1–5] Noteworthy is the placement of anusvāra (*ṁ*) with spirants.

Notes:

1. Vowels include prolonged lengths called *pluta;* three pitches *udātta, anudātta, svarita;* and nasalized variants.
2. Semivowels *y, l, v* include nasal variants *ỹ, l̃, ṽ.*
3. Four additional nasals *k̃, k̃h, g̃,* and *g̃h,* called *yama,* occur instead of non-nasal stops before nasals. A nasal fricative *h̃* occurs after *h* before *ṇ, n, m.*
4. Unaspirated and aspirated retroflex lateral flaps written ळ *ḷ* and ळ्ह *ḷh* occur intervocalically instead of *ḍ* and *ḍh,* according to Vedamitra (1.51).
5. Anusvāra is lengthened by $\frac{1}{4}$ mora to $\frac{3}{4}$ mora after short vowels and is shortened $\frac{1}{4}$ mora to $\frac{1}{4}$ mora after long vowels.

TABLE 7: Sanskrit phonetics according to Śaunaka

	CONSONANTS								VOWELS[1]			
	stops					semivowels[2]	spirants		simple		complex	
	incontinuously contacted					*slightly cont.*	*continuously open*		*continuously open*		*continuously open*	
	UNVOICED		VOICED			VOICED	UNVD.	VD.	VOICED		VOICED	
	unasp.	asp.	unasp.	asp.	nasal[3]				short	long	long, fused	diphthong
GUTTURAL							: *ḥ*	ह् *h*	अ *a*	आ *ā*		
VELAR	क् *k*	ख् *kh*	ग् *g*	घ् *gh*	ङ् *ṅ*		≍ *ẖ*					
PALATAL	च् *c*	छ् *ch*	ज् *j*	झ् *jh*	ञ् *ñ*	य् *y*	श् *ś*		इ *i*	ई *ī*	ए *e*	ऐ *ai*
RETROFLEX[4]	ट् *ṭ*	ठ् *ṭh*	ड् *ḍ*	ढ् *ḍh*	ण् *ṇ*	र् *r*	ष् *ṣ*		ऋ *ṛ*	ॠ *ṝ*		
DENTAL	त् *t*	थ् *th*	द् *d*	ध् *dh*	न् *n*	ल् *l*	स् *s*		ऌ *ḷ*	ॡ *ḹ*		
LABIAL	प् *p*	फ् *ph*	ब् *b*	भ् *bh*	म् *m*	व् *v*	≍ *ḫ*		उ *u*	ऊ *ū*	ओ *o*	औ *au*
NASAL							*ṁ*[5]					

A.8 Sanskrit phonemics

TABLE 8 shows Sanskrit phonemes according to traditional strict definitions of the concept of a phoneme. The table redisplays Sanskrit phonetic segments shown in TABLE 5, setting phonemes in black and sounds that occur only as allophones in gray. The latter and the marginal phonemes anusvāra and visarga are discussed in the notes.[1–4]

Notes:

1. Visarga, allophone of *s in pausa* becomes a phonetic variant of jihvāmūlīya and upadhmānīya before unvoiced velar and labial stops and of sibilants before the same sibilant. It contrasts with *s* < *k, p;* e. g. *paspaśa* : *antaḥpura, paraspara* : *saraḥpadma, antaḥkaraṇa* : *uraska.*
2. Anusvāra, generally an allophone of morpheme-final *m* before a semivowel or spirant, and word-final before a non-labial stop, is a phonetic variant of *m* before a labial stop. It contrasts with *m* in *samrāt, samyak, amlāna, āmreḍita.*
3. Jihvāmūlīya and upadhmānīya are allophones of *s* word-finally before unvoiced velar and labial stops, respectively.
4. The palatal nasal is an allophone of *n* before a palatal stop and is an allophone of *m* and phonetic variant of anusvāra in the same context.

TABLE 8: Sanskrit phonemics

	CONSONANTS							VOWELS				
	stops					semivowels	spirants					
	contacted					*slightly cont.*	*slightly open*	*open*				
								simply open		more open		most open
	UNVOICED		VOICED			VOICED	UNVOICED	VOICED		VOICED		VOICED
	unasp.	asp.	unasp.	asp.	nasal			short	long	short	long	long
GUTTURAL						ह् *h*	: *ḥ*[1]			अ *a*		आ *ā*
VELAR	क् *k*	ख् *kh*	ग् *g*	घ् *gh*	ङ् *ṅ*	*ṁ*[2]	≍ *ḫ*[3]					
PALATAL	च् *c*	छ् *ch*	ज् *j*	झ् *jh*	ञ् *ñ*[4]	य् *y*	श् *ś*	इ *i*	ई *ī*		ए *e*	ऐ *ai*
RETROFLEX	ट् *ṭ*	ठ् *ṭh*	ड् *ḍ*	ढ् *ḍh*	ण् *ṇ*	र् *r*	ष् *ṣ*	ऋ *ṛ*	ॠ *ṝ*			
DENTAL	त् *t*	थ् *th*	द् *d*	ध् *dh*	न् *n*	ल् *l*	स् *s*	ऌ *ḷ*	ॡ *ḹ*			
LABIAL	प् *p*	फ् *ph*	ब् *b*	भ् *bh*	म् *m*	व् *v*	≍ *ḫ*[3]	उ *u*	ऊ *ū*		ओ *o*	औ *au*

A.9 Sanskrit sounds derived from PIE by Burrow

TABLE 9 redisplays the headings and arrangement of sounds given in TABLE 5 and shows the Proto-Indo-European reconstruction of each Sanskrit sound in the place the Sanskrit sound occupies in TABLE 5. The derivations follow those given in Burrow (1955); for Burrow's reconstruction of PIE phonology see TABLE 10.

Notes:

1. Some voiced aspirates may perhaps be derived from a voiced unaspirated stop + H (ibid, 72).
2. The symbol X^h stands for the voiced aspirated stops g^{wh}, $\acute{g}^h$, d^h, b^h.
3. Labiovelars become palatal before H_1e, $e\mathrm{H}_1$, *i*, *i*H; otherwise they become velar (Burrow, 1955, 74–76).
4. Dental stops become retroflex after *ṣ* or together with preceding *l* (ibid., 96–99).
5. *s* → *ṣ* after *i u r/r̥ k* except before *r/r̥* (ibid., 80).
6. /b/ is rare or non-existent in PIE. Sanskrit *b* may arise from voicing of *p;* a special instance is voicing caused by a laryngeal, thus Skt. *pibati* 'drinks' < **pi-p*H_3*-eti* (ibid., 72–73).

TABLE 9: Derivation of Sanskrit sounds from Proto-Indo-European phonemes according to Burrow

	CONSONANTS							VOWELS				
	stops					semivowels	spirants					
	contacted					*slightly cont.*	*slightly open*	*open*				
								simply open		more open		most open
	UNVOICED		VOICED			VOICED	UNVOICED	VOICED		VOICED		VOICED
	unasp.	asp.	unasp.	asp.[1]	nasal			short	long	short	long	long
GUTTURAL						X^h[2]	s			He		eH
VELAR[3]	k^w	k^wH	g^w	g^{wh}	n	n,m	s					
PALATAL[3]	k^w,$\acute{k}$	k^wH,$\acute{k}$H	g^w,$\acute{g}$	g^{wh},$\acute{g}^h$	n	y	$\acute{k}$	y	yH		Hey	eHy
RETROFLEX[4]	t	tH	d	d^h	n	r,l	$\acute{k}$,s[5]	r	rH			
DENTAL	t	tH	d	d^h	n	r,l	$\acute{k}$,s	l	lH			
LABIAL	p	pH	b,p,pH[6]	b^h	m	w	s	w	wH		Hew	eHw

A.10 PIE phonemics according to Burrow

TABLE 10 shows the Proto-Indo-European phonological system as reconstructed by Burrow (1955). Burrow's exposition is less than pellucid, and his introductory lists of PIE sounds with reflexes in various daughter languages is misleading, since he later vigorously argues against the rationale for a considerable number of these sounds. In part, he is reacting to Edgerton (1946). Burk (1976, 15–18) takes Burrow's tables at face value, and attributes to Burrow a Brugmannesque reconstruction of the consonant system together with 26 (!) vowels and diphthongs.

Notes:

1. Burrow also reconstructs a so-called "laryngeal" H, of unspecified phonetic value (Burrow, 1955, 85–89). He further describes a three-laryngeal theory with H_1, H_2, and H_3 but notes that "the laryngeal theory has not yet acquired a completely satisfactory form" (ibid., 108). He denies that "H in any of its varieties could function as a vowel" (ibid., 107).
2. Burrow dismisses as "without serious foundation" (ibid., 82) the reconstruction of fricatives *þ* and *ð*. On p. 67 he notes a velar nasal and *z* but does not discuss these further.
3. Voiceless aspirated stops are not shown, since Burrow reconstructs these uniformly from voiceless stop + H (ibid., 71–73).
4. Burrow observes that, since the development of the laryngeal theory, the only "purely ... vocalic element" is /e/ (ibid., 108). /a/ and /o/ are to be explained either through qualitative alteration or by the action of H. /i/ and /u/ as well as the syllabic nasals and liquids are allophones of the respective consonant phonemes. Long vowels result uniformly from vowel + H. For a notably lapidary criticism of similar reconstructions, see Velten (1956).
5. The nasal stops and sonorants have syllabic (vocalic) allophones /n̥ m̥ r̥ l̥ i u/ (ibid., 108).
6. Velar stops are shown in gray, since Burrow regards it as "exceedingly doubtful whether three distinct series [i. e. palatal, velar, labiovelar] existed in Indo-European" (ibid., 76).

TABLE 10: Proto-Indo-European phonemics according to Burrow

	CONSONANTS[1,2,3]							VOWELS[4]
	stops				liquids[5]	glides[5]	spirants	
	UNVD.	VOICED			VOICED		UNVD.	VOICED
	unasp.	unasp.	asp.	nasal[5]				
LABIOVELAR	k^w	g^w	g^{wh}					
VELAR[6]	k	g	g^h			w		
PALATAL	ḱ	ǵ	$ǵ^h$		r	y		e
DENTAL	t	d	d^h	n	l		s	
LABIAL	p	b	b^h	m				

A.11 PIE phonemics according to Szemerényi

TABLE 11 shows the Proto-Indo-European phonological system as reconstructed by Szemerényi (1967). This is Szemerényi's proposed "new look" for Indo-European, that is "the linguistic stage which can be reconstructed from the data of the IE languages as their immediate antecedent" (Szemerényi, 1967, 96 n. 90). The primary differences between this reconstruction and Burrow's are as follows: (1) a system of four, rather than three, types of stops is posited in each series of stops; (2) a separate series of "palatal" stops is introduced; (3) only a single laryngeal is given, and it is identified as /h/, a glottal spirant; (4) there are five basic vowel phonemes, which occur both short (/a e o i u/) and long (/ā ē ō ī ū), and also a schwa.

It is worth noting that this analysis resembles, along broad lines, that of Brugmann (1906–1916).

TABLE 11: Proto-Indo-European phonemics according to Szemerényi

	CONSONANTS								VOWELS[1]		
	stops					liquids	glides	spirants	low	mid	high
	UNVOICED		VOICED			VOICED		UNVD.	VOICED		
	unasp.	asp.	unasp.	asp.	nasal						
GLOTTAL								h			
LABIOVELAR	k^w	k^{wh}	g^w	g^{wh}							
VELAR	k	k^h	g	g^w					a		
PALATAL	ḱ	$\acute{k}^h$	ǵ	$\acute{g}^h$		r	y		ə	e	i
DENTAL	t	t^h	d	d^h	n	l		s			
LABIAL	p	p^h	b	b^h	m		w			o	u

A.12 Feature tree after Halle

TABLE 12 shows the feature geometry proposed by Halle (1995). In favor of the interpretation of phonological features as organized in a tree, rather than constituting an unordered list, are the facts that (1) only a substantially restricted combination of features is ever used in phonological rules, and (2) sets of features used in phonological rules share a designated articulator.

TABLE 12: Feature tree after Halle (1995)

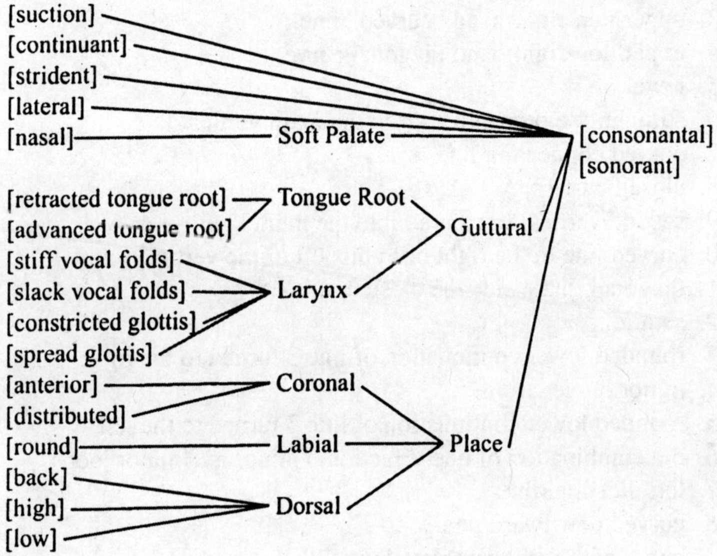

A.13 Graphic features of Devanāgarī according to Ivanov and Toporov

TABLE 13 reproduces the set of distinctive features for graphemes of the Devanāgarī script suggested by Ivanov & Toporov (1968, 27–32):

1. upper horizontal line
2. main vertical line
3. upper non-right-hand "curved" line
4. upper non-right-hand diagonal curve
5. lower quirk
6. straight line perpendicular to the main vertical line
7. curved connecting line
8. closed curve
9. second vertical line parallel to the main line
10. curved line to the right or to the left of the vertical line
11. diagonal line inside the close figure
12. semiloop
13. rounded lower continuation of line 3 turned to the right
14. minor circle
15. rounded lower continuation of line 3 turned to the left
16. the combination of one-directional minor and major loops
17. left diagonal line
18. curved downward line
19. curve with the incomplete loop
20. upper diacritic
21. dot

TABLE 13: Graphic features of Devanāgarī according to Ivanov and Toporov

	अ	आ	इ	ई	उ	ऊ	ऋ	ॠ	ऌ	ॡ	ए	ऐ	ओ	औ	क	ख	ग	घ	ङ	च	छ	ज	झ	ञ	ट	ठ	ड	ढ	ण	त	थ	द	ध	न	प	फ	ब	भ	म	य	र	ल	व	श	ष	स	ह	ं	:
1	+	+	+	+	+	+	+	+	+	+	+	+	+	+	+	+	+	+	+	+	+	+	+	+	+	+	+	+	+	+	+	+	-	+	+	+	+	-	+	+	+	+	+	+	+	+	+	-	-
2	+	+	-	-	-	-	+	+	+	+	-	-	+	+	+	+	+	+	-	+	-	+	+	+	-	-	-	-	+	+	+	-	+	+	+	+	+	+	+	+	-	+	+	+	+	+	-	-	-
3	-	-	+	+	+	+	-	-	-	-	-	-	-	-	-	-	-	-	+	-	-	-	+	-	+	+	+	+	-	-	+	+	-	-	-	-	-	-	-	+	-	-	-	-	-	-	+	-	-
4	-	-	-	-	-	-	-	-	-	-	-	-	-	-	-	+	+	-	-	-	-	-	-	-	-	-	-	-	+	-	-	-	-	-	-	-	-	+	+	-	+	-	-	-	-	+	-	-	-
5	-	-	+	+	-	-	-	-	-	-	+	+	-	-	-	+	-	-	-	-	-	-	+	-	-	-	-	-	+	-	-	+	-	-	-	-	-	-	-	-	+	-	-	+	-	+	-	-	-
6	-	-	-	-	-	-	+	+	-	-	-	-	-	-	-	-	-	-	-	+	-	-	+	-	-	-	-	-	-	-	-	-	-	-	-	-	-	+	+	-	-	-	-	-	-	+	-	-	-
7	-	-	-	-	-	-	-	-	-	-	-	-	-	-	-	-	-	-	-	-	-	-	-	-	-	-	-	-	-	-	+	-	-	-	+	+	-	-	-	+	-	-	-	-	+	-	-	-	-
8	-	-	-	-	-	-	-	-	-	-	+	-	-	-	+	+	-	-	-	-	+	-	-	-	-	-	-	-	-	-	-	-	-	-	-	-	+	-	-	-	-	-	+	-	-	-	-	-	-
9	-	+	-	-	-	-	+	+	-	-	-	-	+	+	-	-	-	-	-	-	-	-	-	-	-	-	-	-	+	-	-	-	-	-	-	-	-	-	-	-	-	-	-	-	-	-	-	-	-
10	-	-	-	-	-	+	-	-	-	-	-	-	-	-	+	-	-	-	-	-	-	-	-	-	-	-	-	-	-	-	-	-	-	-	-	+	-	-	-	-	-	-	-	-	-	-	-	-	-
11	-	-	-	-	-	-	-	-	-	-	-	-	-	-	-	-	-	-	-	-	-	-	-	-	-	-	-	-	-	+	-	-	-	+	-	-	+	-	-	-	-	-	-	-	+	-	-	-	-
12	-	-	-	+	-	-	+	+	+	+	-	-	-	-	-	-	-	-	-	+	-	+	-	+	-	-	-	-	-	-	-	-	-	-	-	-	-	-	-	-	-	-	-	-	-	-	-	-	-
13	-	-	-	-	-	-	-	-	-	-	-	-	-	-	-	-	-	-	-	-	-	-	-	-	+	+	-	+	-	-	-	-	-	-	-	-	-	-	-	-	-	-	-	-	-	-	+	-	-
14	-	-	-	-	-	-	-	-	-	-	-	-	-	-	-	-	-	-	-	-	-	-	-	-	-	-	-	+	-	-	+	-	-	-	-	-	-	-	-	-	-	-	-	+	-	-	-	-	-
15	-	-	+	+	-	-	-	-	-	-	-	-	-	-	-	-	-	-	+	-	-	-	+	-	-	-	+	-	-	-	-	-	-	-	-	-	-	-	-	-	-	-	-	-	-	-	-	-	-
16	-	-	-	-	-	-	-	-	+	+	-	-	-	-	-	-	-	+	-	-	+	-	-	-	-	-	-	-	-	-	-	-	+	-	-	-	-	-	-	-	-	-	-	-	-	-	-	-	-
17	+	+	+	-	-	-	+	+	-	-	-	-	+	+	-	-	-	-	-	-	-	-	-	-	-	-	-	-	-	-	-	-	-	-	-	-	-	-	-	-	-	-	-	-	-	-	-	-	-
18	+	+	-	-	-	-	-	-	-	-	-	-	-	-	-	-	-	-	-	-	+	-	-	-	-	-	-	-	-	-	-	-	-	-	-	-	-	-	-	-	-	-	-	-	-	-	-	-	-
19	-	-	-	-	+	+	-	-	-	-	-	-	-	-	-	-	-	-	-	-	-	-	-	-	-	-	-	-	-	-	-	-	-	-	-	-	-	-	-	-	-	-	-	-	-	+	-	-	-
20	-	-	-	-	-	-	-	-	-	-	+	+	+	-	-	-	-	-	-	-	-	-	-	-	-	-	-	-	-	-	-	-	-	-	-	-	-	-	-	-	-	-	-	-	-	-	-	-	-
21	-	-	-	-	-	-	-	-	-	-	-	-	-	-	-	-	-	-	+	-	-	-	-	-	-	-	-	-	-	-	-	-	-	-	-	-	-	-	-	-	-	-	-	-	-	-	-	+	+

Appendix B

Sanskrit Library Phonetic Basic

The Sanskrit Library Phonetic Basic encoding scheme (SLP1) attempts to meet high standards of unambiguous encoding while restricting encoding to 76 codepoints in the ASCII character set. SLP1 utilizes 58 codepoints to encode segments: 53 to represent phonetic segments and five to represent punctuation ⟨' . ? - ␣⟩. In addition SLP1 utilizes 18 codepoints to encode phonetic features: three to indicate stricture, six to indicate length, eight to indicate tone, and one to indicate nasalization. Although certain features are indicated by a sequence of codepoints, no codepoints double as both segments and features. While useful, SLP1 is not an ideal encoding. To its credit it is consistent in that it consistently encodes phonetic rather than graphic elements (with the exception of the punctuation signs). Yet it does not maintain a consistent basis of encoding because it mixes the encoding of phonetic segments and phonetic features. Nor does it satisfy the Fano condition because it utilizes a few codepoints as prefixes in code sequences. For example, the forward slash ⟨/⟩, back slash ⟨\⟩, and caret ⟨^⟩ indicate udātta, anudātta, and independent svarita accents by themselves but also serve as the prefixes in several sequences that indicate particular tones and tonal sequences realized in various Vedic traditions; and the digit ⟨1⟩, which by itself indicates short length, is used as a prefix in a sequence that serves to indicate length of $1\frac{1}{2}$ morae. Nevertheless, single codepoints capture most phonetic segments commonly used in classical Sanskrit. The only commonly occurring phonetic segment that requires a sequence is nasalized *l*, i.e. ⟨`l~`⟩. Moreover, SLP1 does clearly define single codepoints or code sequences to capture a comprehensive set of phonetic distinctions in classical and Vedic Sanskrit.

B.1 Basic Segments

अ a `a`	आ ā `A`	इ i `i`	ई ī `I`	उ u `u`	ऊ ū `U`

ऋ ṛ `f`	ॠ ṝ `F`	ऌ ḷ `x`	ॡ ḹ `X`
ए e `e`	ऐ ai `E`	ओ o `o`	औ au `O`

क् k `k`	ख् kh `K`	ग् g `g`	घ् gh `G`	ङ् ṅ `N`
च् c `c`	छ् ch `C`	ज् j `j`	झ् jh `J`	ञ् ñ `Y`
ट् ṭ `w`	ठ् ṭh `W`	ड् ḍ `q`	ढ् ḍh `Q`	ण् ṇ `R`
		ळ् ḷ `L`	ळ्ह् ḷh `|`	
त् t `t`	थ् th `T`	द् d `d`	ध् dh `D`	न् n `n`
प् p `p`	फ् ph `P`	ब् b `b`	भ् bh `B`	म् m `m`

य् y `y`	र् r `r`	ल् l `l`	व् v `v`
श् ś `S`	ष् ṣ `z`	स् s `s`	ह् h `h`
ः ḥ `H`	≍ ẖ `Z`	≍ ḫ `V`	ṁ `M`

B.2 Punctuation

Although punctuation does not properly belong to a phonetic encoding, a limited number of punctuation tokens are supported in this encoding, since they can be used to provide basic segmentation information. The question mark is used to indicate inaudible or illegible characters in transcription.

ऽ '	। .	?	--	□ ␣
'	.	?	-	␣
avagraha	danda	question	hyphen	space

B.3 Modifiers

Modifiers are added after a character to indicate variations in segment stricture, length, accent, and nasalization, in the order stated. Prolonged length, accent, and nasalization occur in classical Sanskrit as well as Vedic. Modifiers are used in combination to indicate special features of stricture, length, accent, and nasalization in Vedic.

B.3.1 Stricture

_ heaviness [used for semivowels *y* or *v*]
= lightness [used for semivowels *y* or *v*]
! lack of release (*abhinidhāna*) [used for stops or semivowels *y*, *v*, or *l*]

B.3.2 Length

* subsegmental epenthetic vowel (*svarabhakti*)
# length of half a mora
1 length of one mora [used in Vedic after short agitated *kampa;* short *e, o;* and heavy *anusvāra*]
1# slightly lengthened
2 length of two morae [used for *dvimātra anusvāra* in Vedic]

- 3 prolonged length of three morae [used for *pluta* vowels]
- 4 prolonged length of four or more morae [used in *raṅga*]

B.3.3 Accent

- / high pitch
- \ low pitch
- ^ circumflex
- 6 extra low tone
- 7 low tone
- 8 high tone
- 9 extra high tone
- + sharpness

B.3.4 Nasalization

- ~ nasalization

B.4 Modifier combinations and usage notes

B.4.1 Stricture

- `y_` heavy *y*
- `v_` heavy *v*
- `y=` light *y*
- `v=` light *v*
- `k!` unreleased (*abhinidhāna*) *k*
- `g!` unreleased (*abhinidhāna*) *g*
- . . . *similarly for other unreleased stops*
- `y!` unreleased (*abhinidhāna*) *y*
- `v!` unreleased (*abhinidhāna*) *v*
- `l!` unreleased (*abhinidhāna*) *l*

B.4.2 Length

`a*`	epenthetic *a*
`i*`	epenthetic *i*
`u*`	epenthetic *u*
`f*`	epenthetic *ṛ*
`x*`	epenthetic *ḷ*
`e*`	epenthetic *e*
`e1`	short *e*
`o1`	short *o*
`a1#`	slightly lengthened short *a*

... *similarly for other slightly lengthened short vowels*

B.4.3 Surface accent

Tonal contours in Vedic have numerous distinct varieties described in *Prātiśākhyas*. The indication of these requires the use of the accent signs for high pitch, low pitch, and circumflex (**/**, ****, and **^**) in conjunction with tonal modifiers **6**, **7**, **8**, **9** that indicate the features *extra low, low, high,* and *extra high* pitch respectively. The additional modifier **+** is used to indicate a distinction in sharpness or effort of uncertain phonetic significance described in the *Vājasaneyi* (1.125) and *Taittirīya* (20.9-12) *Prātiśākhyas*, in spite of the same length of vowel and same beginning and end pitches. The term 'aggravation' below translates *kampa:* 'aggravated' means with *kampa;* 'unaggravated' means without *kampa.* The following modifier sequences are used to indicate the tonal features described to their right:

/8	high tone (*udātta*)
\\7	low tone (*anudātta*)
\\6	extra low tone (*sannatara*)
^98	declining tone from extra high to high (dependent and unaggravated independent *svarita* according to the *Ṛkprātiśākhya*)
^97	declining tone from extra high to low (aggravated independent *svarita* according to the *Ṛkprātiśākhya*)

`^87`	declining tone from high to low (dependent *svarita* according to the *Vājasaneyi* (1.125) and *Taittirīya* (20.9–12) *Prātiśākhyas*)
`^87+`	sharp declining tone from high to low (independent *svarita* according to the *Vājasaneyi* (1.125) and *Taittirīya* (20.9–12) *Prātiśākhyas*)
`^86`	declining tone from high to extra low (aggravated independent svarita according to the *Vājasaneyi-prātiśākhya*)

Vowel accent examples

`a/8`	high toned vowel *a*
`a^97`	the vowel *a* with short agitated circumflex as described in the *Ṛkprātiśākhya*
`a3^97`	the vowel *a* with prolonged agitated circumflex as described in the *Ṛkprātiśākhya*

B.4.4 Syllabified visarga and anusvāra accent

`H/`	high-pitched *visarga*
`H\`	low-pitched *visarga*
`H^`	*svarita visarga*
`M\`	low-pitched *anusvāra*

B.4.5 Nasals

Nasalization

Both SLP1 and SLP2 include means to encode 20 yamas (**`k~`**, **`kh~`**, ..., **`b~`**, **`bh~`**) considered, on phonetic grounds, to be epenthetic nasalized segments that adopt features of both of the preceding stop and of the following nasal. Yet the preferred method of encoding yamas, in accordance with the phonological analysis of most ancient Indian phonetic treatises, is to employ characters for just four epenthetic nasals (**`k~`**, **`kh~`**, **`g~`**, **`gh~`**), or, on the minority view of the *Ṛkprātiśākhya*, to employ yamas (`k~`, `kh~`, . . . , `b~`, `bh~`) in place of the non-nasal stop that precedes the nasal. (See p. 63 and p. 72 for discussion.)

`l~`	nasalized *l*
`y~`	nasalized *y*
`v~`	nasalized *v*
`k~`	nasalized offset (*yama*), after unvoiced unaspirated non-nasal stop when followed by a nasal stop
`K~`	nasalized offset (*yama*), after unvoiced aspirated non-nasal stop when followed by a nasal stop
`g~`	nasalized offset (*yama*), after voiced unaspirated non-nasal stop when followed by a nasal stop
`G~`	nasalized offset (*yama*), after voiced aspirated non-nasal stop when followed by a nasal stop
`h~`	nasalized offset (*nāsikya*), after *h* when followed by a nasal stop

Anusvāra

`M#`	short *anusvāra* (which follows a long vowel according to the *Ṛk* and *Vājasaneyi Prātiśākhyas*: *ṚPr.* 13.22, 13.29, 13.32–33; *VPr.* 4.148–149; the short *anusvāra* measures half a mora while the preceding vowel measures 1.5 morae)
`M1#`	long *anusvāra* (which follows a short vowel according to the *Ṛk* and *Vājasaneyi Prātiśākhyas*; the long *anusvāra* measures 1.5 morae while the preceding vowel measures 0.5 morae)
`M1`	heavy *anusvāra* (which is usually called *guru* and also by some *hrasva* and which occurs before a conjunct consonant according to Śikṣās)
`M2`	two-mora *anusvāra* (which is called *dvimātra* and occurs before a consonant followed by *ṛ* according to Śikṣās)

Raṅga

2~	two-mora *raṅga* (vowel two *mātras* in length nasalized for the last half *mātra* with *kampa* in the middle according to *Pāṇinīyaśikṣā* 26–30)
4~	*raṅga* (nasalized vowel four *mātras* in length followed by a break according to *Mallaśarmakṛtaśikṣā*; texts show a double danda to mark the break

Appendix C

Sanskrit Library Phonetic Segmental

The Sanskrit Library Phonetic Segmental encoding scheme (SLP2) adheres to the most rigorous standards of unambiguous encoding described in Chapter 4. It utilizes a consistent basis for encoding, namely broadly defined phonemes, and it creates a one-to-one correspondence between codepoints and items encoded. In terms of the three axes of encoding, SLP2 encodes phonetics rather than graphics, segments rather than features, and contrastive rather than complementary units. It encodes Sanskrit phonetic segments by assigning one codepoint to each phoneme broadly defined, that is, to each segment that is minimally contrastive in the sense concluded in sections 6.1.5 and 6.1.6.

In column 1 the unique codepoints of SLP2 are shown in hexadecimal notation. In column 2 the equivalent encoding in SLP1 is given. In columns 3 and 4 Devanāgarī and Roman representations are given. In column 5 an IPA transcription of the encoded sound is given.

Devanāgarī

Often several options are given for the marking of Vedic accentuation in Devanāgarī, including those used in the following traditions:

1. *Śākalasaṁhitā* of the *Ṛgveda*

2. *Vājasaneyisaṁhitā* of the *Śuklayajurveda*

3. *Taittirīyasaṁhitā* of the *Kṛṣṇayajurveda*

4. *Śaunakīyasaṁhitā* of the *Atharvaveda*

5. *Maitrāyaṇīsaṁhitā* of the *Kṛṣṇayajurveda*, *Ṛgveda khilāni*, and Kashmiri mss. of #2

6. *Kāṭhakasaṁhitā* of the *Kṛṣṇayajurveda*

7. *Paippalādasaṁhitā* of the *Atharvaveda*

8. *Sāmavedasaṁhitā* in the *Kauthuma śakhā*

9. *Śatapathabrāhmaṇa*

Superscript numerals given in the table refer to these nine traditions. The options are illustrative rather than comprehensive for two reasons: First, correlating the precise phonetics of various traditions of Vedic recitation with graphic signs used in manuscripts requires further research and may never be determined completely. The association of svarita marks with particular surface tonal sequences in 012-017, for instance, is merely suggestive based on the division into dependent (012-013), independent (014-015), and aggravated independent svaritas (016-017) for traditions in which the *udātta* is the highest tone (5-7). Second, at the time of writing, even sophisticated typesetting software does not permit representation of all the graphic signs used in various Vedic traditions. Among svaritas not shown is Maitrāyaṇī dependent svarita, marked with a horizontal stroke at mid-height through a character. Besides the marks that represent the independent svarita shown at 006, 010 and 058, 014, and 016, there is, for example, अ॒ used in the *Śaunakīyasaṁhitā* of the *Atharvaveda*. The Vedic Unicode Character Phonetic Value Table linked to the Sanskrit Library Vedic Unicode page correlates most of the new characters included in the Devanagari Extended and Vedic Extensions blocks with the Sanskrit Library Phonetic encoding (SLP1) and demonstrates which are used in which Vedic traditions.

IPA transcription

The IPA transcription given in column 5 is for reference; it does not necessarily represent the only historically correct reconstruction for the sound in question. Surface tones are indicated using the tone-letter system of Chao (1930). Underlying tones are indicated using the *grave accent, acute accent,* and *circumflex accent* with their standard IPA (1949–1996) meanings.

The short *a* [ɐ] in Sanskrit, although described as close in comparison with *ā* [ɑː], is yet more open than schwa [ə].

The diphthongs *ai* and *au* in the modern pronunciation of Sanskrit use the close *a* [ɐ] at the onset but preserve the same sounds as the corresponding vowels *i* [i] and *u* [u] at the offset. The vowels represented by *i* and *u* are the most front and most back vowels shown in the IPA chart; they never represent [ɪ] as in 'pin' or [ʊ] as in 'book'.

We use the true palatal symbols for the palatal series of stops *c ch j jh* [c c^{h} ɟ ɟ^{h}] and a palatal spirant *ś* [ç] rather than alveolar fricatives [ʧ ʧ^{h} ʤ ʤ^{h}].

SLP2	SLP1	DEVANĀGARĪ	ROMAN	IPA
000	a	अ	a	ɐ
001	a~	अँ	ã	ɐ̃
002	a/	अ[1–4] / अ॑[5–7] / अ॑[8]	á	ɐ́
003	a/~	अँ[1–4] / अँ॑[5–7] / अँ॑[8]	ã́	ɐ̃́
004	a\	अ॒[1–5] / अ़[6,7] / अ᳚[8]	a/a̱	ɐ̀
005	a\~	अँ॒[1–5] / अँ़[6,7] / अँ᳚[8]	ã/ã̱	ɐ̃̀
006	a^	अ॑[1,3] / अ᳙[2] / अ᳛[8]	à	ɐ̂
007	a^~	अँ॑[1,3] / अँ᳙[2] / अँ᳛[8]	ã̀	ɐ̃̂
008	a/8	अ[1–4] / अ॑[5–7]		ɐ˥
009	a/8~	अँ[1–4] / अँ॑[5–7]		ɐ̃˥
00A	a\7	अ॒[1–4] / अ[5–6] / अ़[7]		ɐ˧
00B	a\7~	अँ॒[1–4] / अँ[5–6] / अँ़[7]		ɐ̃˧
00C	a\6	अ॒[5] / अ़[6,7]		ɐ˨
00D	a\6~	अँ॒[5] / अँ़[6,7]		ɐ̃˨
00E	a^98	अ॑[1–4]		ɐ˥˩
00F	a^98~	अँ॑[1–4]		ɐ̃˥˩
010	a^97	अ१॑[1,4]		ɐ˥˧
011	a^97~	अँ१॑[1,4]		ɐ̃˥˧
012	a^87	अँ᳜[5] / अ़[6,7]		ɐ˦˧
013	a^87~	अँ᳜[5] / अँ़[6,7]		ɐ̃˦˧
014	a^87+	अ᳘[5,6] / अ᳘[7]		ɐ˦˧
015	a^87+~	अँ᳘[5,6] / अँ᳘[7]		ɐ̃˦˧
016	a^86	३अ॒[5] / अ᳐[6]		ɐ˦˨

SLP2	SLP1	Devanāgarī	Roman	IPA
017	a^86~	३अँ॒[5] / अँ॒[6]		ɐ̃˧˦˧
018	a1#	अ	a	ɐˑ
019	a1#~	अँ	ã	ɐ̃ˑ
01A	a1#/	अ[1-4] / अ॑[5-7] / अ॑[8]	á	ɐ́ˑ
01B	a1#/~	अँ[1-4] / अँ॑[5-7] / अँ॑[8]	ã́	ɐ̃́ˑ
01C	a1#\	अ॒[1-5] / अ॒[6,7] / अ॑[8]	a/a̱	ɐ̀ˑ
01D	a1#\~	अँ॒[1-5] / अँ॒[6,7] / अँ॑[8]	ã/ã̱	ɐ̃̀ˑ
01E	a1#^	अ॑[1,3] / अ॒[2] / अ॑[8]	à	ɐ̂ˑ
01F	a1#^~	अँ॑[1,3] / अँ॒[2] / अँ॑[8]	ã̀	ɐ̃̂ˑ
020	a1#/8	अ[1-4] / अ॑[5-7]		ɐˑ˥
021	a1#/8~	अँ[1-4] / अँ॑[5-7]		ɐ̃ˑ˥
022	a1#\7	अ॒[1-4] / अ[5-6] / अ॒[7]		ɐˑ˧
023	a1#\7~	अँ॒[1-4] / अँ[5-6] / अँ॒[7]		ɐ̃ˑ˧
024	a1#\6	अ॒[5] / अ॒[6,7]		ɐˑ˨
025	a1#\6~	अँ॒[5] / अँ॒[6,7]		ɐ̃ˑ˨
026	a1#^98	अ॑[1-4]		ɐˑ˥˦
027	a1#^98~	अँ॑[1-4]		ɐ̃ˑ˥˦
028	a1#^97	अ१॒॑[1,4]		ɐˑ˥˧
029	a1#^97~	अँ१॒॑[1,4]		ɐ̃ˑ˥˧
02A	a1#^87	अ᳚[5] / अ॒[6,7]		ɐˑ˧˦˧
02B	a1#^87~	अँ᳚[5] / अँ॒[6,7]		ɐ̃ˑ˧˦˧
02C	a1#^87+	अ॒[5,6] / अ॒[7]		ɐˑ˧˦˧
02D	a1#^87+~	अँ॒[5,6] / अँ॒[7]		ɐ̃ˑ˧˦˧

SLP2	SLP1	DEVANĀGARĪ	ROMAN	IPA
02E	a1#^86	३अ॒[5] / अ॒॒[6]		ɐˑ˧˥
02F	a1#^86~	३अँ॒[5] / अँ॒॒[6]		ɐ̃ˑ˧˥
030	A	आ	ā	ɑː
031	A~	आँ	ā̃	ɑ̃ː
032	A/	आ[1–4] / आ॑[5–7] / आ॑[8]	á̄	ɑ́ː
033	A/~	आँ[1–4] / आँ॑[5–7] / आँ॑[8]	á̄̃	ɑ̃́ː
034	A\	आ॒[1–5] / आ̩[6,7] / आ᳚[8]	ā/ā̱	ɑ̀ː
035	A\~	आँ॒[1–5] / आँ̩[6,7] / आँ᳚[8]	ā̃/ā̱̃	ɑ̃̀ː
036	A^	आ॑[1,3] / आ॒[2] / आ᳚[8]	ā̀	ɑ̂ː
037	A^~	आँ॑[1,3] / आँ॒[2] / आँ᳚[8]	ā̃̀	ɑ̃̂ː
038	A/8	आ[1–4] / आ॑[5–7]		ɑː˥
039	A/8~	आँ[1–4] / आँ॑[5–7]		ɑ̃ː˥
03A	A\7	आ॒[1–4] / आ[5–6] / आ̣[7]		ɑː˧
03B	A\7~	आँ॒[1–4] / आँ[5–6] / आँ̣[7]		ɑ̃ː˧
03C	A\6	आ॒[5] / आ̩[6,7]		ɑː˨
03D	A\6~	आँ॒[5] / आँ̩[6,7]		ɑ̃ː˨
03E	A^98	आ॑[1–4]		ɑː˥˦
03F	A^98~	आँ॑[1–4]		ɑ̃ː˥˦
040	A^97	आ॒३॒॑[1,4]		ɑː˥˧
041	A^97~	आँ॒३॒॑[1,4]		ɑ̃ː˥˧
042	A^87	आ᳡[5] / आ̣[6,7]		ɑː˦˧
043	A^87~	आँ᳡[5] / आँ̣[6,7]		ɑ̃ː˦˧
044	A^87+	आ᳙[5,6] / आ᳙[7]		ɑː˦˧

SLP2	SLP1	Devanāgarī	Roman	IPA
045	`A^87+~`	आँ̱ [5,6] / आँ᳚ [7]		ã:˦˨
046	`A^86`	३आ̱ [5] / आ᳚ [6]		ɑ:˦˨
047	`A^86~`	३आँ̱ [5] / आँ᳚ [6]		ã:˦˨
048	`a3`	अ३	a3	ɑ::
049	`a3~`	अँ३	ã3	ã::
04A	`a3/`	अ३ [1–4] / अ॑३ [5–7] / अ॑३ [8]	á3	á::
04B	`a3/~`	अँ३ [1–4] / अँ॑३ [5–7] / अँ॑३ [8]	ã́3	ã́::
04C	`a3\`	अ̱३ [1–7] / अ॒३ [8]	a3/a̱3	ɑ̀::
04D	`a3\~`	अँ̱३ [1–7] / अँ॒३ [8]	ã3/ã̱3	ɑ̃̀::
04E	`a3^`	अ॑३ [1,3] / अ̱३ [2] / अ॑३ [8]	à3	ɑ̂::
04F	`a3^~`	अँ॑३ [1,3] / अँ̱३ [2] / अँ॑३ [8]	ã̀3	ɑ̃̂::
050	`a3/8`	अ३ [1–4] / अ॑३ [5–7]		ɑ::˥
051	`a3/8~`	अँ३ [1–4] / अँ॑३ [5–7]		ã::˥
052	`a3\7`	अ̱३ [1–4] / अ३ [5–7]		ɑ::˧
053	`a3\7~`	अँ̱३ [1–4] / अँ३ [5–7]		ã::˧
054	`a3\6`	अ̱३ [5] / अ॒३ [6,7]		ɑ::˨
055	`a3\6~`	अँ̱३ [5] / अँ॒३ [6,7]		ã::˨
056	`a3^98`	अ॑३ [1–4]		ɑ::˥˦
057	`a3^98~`	अँ॑३ [1–4]		ã::˥˦
058	`a3^97`	अ̱३̱॑ [1,4]		ɑ::˦˧
059	`a3^97~`	अँ̱३̱॑ [1,4]		ã::˦˧
05A	`a3^87`	अँ᳚३ [5] / अ॒३ [6,7]		ɑ::˦˧
05B	`a3^87~`	अँ᳚३ [5] / अँ॒३ [6,7]		ã::˦˧

SLP2	SLP1	Devanāgarī	Roman	IPA
05C	a3^87+	अ॒३ 5,6 / अ॒३ 7		ɑ::˥˧
05D	a3^87+~	अँ॒३ 5,6 / अँ॒३ 7		ɑ̃::˥˧
05E	a3^86	३अ॒३ 5 / अ॒३ 6		ɑ::˥˩
05F	a3^86~	३अँ॒३ 5 / अँ॒३ 6		ɑ̃::˥˩
060	a4~	अँ४	ã4	ɑ̃:::
061	a4/~	अँ४ 1–4 / अँ॑४ 5–7 / अँ॑४ 8	ã́4	ɑ̃́:::
062	a4\~	अँ॒४ 1–7 / अँ॑४ 8	ã4/ã̱4	ɑ̃̀:::
063	a4^~	अँ॑४ 1,3 / अँ॒४ 2 / अँ॑४ 8	ã̀4	ɑ̃̂:::
064	a4/8~	अँ४ 1–4 / अँ॑४ 5–7		ɑ̃:::˦
065	a4\7~	अँ॒४ 1–4 / अँ४ 5–7		ɑ̃:::˧
066	a4\6~	अँ॒४ 5 / अँ॒४ 6,7		ɑ̃:::˨
067	a4^98~	अँ॑४ 1–4		ɑ̃:::˥
068	a4^97~			ɑ̃:::˥˧
069	a4^87~	अँ॑४ 5 / अँ़४ 6,7		ɑ̃:::˦˧
06A	a4^87+~	अँ॒४ 5,6 / अँ॒४ 7		ɑ̃:::˦˧
06B	a4^86~	३अँ॒४ 5 / अँ॒४ 6		ɑ̃:::˦˨
06C	a*		a	ɐ̆
080	i	इ	i	i
081	i~	इँ	ĩ	ĩ
082	i/	इ 1–4 / इ॑ 5–7 / इ॑ 8	í	í
083	i/~	इँ 1–4 / इँ॑ 5–7 / इँ॑ 8	ĩ́	ĩ́
084	i\	इ॒ 1–5 / इ॒ 6,7 / इ॑ 8	i/i̱	ì
085	i\~	इँ॒ 1–5 / इँ॒ 6,7 / इँ॑ 8	ĩ/ĩ̱	ĩ̀

SLP2	SLP1	DEVANĀGARĪ	ROMAN	IPA
086	`i^`	इ॑^{1,3} / इ॒^{2} / इ꣢^{8}	ì	î
087	`i^~`	इँ॑^{1,3} / इँ॒^{2} / इँ꣢^{8}	ì̃	î̃
088	`i/8`	इ$^{1-4}$ / इ॑$^{5-7}$		i˦
089	`i/8~`	इँ$^{1-4}$ / इँ॑$^{5-7}$		ĩ˦
08A	`i\7`	इ॒$^{1-4}$ / इ$^{5-6}$ / इ़^{7}		i˧
08B	`i\7~`	इँ॒$^{1-4}$ / इँ$^{5-6}$ / इँ़^{7}		ĩ˧
08C	`i\6`	इ॒^{5} / इ᳭^{6,7}		i˨
08D	`i\6~`	इँ॒^{5} / इँ᳭^{6,7}		ĩ˨
08E	`i^98`	इ॑$^{1-4}$		i˥˧
08F	`i^98~`	इँ॑$^{1-4}$		ĩ˥˧
090	`i^97`	इ१॒॑^{1,4}		i˥˨
091	`i^97~`	इँ१॒॑^{1,4}		ĩ˥˨
092	`i^87`	इ᳛^{5} / इ़^{6,7}		i˦˧
093	`i^87~`	इँ᳛^{5} / इँ़^{6,7}		ĩ˦˧
094	`i^87+`	इ᳕^{5,6} / इ॒^{7}		i˦˧
095	`i^87+~`	इँ᳕^{5,6} / इँ॒^{7}		ĩ˦˧
096	`i^86`	३इ॒^{5} / इ᳖^{6}		i˦˨
097	`i^86~`	३इँ॒^{5} / इँ᳖^{6}		ĩ˦˨
098	`i1#`	इ	i	iˑ
099	`i1#~`	इँ	ĩ	ĩˑ
09A	`i1#/`	इ$^{1-4}$ / इ॑$^{5-7}$ / इ꣡^{8}	í	íˑ
09B	`i1#/~`	इँ$^{1-4}$ / इँ॑$^{5-7}$ / इँ꣡^{8}	í̃	í̃ˑ
09C	`i1#\`	इ॒$^{1-5}$ / इ᳭^{6,7} / इ॓^{8}	i/i̲	ìˑ

SLP2	SLP1	Devanāgarī	Roman	IPA
09D	i1#\~	ई॒ँ[1–5] / ईँ̣[6,7] / ईँ᳚[8]	ĩ/ḭ̃	ì̃ˑ
09E	i1#^	ई॑[1,3] / ई॒[2] / ई᳚[8]	ì	îˑ
09F	i1#^~	ईँ॑[1,3] / ई॒ँ[2] / ईँ᳚[8]	ì̃	î̃ˑ
0A0	i1#/8	ई[1–4] / ई॑[5–7]		iˑ˥
0A1	i1#/8~	ईँ[1–4] / ईँ॑[5–7]		ĩˑ˥
0A2	i1#\7	ई॒[1–4] / ई[5–6] / ई̣[7]		iˑ˧
0A3	i1#\7~	ई॒ँ[1–4] / ईँ[5–6] / ईँ̣[7]		ĩˑ˧
0A4	i1#\6	ई॒[5] / ई̣[6,7]		iˑ˨
0A5	i1#\6~	ई॒ँ[5] / ईँ̣[6,7]		ĩˑ˨
0A6	i1#^98	ई॑[1–4]		iˑ˥˧
0A7	i1#^98~	ईँ॑[1–4]		ĩˑ˥˧
0A8	i1#^97	ई३॒॑[1,4]		iˑ˨˥
0A9	i1#^97~	ईँ३॒॑[1,4]		ĩˑ˨˥
0AA	i1#^87	ई᳛[5] / ई̣[6,7]		iˑ˧˥
0AB	i1#^87~	ईँ᳛[5] / ईँ̣[6,7]		ĩˑ˧˥
0AC	i1#^87+	ई॒[5,6] / ई॒[7]		iˑ˧˥
0AD	i1#^87+~	ईँ॒[5,6] / ईँ॒[7]		ĩˑ˧˥
0AE	i1#^86	३ई॒[5] / ई॒[6]		iˑ˨˦
0AF	i1#^86~	३ईँ॒[5] / ईँ॒[6]		ĩˑ˨˦
0B0	I	ई	ī	iː
0B1	I~	ईँ	ī̃	ĩː
0B2	I/	ई॑[1–4] / ई॑[5–7] / ई॑[8]	ī́	íː
0B3	I/~	ईँ॑[1–4] / ईँ॑[5–7] / ईँ॑[8]	ī̃́	í̃ː

SLP2	SLP1	DEVANĀGARĪ	ROMAN	IPA
0B4	`I\`	ई॒[1–5] / ई॒[6,7] / ई॑[8]	ī/ī̱	ì:
0B5	`I\~`	ईँ॒[1–5] / ईँ॒[6,7] / ईँ॑[8]	ī̃/ī̱̃	ĩ̀:
0B6	`I^`	ई॑[1,3] / ई॒[2] / ई॑[8]	ī̀	î:
0B7	`I^~`	ईँ॑[1,3] / ईँ॒[2] / ईँ॑[8]	ī̃̀	ĩ̂:
0B8	`I/8`	ई[1–4] / ई॑[5–7]		i:˥
0B9	`I/8~`	ईँ[1–4] / ईँ॑[5–7]		ĩ:˥
0BA	`I\7`	ई॒[1–4] / ई॒[5–6] / ई॒[7]		i:˧
0BB	`I\7~`	ईँ॒[1–4] / ईँ॒[5–6] / ईँ॒[7]		ĩ:˧
0BC	`I\6`	ई॒[5] / ई॒[6,7]		i:˨
0BD	`I\6~`	ईँ॒[5] / ईँ॒[6,7]		ĩ:˨
0BE	`I^98`	ई॑[1–4]		i:˥˦
0BF	`I^98~`	ईँ॑[1–4]		ĩ:˥˦
0C0	`I^97`	ई॒३॑[1,4]		i:˥˧
0C1	`I^97~`	ईँ॒३॑[1,4]		ĩ:˥˧
0C2	`I^87`	ई॑[5] / ई॒[6,7]		i:˦˧
0C3	`I^87~`	ईँ॑[5] / ईँ॒[6,7]		ĩ:˦˧
0C4	`I^87+`	ई॒[5,6] / ई॒[7]		i:˦˧
0C5	`I^87+~`	ईँ॒[5,6] / ईँ॒[7]		ĩ:˦˧
0C6	`I^86`	३ई॒[5] / ई॒[6]		i:˦˨
0C7	`I^86~`	३ईँ॒[5] / ईँ॒[6]		ĩ:˦˨
0C8	`i3`	इ३	i3	iːː
0C9	`i3~`	इँ३	ĩ3	ĩːː
0CA	`i3/`	इ३[1–4] / इ॑३[5–7] / इ॑३[8]	í3	íːː

SLP2	SLP1	Devanāgarī	Roman	IPA
0CB	i3/~	ईँ३ [1–4] / ईँ३ [5–7] / ईँ३ [8]	ĩ́3	ĩ́::
0CC	i3\	इ३ [1–7] / इ३ [8]	ì3/i̱3	ì::
0CD	i3\~	इँ३ [1–7] / इँ३ [8]	ĩ̀3/ĩ̱3	ĩ̀::
0CE	i3^	इ३ [1,3] / इ३ [2] / इ३ [8]	ȋ3	î::
0CF	i3^~	इँ३ [1,3] / इँ३ [2] / इँ३ [8]	ȋ̃3	ĩ̂::
0D0	i3/8	इ३ [1–4] / इ३ [5–7]		i::˥
0D1	i3/8~	इँ३ [1–4] / इँ३ [5–7]		ĩ::˥
0D2	i3\7	इ३ [1–4] / इ३ [5–7]		i::˧
0D3	i3\7~	इँ३ [1–4] / इँ३ [5–7]		ĩ::˧
0D4	i3\6	इ३ [5] / इ३ [6,7]		i::˨
0D5	i3\6~	इँ३ [5] / इँ३ [6,7]		ĩ::˨
0D6	i3^98	इ३ [1–4]		i::˥˦
0D7	i3^98~	इँ३ [1–4]		ĩ::˥˦
0D8	i3^97	इ३ [1,4]		i::˧˥
0D9	i3^97~	इँ३ [1,4]		ĩ::˧˥
0DA	i3^87	इ३ [5] / इ३ [6,7]		i::˧˦
0DB	i3^87~	इँ३ [5] / इँ३ [6,7]		ĩ::˧˦
0DC	i3^87+	इ३ [5,6] / इ३ [7]		i::˧˦
0DD	i3^87+~	इँ३ [5,6] / इँ३ [7]		ĩ::˧˦
0DE	i3^86	३इ३ [5] / इ३ [6]		i::˨˦
0DF	i3^86~	३इँ३ [5] / इँ३ [6]		ĩ::˨˦
0E0	i4~	इँ४	ĩ4	ĩ:::
0E1	i4/~	इँ४ [1–4] / इँ४ [5–7] / इँ४ [8]	ĩ́4	ĩ́:::

SLP2	SLP1	DEVANĀGARĪ	ROMAN	IPA
0E2	i4\~	ई॒ँ३ [1–7] / ई॑ँ३ [8]	ĩ4/ĩ̱4	ĩ̀:::
0E3	i4^~	ई᳚ँ३ [1,3] / ई॒ँ३ [2] / ई॑ँ३ [8]	ĩ̀4	ĩ̂:::
0E4	i4/8~	ईँ३ [1–4] / ई॑ँ३ [5–7]		ĩ:::˥
0E5	i4\7~	ई॒ँ३ [1–4] / ई॒ँ३ [5–7]		ĩ:::˧
0E6	i4\6~	ई॒ँ३ [5] / ई॒ँ३ [6,7]		ĩ:::˨
0E7	i4^98~	ई॑ँ३ [1–4]		ĩ:::˥˦
0E8	i4^97~			ĩ:::˥˧
0E9	i4^87~	ईँ३ [5] / ई॒ँ३ [6,7]		ĩ:::˦˧
0EA	i4^87+~	ई॒ँ३ [5,6] / ई॒ँ३ [7]		ĩ:::˦˧
0EB	i4^86~	३ई॒ँ३ [5] / ई॒ँ३ [6]		ĩ:::˦˨
0EC	i*		i	ĭ
100	u	उ	u	u
101	u~	उँ	ũ	ũ
102	u/	उ [1–4] / उ॑ [5–7] / उ॑ [8]	ú	ú
103	u/~	उँ [1–4] / उ॑ँ [5–7] / उ॑ँ [8]	ű	ű
104	u\	उ॒ [1–5] / उ॒ [6,7] / उ॑ [8]	u/u̱	ù
105	u\~	उ॒ँ [1–5] / उ॒ँ [6,7] / उ॑ँ [8]	ũ/ũ̱	ũ̀
106	u^	उ॑ [1,3] / उ॒ [2] / उ᳚ [8]	ù	û
107	u^~	उ॑ँ [1,3] / उ॒ँ [2] / उ᳚ँ [8]	ũ̀	ũ̂
108	u/8	उ [1–4] / उ॑ [5–7]		u˥
109	u/8~	उँ [1–4] / उ॑ँ [5–7]		ũ˥
10A	u\7	उ॒ [1–4] / उ [5–6] / उ॒ [7]		u˧
10B	u\7~	उ॒ँ [1–4] / उँ [5–6] / उ॒ँ [7]		ũ˧

SLP2	SLP1	DEVANĀGARĪ	ROMAN	IPA
10C	u\6	उ॒[5] / उ᳭[6,7]		u˧
10D	u\6~	उँ॒[5] / उँ᳭[6,7]		ũ˧
10E	u^98	उ॑[1-4]		u˥
10F	u^98~	उँ॑[1-4]		ũ˥
110	u^97	उ१॒॑[1,4]		u˥˦
111	u^97~	उँ१॒॑[1,4]		ũ˥˦
112	u^87	उ᳚[5] / उ᳭[6,7]		u˦˧
113	u^87~	उँ᳚[5] / उँ᳭[6,7]		ũ˦˧
114	u^87+	उ॒[5,6] / उ॒[7]		u˦˧
115	u^87+~	उँ॒[5,6] / उँ॒[7]		ũ˦˧
116	u^86	ꣳउ॒[5] / उ॒[6]		u˦˨
117	u^86~	ꣳउँ॒[5] / उँ॒[6]		ũ˦˨
118	u1#	उ	u	uˑ
119	u1#~	उँ	ũ	ũˑ
11A	u1#/	उ[1-4] / उ॑[5-7] / उ॑[8]	ú	úˑ
11B	u1#/~	उँ[1-4] / उँ॑[5-7] / उँ॑[8]	ű	űˑ
11C	u1#\	उ॒[1-5] / उ᳭[6,7] / उ॑[8]	u/u̲	ùˑ
11D	u1#\~	उँ॒[1-5] / उँ᳭[6,7] / उँ॑[8]	ũ/ũ̲	ȕˑ
11E	u1#^	उ॑[1,3] / उ॒[2] / उ᳒[8]	ù	ûˑ
11F	u1#^~	उँ॑[1,3] / उँ॒[2] / उँ᳒[8]	ȕ	û̃ˑ
120	u1#/8	उ[1-4] / उ॑[5-7]		uˑ˥
121	u1#/8~	उँ[1-4] / उँ॑[5-7]		ũˑ˥
122	u1#\7	उ॒[1-4] / उ[5-6] / उ᳭[7]		uˑ˧

SLP2	SLP1	DEVANĀGARĪ	ROMAN	IPA
123	`u1#\7~`	उँ॒[1–4] / उँ॒[5–6] / उँ़[7]		ũ·˧
124	`u1#\6`	उ॒[5] / उ᳭[6,7]		u·˨
125	`u1#\6~`	उँ॒[5] / उँ᳭[6,7]		ũ·˨
126	`u1#^98`	उ॑[1–4]		u·˥
127	`u1#^98~`	उँ॑[1–4]		ũ·˥
128	`u1#^97`	उ१॒॑ [1,4]		u·˥˧
129	`u1#^97~`	उँ१॒॑ [1,4]		ũ·˥˧
12A	`u1#^87`	उ᳚[5] / उ़[6,7]		u·˧˦
12B	`u1#^87~`	उँ᳚[5] / उँ़[6,7]		ũ·˧˦
12C	`u1#^87+`	उ᳕[5,6] / उ᳕[7]		u·˧˦
12D	`u1#^87+~`	उँ᳕[5,6] / उँ᳕[7]		ũ·˧˦
12E	`u1#^86`	३उ॒[5] / उ᳕[6]		u·˨˦
12F	`u1#^86~`	३उँ॒[5] / उँ᳕[6]		ũ·˨˦
130	`U`	ऊ	ū	uː
131	`U~`	ऊँ	ū̃	ũː
132	`U/`	ऊ[1–4] / ऊ॑[5–7] / ऊ॑[8]	ū́	úː
133	`U/~`	ऊँ[1–4] / ऊँ॑[5–7] / ऊँ॑[8]	ū̃́	ṹː
134	`U\`	ऊ॒[1–5] / ऊ᳭[6,7] / ऊ॑[8]	ū/ū̱	ùː
135	`U\~`	ऊँ॒[1–5] / ऊँ᳭[6,7] / ऊँ॑[8]	ū̃/ū̱̃	ũ̀ː
136	`U^`	ऊ॑[1,3] / ऊ᳕[2] / ऊ᳒[8]	ū̀	ûː
137	`U^~`	ऊँ॑[1,3] / ऊँ᳕[2] / ऊँ᳒[8]	ū̃̀	ũ̂ː
138	`U/8`	ऊ[1–4] / ऊ॑[5–7]		uː˦
139	`U/8~`	ऊँ[1–4] / ऊँ॑[5–7]		ũː˦

SLP2	SLP1	Devanāgarī	Roman	IPA
13A	U\7	ऊ॒[1–4] / ऊ[5–6] / ऊ़[7]		u:˧
13B	U\7~	ऊँ॒[1–4] / ऊँ[5–6] / ऊँ़[7]		ũ:˧
13C	U\6	ऊ॒[5] / ऊ᳭[6,7]		u:˧
13D	U\6~	ऊँ॒[5] / ऊँ᳭[6,7]		ũ:˧
13E	U^98	ऊ॑[1–4]		u:˥
13F	U^98~	ऊँ॑[1–4]		ũ:˥
140	U^97	ऊ॒३॒॑[1,4]		u:˥˧
141	U^97~	ऊँ॒३॒॑[1,4]		ũ:˥˧
142	U^87	ऊ᳛[5] / ऊ़[6,7]		u:˦˧
143	U^87~	ऊँ᳛[5] / ऊँ़[6,7]		ũ:˦˧
144	U^87+	ऊ᳘[5,6] / ऊ᳘[7]		u:˦˧
145	U^87+~	ऊँ᳘[5,6] / ऊँ᳘[7]		ũ:˦˧
146	U^86	३ऊ॒[5] / ऊ᳙[6]		u:˦˨
147	U^86~	३ऊँ॒[5] / ऊँ᳙[6]		ũ:˦˨
148	u3	उ३	u3	u::
149	u3~	उँ३	ũ3	ũ::
14A	u3/	उ३[1–4] / उ॑३[5–7] / उ॑३[8]	ú3	ú::
14B	u3/~	उँ३[1–4] / उँ॑३[5–7] / उँ॑३[8]	ṹ3	ṹ::
14C	u3\	उ॒३[1–7] / उ॑३[8]	u3/u̱3	ù::
14D	u3\~	उँ॒३[1–7] / उँ॑३[8]	ũ3/ũ̱3	ũ̀::
14E	u3^	उ॑३[1,3] / उ᳘३[2] / उ꣢३[8]	ù3	û::
14F	u3^~	उँ॑३[1,3] / उँ᳘३[2] / उँ꣢३[8]	ũ̀3	ũ̂::
150	u3/8	उ३[1–4] / उ॑३[5–7]		u::˥

SLP2	SLP1	DEVANĀGARĪ	ROMAN	IPA
151	u3/8~	उँ३ [1–4] / उँ॑३ [5–7]		ũ::˥
152	u3\7	उ॒३ [1–4] / उ३ [5–7]		u::˧
153	u3\7~	उँ॒३ [1–4] / उँ३ [5–7]		ũ::˧
154	u3\6	उ॒३ [5] / उ᳭३ [6,7]		u::˨
155	u3\6~	उँ॒३ [5] / उँ᳭३ [6,7]		ũ::˨
156	u3^98	उ॑३ [1–4]		u::˥˦
157	u3^98~	उँ॑३ [1–4]		ũ::˥˦
158	u3^97	उ॒३॒॑ [1,4]		u::˧˥
159	u3^97~	उँ॒३॒॑ [1,4]		ũ::˧˥
15A	u3^87	उ᳚३ [5] / उ᳭३ [6,7]		u::˦˥
15B	u3^87~	उँ᳚३ [5] / उँ᳭३ [6,7]		ũ::˦˥
15C	u3^87+	उ᳖३ [5,6] / उ᳖३ [7]		u::˨˦
15D	u3^87+~	उँ᳖३ [5,6] / उँ᳖३ [7]		ũ::˨˦
15E	u3^86	३उ॒३ [5] / उ᳘३ [6]		u::˨˥
15F	u3^86~	३उँ॒३ [5] / उँ᳘३ [6]		ũ::˨˥
160	u4~	उँ४	ũ4	ũ:::
161	u4/~	उँ४ [1–4] / उँ॑४ [5–7] / उँ॑४ [8]	ṹ4	ṹ:::
162	u4\~	उँ॒४ [1–7] / उँ॑४ [8]	ũ4/ũ̱4	ũ̀:::
163	u4^~	उ॑४ [1,3] / उँ॒४ [2] / उँ॑४ [8]	ũ̀4	ũ̂:::
164	u4/8~	उँ४ [1–4] / उँ॑४ [5–7]		ũ:::˥
165	u4\7~	उँ॒४ [1–4] / उँ४ [5–7]		ũ:::˧
166	u4\6~	उँ॒४ [5] / उँ᳭४ [6,7]		ũ:::˨
167	u4^98~	उँ॑४ [1–4]		ũ:::˥˦

SLP2	SLP1	Devanāgarī	Roman	IPA
168	u4^97~			ũ:::˦˨
169	u4^87~	उँ४[5] / उँ४[6,7]		ũ:::˦˨
16A	u4^87+~	उँ४[5,6] / उँ४[7]		ũ:::˦˨
16B	u4^86~	३उँ४[5] / उँ४[6]		ũ:::˦˨
16C	u*		u	ŭ
180	f	ऋ	r̥	ɹ̩
181	f~	ऋँ	r̥̃	ɹ̩̃
182	f/	ऋ[1-4] / ऋ॑[5-7] / ऋ॑[8]	ŕ̥	ɹ̩́
183	f/~	ऋँ[1-4] / ऋँ॑[5-7] / ऋँ॑[8]	ŕ̥̃	ɹ̩̃́
184	f\	ऋ॒[1-5] / ऋ॒[6,7] / ऋ॒[8]	r̥/r̥̱	ɹ̩̀
185	f\~	ऋँ॒[1-5] / ऋँ॒[6,7] / ऋँ॒[8]	r̥̃/r̥̱̃	ɹ̩̃̀
186	f^	ऋ॑[1,3] / ऋ॒[2] / ऋ॑[8]	r̥̂	ɹ̩̂
187	f^~	ऋँ॑[1,3] / ऋँ॒[2] / ऋँ॑[8]	r̥̂̃	ɹ̩̂̃
188	f/8	ऋ[1-4] / ऋ॑[5-7]		ɹ̩˥˩
189	f/8~	ऋँ[1-4] / ऋँ॑[5-7]		ɹ̩̃˥˩
18A	f\7	ऋ॒[1-4] / ऋ[5-6] / ऋ॒[7]		ɹ̩˧˩
18B	f\7~	ऋँ॒[1-4] / ऋँ[5-6] / ऋँ॒[7]		ɹ̩̃˧˩
18C	f\6	ऋ॒[5] / ऋ[6,7]		ɹ̩˧˩
18D	f\6~	ऋँ॒[5] / ऋँ[6,7]		ɹ̩̃˧˩
18E	f^98	ऋ॑[1-4]		ɹ̩˥˨
18F	f^98~	ऋँ॑[1-4]		ɹ̩̃˥˨
190	f^97	ऋ१॒[1,4]		ɹ̩˦˨
191	f^97~	ऋँ१॒[1,4]		ɹ̩̃˦˨

SLP2	SLP1	Devanāgarī	Roman	IPA
192	f^87	ऋ[5] / ऋ[6,7]		ɻ̩˩˥
193	f^87~	ऋ[5] / ऋ[6,7]		ɻ̩̃˩˥
194	f^87+	ऋ[5,6] / ऋ[7]		ɻ̩˩˥
195	f^87+~	ऋ[5,6] / ऋ[7]		ɻ̩̃˩˥
196	f^86	३ऋ[5] / ऋ[6]		ɻ̩˨˥
197	f^86~	३ऋ[5] / ऋ[6]		ɻ̩̃˨˥
198	f1#	ऋ	r̥	ɻ̩ˑ
199	f1#~	ऋ	r̥̃	ɻ̩̃ˑ
19A	f1#/	ऋ[1–4] / ऋ[5–7] / ऋ[8]	ŕ̥	ɻ̩́ˑ
19B	f1#/~	ऋ[1–4] / ऋ[5–7] / ऋ[8]	ŕ̥̃	ɻ̩̃́ˑ
19C	f1#\	ऋ[1–5] / ऋ[6,7] / ऋ[8]	r̥/r̥̱	ɻ̩̀ˑ
19D	f1#\~	ऋ[1–5] / ऋ[6,7] / ऋ[8]	r̥̃/r̥̱̃	ɻ̩̃̀ˑ
19E	f1#^	ऋ[1,3] / ऋ[2] / ऋ[8]	r̥̀	ɻ̩̂ˑ
19F	f1#^~	ऋ[1,3] / ऋ[2] / ऋ[8]	r̥̃̀	ɻ̩̃̂ˑ
1A0	f1#/8	ऋ[1–4] / ऋ[5–7]		ɻ̩ˑ˥
1A1	f1#/8~	ऋ[1–4] / ऋ[5–7]		ɻ̩̃ˑ˥
1A2	f1#\7	ऋ[1–4] / ऋ[5–6] / ऋ[7]		ɻ̩ˑ˧
1A3	f1#\7~	ऋ[1–4] / ऋ[5–6] / ऋ[7]		ɻ̩̃ˑ˧
1A4	f1#\6	ऋ[5] / ऋ[6,7]		ɻ̩ˑ˨
1A5	f1#\6~	ऋ[5] / ऋ[6,7]		ɻ̩̃ˑ˨
1A6	f1#^98	ऋ[1–4]		ɻ̩ˑ˥˩
1A7	f1#^98~	ऋ[1–4]		ɻ̩̃ˑ˥˩
1A8	f1#^97	ऋ[1,4]		ɻ̩ˑ˦˥

SLP2	SLP1	DEVANĀGARĪ	ROMAN	IPA
1A9	f1#^97~	ॠँ१ [1,4]		ɹ̩̃ˑ˦˥
1AA	f1#^87	ॠ॒ [5] / ॠ॒ [6,7]		ɹ̩ˑ˦˥
1AB	f1#^87~	ॠँ [5] / ॠँ [6,7]		ɹ̩̃ˑ˦˥
1AC	f1#^87+	ॠ᳚ [5,6] / ॠ᳚ [7]		ɹ̩ˑ˦˥
1AD	f1#^87+~	ॠँ [5,6] / ॠँ [7]		ɹ̩̃ˑ˦˥
1AE	f1#^86	३ ॠ॒ [5] / ॠ [6]		ɹ̩ˑ˦˥
1AF	f1#^86~	३ ॠँ [5] / ॠँ [6]		ɹ̩̃ˑ˦˥
1B0	F	ॠ	r̥̄	ɹ̩ː
1B1	F~	ॠँ	r̥̄̃	ɹ̩̃ː
1B2	F/	ॠ [1-4] / ॠ॑ [5-7] / ॠ॑ [8]	r̥̄́	ɹ̩́ː
1B3	F/~	ॠँ [1-4] / ॠँ॑ [5-7] / ॠँ॑ [8]	r̥̄̃́	ɹ̩̃́ː
1B4	F\	ॠ॒ [1-5] / ॠ [6,7] / ॠ॑ [8]	r̥̄/r̥̱̄	ɹ̩̀ː
1B5	F\~	ॠँ॒ [1-5] / ॠँ [6,7] / ॠँ॑ [8]	r̥̄̃/r̥̱̄̃	ɹ̩̃̀ː
1B6	F^	ॠ॑ [1,3] / ॠ᳚ [2] / ॠ [8]	r̥̄̂	ɹ̩̂ː
1B7	F^~	ॠँ॑ [1,3] / ॠँ [2] / ॠँ [8]	r̥̄̃̂	ɹ̩̃̂ː
1B8	F/8	ॠ [1-4] / ॠ॑ [5-7]		ɹ̩ː˥
1B9	F/8~	ॠँ [1-4] / ॠँ॑ [5-7]		ɹ̩̃ː˥
1BA	F\7	ॠ॒ [1-4] / ॠ [5-6] / ॠ [7]		ɹ̩ː˧
1BB	F\7~	ॠँ॒ [1-4] / ॠँ [5-6] / ॠँ [7]		ɹ̩̃ː˧
1BC	F\6	• ॠ॒ [5] / ॠ [6,7]		ɹ̩ː˧
1BD	F\6~	ॠँ॒ [5] / ॠँ [6,7]		ɹ̩̃ː˧
1BE	F^98	ॠ॑ [1-4]		ɹ̩ː˥˦
1BF	F^98~	ॠँ॑ [1-4]		ɹ̩̃ː˥˦

SLP2	SLP1	DEVANĀGARĪ	ROMAN	IPA
1C0	F^97	ऋ॒३॑ [1,4]		ɻ̩ː˧˥
1C1	F^97~	ऋँ॒३॑ [1,4]		ɻ̩̃ː˧˥
1C2	F^87	ऋ᳚ [5] / ऋ᳭ [6,7]		ɻ̩ː˧˥
1C3	F^87~	ऋँ᳚ [5] / ऋँ᳭ [6,7]		ɻ̩̃ː˧˥
1C4	F^87+	ऋ᳕ [5,6] / ऋ॒ [7]		ɻ̩ː˧˥
1C5	F^87+~	ऋँ᳕ [5,6] / ऋँ॒ [7]		ɻ̩̃ː˧˥
1C6	F^86	३ऋ॒ [5] / ऋ᳕ [6]		ɻ̩ː˨˥
1C7	F^86~	३ऋँ॒ [5] / ऋँ᳕ [6]		ɻ̩̃ː˨˥
1C8	f3	ऋ३	r̥3	ɻ̩ːː
1C9	f3~	ऋँ३	r̥̃3	ɻ̩̃ːː
1CA	f3/	ऋ३ [1-4] / ऋ॑३ [5-7] / ऋ॑३ [8]	ŕ̥3	ɻ̩́ːː
1CB	f3/~	ऋँ३ [1-4] / ऋँ॑३ [5-7] / ऋँ॑३ [8]	ŕ̥̃3	ɻ̩̃́ːː
1CC	f3\	ऋ॒३ [1-7] / ऋ॑३ [8]	r̥3/r̥̱3	ɻ̩̀ːː
1CD	f3\~	ऋँ॒३ [1-7] / ऋँ॑३ [8]	r̥̃3/r̥̱̃3	ɻ̩̃̀ːː
1CE	f3^	ऋ॑३ [1,3] / ऋ॒३ [2] / ऋ॑३ [8]	r̥̀3	ɻ̩̂ːː
1CF	f3^~	ऋँ॑३ [1,3] / ऋँ॒३ [2] / ऋँ॑३ [8]	r̥̃̀3	ɻ̩̃̂ːː
1D0	f3/8	ऋ३ [1-4] / ऋ॑३ [5-7]		ɻ̩ːː˥
1D1	f3/8~	ऋँ३ [1-4] / ऋँ॑३ [5-7]		ɻ̩̃ːː˥
1D2	f3\7	ऋ॒३ [1-4] / ऋ३ [5-7]		ɻ̩ːː˧
1D3	f3\7~	ऋँ॒३ [1-4] / ऋँ३ [5-7]		ɻ̩̃ːː˧
1D4	f3\6	ऋ॒३ [5] / ऋ᳭३ [6,7]		ɻ̩ːː˧
1D5	f3\6~	ऋँ॒३ [5] / ऋँ᳭३ [6,7]		ɻ̩̃ːː˧
1D6	f3^98	ऋ॑३ [1-4]		ɻ̩ːː˥

SLP2	SLP1	Devanāgarī	Roman	IPA
1D7	f3^98~	ॠ३ [1–4]		ɻ̩̃ːː˥
1D8	f3^97	ॠ३ [1,4]		ɻ̩ːː˧˥
1D9	f3^97~	ॠ३ [1,4]		ɻ̩̃ːː˧˥
1DA	f3^87	ॠ३ [5] / ॠ३ [6,7]		ɻ̩ːː˧˥
1DB	f3^87~	ॠ३ [5] / ॠ३ [6,7]		ɻ̩̃ːː˥
1DC	f3^87+	ॠ३ [5,6] / ॠ३ [7]		ɻ̩ːː˥
1DD	f3^87+~	ॠ३ [5,6] / ॠ३ [7]		ɻ̩̃ːː˥
1DE	f3^86	३ॠ३ [5] / ॠ३ [6]		ɻ̩ːː˧˥
1DF	f3^86~	३ॠ३ [5] / ॠ३ [6]		ɻ̩̃ːː˧˥
1E0	f4~	ॠ४	r̥̃4	ɻ̩̃ːːː
1E1	f4/~	ॠ४ [1–4] / ॠ४ [5–7] / ॠ४ [8]	ŕ̥4	ɻ̩̃́ːːː
1E2	f4\~	ॠ४ [1–7] / ॠ४ [8]	r̥̃4/r̥̱̃4	ɻ̩̃̀ːːː
1E3	f4^~	ॠ४ [1,3] / ॠ४ [2] / ॠ४ [8]	r̥̀4	ɻ̩̂ːːː
1E4	f4/8~	ॠ४ [1–4] / ॠ४ [5–7]		ɻ̩̃ːːː˥
1E5	f4\7~	ॠ४ [1–4] / ॠ४ [5–7]		ɻ̩̃ːːː˧
1E6	f4\6~	ॠ४ [5] / ॠ४ [6,7]		ɻ̩̃ːːː˧
1E7	f4^98~	ॠ४ [1–4]		ɻ̩̃ːːː˥
1E8	f4^97~			ɻ̩̃ːːː˧˥
1E9	f4^87~	ॠ४ [5] / ॠ४ [6,7]		ɻ̩̃ːːː˧˥
1EA	f4^87+~	ॠ४ [5,6] / ॠ४ [7]		ɻ̩̃ːːː˧˥
1EB	f4^86~	३ॠ४ [5] / ॠ४ [6]		ɻ̩̃ːːː˧˥
1EC	f*		r̆	ɻ̩̆
200	x	ऌ	l̥	l̩

SLP2	SLP1	DEVANĀGARĪ	ROMAN	IPA
201	x~	ऌँ	l̥̃	l̩̃
202	x/	ऌ[1–4] / ऌ॑[5–7] / ऌ॑[8]	ĺ̥	ĺ̩
203	x/~	ऌँ[1–4] / ऌँ॑[5–7] / ऌँ॑[8]	ĺ̥̃	ĺ̩̃
204	x\	ऌ॒[1–5] / ऌ᳭[6,7] / ऌ॑[8]	l̥/l̥̱	l̩̀
205	x\~	ऌँ॒[1–5] / ऌँ᳭[6,7] / ऌँ॑[8]	l̥̃/l̥̱̃	l̩̀̃
206	x^	ऌ॑[1,3] / ऌ॒[2] / ऌ᳚[8]	l̥̀	l̩̂
207	x^~	ऌँ॑[1,3] / ऌँ॒[2] / ऌँ᳚[8]	l̥̀̃	l̩̂̃
208	x/8	ऌ[1–4] / ऌ॑[5–7]		l̩˥
209	x/8~	ऌँ[1–4] / ऌँ॑[5–7]		l̩̃˥
20A	x\7	ऌ॒[1–4] / ऌ[5–6] / ऌ᳭[7]		l̩˧
20B	x\7~	ऌँ॒[1–4] / ऌँ[5–6] / ऌँ᳭[7]		l̩̃˧
20C	x\6	ऌ॒[5] / ऌ᳭[6,7]		l̩˩
20D	x\6~	ऌँ॒[5] / ऌँ᳭[6,7]		l̩̃˩
20E	x^98	ऌ॑[1–4]		l̩˥˦
20F	x^98~	ऌँ॑[1–4]		l̩̃˥˦
210	x^97	ऌ१॑[1,4]		l̩˥˧
211	x^97~	ऌँ१॑[1,4]		l̩̃˥˧
212	x^87	ऌ᳚[5] / ऌ᳭[6,7]		l̩˦˧
213	x^87~	ऌँ᳚[5] / ऌँ᳭[6,7]		l̩̃˦˧
214	x^87+	ऌ᳕[5,6] / ऌ॒[7]		l̩˦˨
215	x^87+~	ऌँ᳕[5,6] / ऌँ॒[7]		l̩̃˦˨
216	x^86	३ऌ॒[5] / ऌ᳕[6]		l̩˧˩
217	x^86~	३ऌँ॒[5] / ऌँ᳕[6]		l̩̃˧˩

SLP2	SLP1	DEVANĀGARĪ	ROMAN	IPA
218	x1#	ऌ	l̥	l̩·
219	x1#~	ऌँ	l̥̃	l̩̃·
21A	x1#/	ऌ[1–4] / ऌ॑[5–7] / ऌ॑[8]	ĺ̥	ĺ̩·
21B	x1#/~	ऌँ[1–4] / ऌँ॑[5–7] / ऌँ॑[8]	l̥̃́	l̩̃́·
21C	x1#\	ऌ॒[1–5] / ऌ॒[6,7] / ऌ॑[8]	l̥/l̥̱	l̩̀·
21D	x1#\~	ऌँ॒[1–5] / ऌँ॒[6,7] / ऌँ॑[8]	l̥̃/l̥̱̃	l̩̃̀·
21E	x1#^	ऌ॑[1,3] / ऌ॒[2] / ऌ॑[8]	l̥̂	l̩̂·
21F	x1#^~	ऌँ॑[1,3] / ऌँ॒[2] / ऌँ॑[8]	l̥̃̂	l̩̃̂·
220	x1#/8	ऌ[1–4] / ऌ॑[5–7]		l̩·˥
221	x1#/8~	ऌँ[1–4] / ऌँ॑[5–7]		l̩̃·˥
222	x1#\7	ऌ॒[1–4] / ऌ[5–6] / ऌ॒[7]		l̩·˧
223	x1#\7~	ऌँ॒[1–4] / ऌँ[5–6] / ऌँ॒[7]		l̩̃·˧
224	x1#\6	ऌ॒[5] / ऌ॒[6,7]		l̩·˨
225	x1#\6~	ऌँ॒[5] / ऌँ॒[6,7]		l̩̃·˨
226	x1#^98	ऌ॑[1–4]		l̩·˥˦
227	x1#^98~	ऌँ॑[1–4]		l̩̃·˥˦
228	x1#^97	ऌ१॑[1,4]		l̩·˥˧
229	x1#^97~	ऌँ१॑[1,4]		l̩̃·˥˧
22A	x1#^87	ऌँ[5] / ऌ॒[6,7]		l̩·˦˧
22B	x1#^87~	ऌँ[5] / ऌँ॒[6,7]		l̩̃·˦˧
22C	x1#^87+	ऌ॒[5,6] / ऌ॒[7]		l̩·˦˧
22D	x1#^87+~	ऌँ॒[5,6] / ऌँ॒[7]		l̩̃·˦˧
22E	x1#^86	३ऌ॒[5] / ऌ॒[6]		l̩·˦˨

SLP2	SLP1	DEVANĀGARĪ	ROMAN	IPA
22F	x1#^86~	३ॡँ॒[5] / ॡँ॒[6]		l̩̃·˧˦
230	X	ॡ	l̥̄	l̩ː
231	X~	ॡँ	l̥̄̃	l̩̃ː
232	X/	ॡ[1–4] / ॡ॑[5–7] / ॡ॑[8]	ĺ̥̄	ĺ̩ː
233	X/~	ॡँ[1–4] / ॡँ॑[5–7] / ॡँ॑[8]	l̥̄̃́	l̩̃́ː
234	X\	ॡ॒[1–5] / ॡ॒[6,7] / ॡ॑[8]	l̥̄/l̥̱̄	l̩̀ː
235	X\~	ॡँ॒[1–5] / ॡँ॒[6,7] / ॡँ॑[8]	l̥̄̃/l̥̱̄̃	l̩̃̀ː
236	X^	ॡ॑[1,3] / ॡ॒[2] / ॡ॑[8]	l̥̄̀	l̩̂ː
237	X^~	ॡँ॑[1,3] / ॡँ॒[2] / ॡँ॑[8]	l̥̄̃̀	l̩̃̂ː
238	X/8	ॡ[1–4] / ॡ॑[5–7]		l̩ː˥
239	X/8~	ॡँ[1–4] / ॡँ॑[5–7]		l̩̃ː˥
23A	X\7	ॡ॒[1–4] / ॡ[5–6] / ॡ॒[7]		l̩ː˧
23B	X\7~	ॡँ॒[1–4] / ॡँ[5–6] / ॡँ॒[7]		l̩̃ː˧
23C	X\6	ॡ॒[5] / ॡ॒[6,7]		l̩ː˨
23D	X\6~	ॡँ॒[5] / ॡँ॒[6,7]		l̩̃ː˨
23E	X^98	ॡ॑[1–4]		l̩ː˥˦
23F	X^98~	ॡँ॑[1–4]		l̩̃ː˥˦
240	X^97	ॡ॒३॒॑[1,4]		l̩ː˧˦
241	X^97~	ॡँ॒३॒॑[1,4]		l̩̃ː˧˦
242	X^87	ॡ᳚[5] / ॡ॒[6,7]		l̩ː˧˥
243	X^87~	ॡँ᳚[5] / ॡँ॒[6,7]		l̩̃ː˧˥
244	X^87+	ॡ॒[5,6] / ॡ॒[7]		l̩ː˧˥
245	X^87+~	ॡँ॒[5,6] / ॡँ॒[7]		l̩̃ː˧˥

SLP2	SLP1	DEVANĀGARĪ	ROMAN	IPA
246	**X^86**	३ॡ[5] / ॡ[6]		l̩ː˨˦˨
247	**X^86~**	३ॡँ[5] / ॡँ[6]		l̩̃ː˨˦˨
248	**x3**	ऌ३	ḷ3	l̩ːː
249	**x3~**	ऌँ३	ḷ̃3	l̩̃ːː
24A	**x3/**	ऌ३[1–4] / ऌ॑३[5–7] / ऌ॑३[8]	ḷ́3	ĺ̩ːː
24B	**x3/~**	ऌँ३[1–4] / ऌँ॑३[5–7] / ऌँ॑३[8]	ḷ̃́3	l̩̃́ːː
24C	**x3**	ऌ॒३[1–7] / ऌ॑३[8]	ḷ3/ḷ̱3	l̩̀ːː
24D	**x3\\~**	ऌँ॒३[1–7] / ऌँ॑३[8]	ḷ̃3/ḷ̱̃3	l̩̃̀ːː
24E	**x3^**	ऌ॑३[1,3] / ऌ॒३[2] / ऌ॑३[8]	ḷ̀3	l̩̂ːː
24F	**x3^~**	ऌँ॑३[1,3] / ऌँ॒३[2] / ऌँ॑३[8]	ḷ̃̀3	l̩̃̂ːː
250	**x3/8**	ऌ३[1–4] / ऌ॑३[5–7]		l̩ːː˥
251	**x3/8~**	ऌँ३[1–4] / ऌँ॑३[5–7]		l̩̃ːː˥
252	**x3\\7**	ऌ॒३[1–4] / ऌ३[5–7]		l̩ːː˧
253	**x3\\7~**	ऌँ॒३[1–4] / ऌँ३[5–7]		l̩̃ːː˧
254	**x3\\6**	ऌ॒३[5] / ऌ३[6,7]		l̩ːː˨
255	**x3\\6~**	ऌँ॒३[5] / ऌँ३[6,7]		l̩̃ːː˨
256	**x3^98**	ऌ॑३[1–4]		l̩ːː˥˧
257	**x3^98~**	ऌँ॑३[1–4]		l̩̃ːː˥˧
258	**x3^97**	ऌ॒३॑[1,4]		l̩ːː˧˥˧
259	**x3^97~**	ऌँ॒३॑[1,4]		l̩̃ːː˧˥˧
25A	**x3^87**	ऌ॑३[5] / ऌ३[6,7]		l̩ːː˨˦˨
25B	**x3^87~**	ऌँ॑३[5] / ऌँ३[6,7]		l̩̃ːː˨˦˨
25C	**x3^87+**	ऌ३[5,6] / ऌ॒३[7]		l̩ːː˨˦˨

SLP2	SLP1	DEVANĀGARĪ	ROMAN	IPA
25D	x3^87+~	ऌँ३ [5,6] / ऌँ३ [7]		l̩̃ːː˥˩
25E	x3^86	३ऌ३ [5] / ऌ३ [6]		l̩ːː˥˩
25F	x3^86~	३ऌँ३ [5] / ऌँ३ [6]		l̩̃ːː˥˩
260	x4~	ऌँ४	l̥̃4	l̩̃ːːː
261	x4/~	ऌँ४ [1–4] / ऌँ४ [5–7] / ऌँ४ [8]	ĺ̥̃4	ĺ̩̃ːːː
262	x4\~	ऌँ४ [1–7] / ऌँ४ [8]	l̥̃4/l̥̱̃4	l̩̃̀ːːː
263	x4^~	ऌँ४ [1,3] / ऌँ४ [2] / ऌँ४ [8]	l̥̃̀4	l̩̃̂ːːː
264	x4/8~	ऌँ४ [1–4] / ऌँ४ [5–7]		l̩̃ːːː˥
265	x4\7~	ऌँ४ [1–4] / ऌँ४ [5–7]		l̩̃ːːː˧
266	x4\6~	ऌँ४ [5] / ऌँ४ [6,7]		l̩̃ːːː˨
267	x4^98~	ऌँ४ [1–4]		l̩̃ːːː˥˩
268	x4^97~			l̩̃ːːː˥˩
269	x4^87~	ऌँ४ [5] / ऌँ४ [6,7]		l̩̃ːːː˥˩
26A	x4^87+~	ऌँ४ [5,6] / ऌँ४ [7]		l̩̃ːːː˥˩
26B	x4^86~	३ऌँ४ [5] / ऌँ४ [6]		l̩̃ːːː˥˩
26C	x*		l̥	l̩̆
280	e1	ए१	ĕ	e
281	e1~	एँ१	ĕ̃	ẽ
282	e1/	ए१ [1–4] / ए१ [5–7] / ए१ [8]	ĕ́	é
283	e1/~	एँ१ [1–4] / एँ१ [5–7] / एँ१ [8]	ĕ̃́	ẽ́
284	e1\	ए॒१ [1–7] / ए१ [8]	ĕ/ĕ̱	è
285	e1\~	एँ॒१ [1–7] / एँ१ [8]	ĕ̃/ĕ̱̃	ẽ̀
286	e1^	ए१ [1,3] / ए॒१ [2] / ए१ [8]	ĕ̀	ê

SLP2	SLP1	Devanāgarī	Roman	IPA
287	**e1^~**	ए॑ँ१ [1,3] / ए॒ँ१ [2] / ए॑ँ१ [8]	ẽ̂	ê
288	**e1/8**	ए१ [1–4] / ए॑१ [5–7]		e˥
289	**e1/8~**	एँ१ [1–4] / ए॑ँ१ [5–7]		ẽ˥
28A	**e1\7**	ए॒१ [1–4] / ए१ [5–7]		e˧
28B	**e1\7~**	ए॒ँ१ [1–4] / एँ१ [5–7]		ẽ˧
28C	**e1\6**	ए॒१ [5] / ए१ [6,7]		e˨
28D	**e1\6~**	ए॒ँ१ [5] / एँ१ [6,7]		ẽ˨
28E	**e1^98**	ए॑१ [1–4]		e˥˦
28F	**e1^98~**	ए॑ँ१ [1–4]		ẽ˥˦
290	**e1^97**	ए१॒॑ [1,4]		e˦˧
291	**e1^97~**	एँ१॒॑ [1,4]		ẽ˦˧
292	**e1^87**	ए᳚१ [5] / ए१ [6,7]		e˥˧
293	**e1^87~**	ए᳚ँ१ [5] / एँ१ [6,7]		ẽ˥˧
294	**e1^87+**	ए॒१ [5,6] / ए॒१ [7]		e˥˧
295	**e1^87+~**	ए॒ँ१ [5,6] / ए॒ँ१ [7]		ẽ˥˧
296	**e1^86**	३ए॒१ [5] / ए॒१ [6]		e˥˨
297	**e1^86~**	३ए॒ँ१ [5] / ए॒ँ१ [6]		ẽ˥˨
298	**e**	ए	e	eː
299	**e~**	एँ	ẽ	ẽː
29A	**e/**	ए [1–4] / ए॑ [5–7] / ए॑ [8]	é	éː
29B	**e/~**	एँ [1–4] / ए॑ँ [5–7] / ए॑ँ [8]	ẽ́	ẽ́ː
29C	**e**	ए॒ [1–5] / ए [6,7] / ए॑ [8]	e/e̱	èː
29D	**e\\~**	ए॒ँ [1–5] / एँ [6,7] / ए॑ँ [8]	ẽ/ẽ̱	ẽ̀ː

SLP2	SLP1	DEVANĀGARĪ	ROMAN	IPA
29E	**e^**	ए॑[1,3] / ए॒[2] / ए᳚[8]	è	ê:
29F	**e^~**	एँ॑[1,3] / एँ॒[2] / एँ᳚[8]	è̃	ễ:
2A0	**e/8**	ए[1–4] / ए॑[5–7]		e:˥
2A1	**e/8~**	एँ[1–4] / एँ॑[5–7]		ẽ:˥
2A2	**e\7**	ए॒[1–4] / ए[5–6] / ए॒[7]		e:˧
2A3	**e\7~**	एँ॒[1–4] / एँ[5–6] / एँ॒[7]		ẽ:˧
2A4	**e\6**	ए॒[5] / ए[6,7]		e:˨
2A5	**e\6~**	एँ॒[5] / एँ[6,7]		ẽ:˨
2A6	**e^98**	ए॑[1–4]		e:˥˦
2A7	**e^98~**	एँ॑[1–4]		ẽ:˥˦
2A8	**e^97**	ए॒३॑[1,4]		e:˦˥˦
2A9	**e^97~**	एँ॒३॑[1,4]		ẽ:˦˥˦
2AA	**e^87**	ए᳕[5] / ए[6,7]		e:˦˧
2AB	**e^87~**	एँ᳕[5] / एँ[6,7]		ẽ:˦˧
2AC	**e^87+**	ए॒[5,6] / ए॒[7]		e:˧˦
2AD	**e^87+~**	एँ॒[5,6] / एँ॒[7]		ẽ:˧˦
2AE	**e^86**	३ए॒[5] / ए॒[6]		e:˨˦
2AF	**e^86~**	३एँ॒[5] / एँ॒[6]		ẽ:˨˦
2B0	**e3**	ए३	e3	e::
2B1	**e3~**	एँ३	ẽ3	ẽ::
2B2	**e3/**	ए३[1–4] / ए॑३[5–7] / ए॑३[8]	é3	é::
2B3	**e3/~**	एँ३[1–4] / एँ॑३[5–7] / एँ॑३[8]	ẽ́3	ẽ́::
2B4	**e3**	ए॒३[1–7] / ए᳚३[8]	e3/e̲3	è::

SLP2	SLP1	Devanāgarī	Roman	IPA
2B5	e3\~	एँ३ [1–7] / एँ३ [8]	ẽ3/ẽ̱3	ḕ::
2B6	e3^	ए३ [1,3] / ए३ [2] / ए३ [8]	è3	ê::
2B7	e3^~	एँ३ [1,3] / एँ३ [2] / एँ३ [8]	ȅ3	ẽ̂::
2B8	e3/8	ए३ [1–4] / ए३ [5–7]		e::˥
2B9	e3/8~	एँ३ [1–4] / एँ३ [5–7]		ẽ::˥
2BA	e3\7	ए३ [1–4] / ए३ [5–7]		e::˧
2BB	e3\7~	एँ३ [1–4] / एँ३ [5–7]		ẽ::˧
2BC	e3\6	ए३ [5] / ए३ [6,7]		e::˨
2BD	e3\6~	एँ३ [5] / एँ३ [6,7]		ẽ::˨
2BE	e3^98	ए३ [1–4]		e::˥˧
2BF	e3^98~	एँ३ [1–4]		ẽ::˥˧
2C0	e3^97	ए३ [1,4]		e::˧˥˧
2C1	e3^97~	एँ३ [1,4]		ẽ::˧˥˧
2C2	e3^87	एँ३ [5] / ए३ [6,7]		e::˧˥
2C3	e3^87~	एँ३ [5] / एँ३ [6,7]		ẽ::˧˥
2C4	e3^87+	ए३ [5,6] / ए३ [7]		e::˧˦
2C5	e3^87+~	एँ३ [5,6] / एँ३ [7]		ẽ::˧˦
2C6	e3^86	३ए३ [5] / ए३ [6]		e::˨˧
2C7	e3^86~	३एँ३ [5] / एँ३ [6]		ẽ::˨˧
2C8	e4~	एँ४	ẽ4	ẽ:::
2C9	e4/~	एँ४ [1–4] / एँ४ [5–7] / एँ४ [8]	ẽ́4	ẽ́:::
2CA	e4\~	एँ४ [1–7] / एँ४ [8]	ẽ4/ẽ̱4	ḕ:::
2CB	e4^~	एँ४ [1,3] / एँ४ [2] / एँ४ [8]	ȅ4	ẽ̂:::

SLP2	SLP1	DEVANĀGARĪ	ROMAN	IPA
2CC	e4/8~	एँ४ $^{1-4}$ / ए॑ँ४ $^{5-7}$		ẽ:::˥
2CD	e4\7~	ए॒ँ४ $^{1-4}$ / एँ४ $^{5-7}$		ẽ:::˧
2CE	e4\6~	ए॒ँ४ ^{5} / एँ४ ^{6,7}		ẽ:::˨
2CF	e4^98~	ए॑ँ४ $^{1-4}$		ẽ:::˥˧
2D0	e4^97~			ẽ:::˥˨
2D1	e4^87~	एँ४ ^{5} / एँ४ ^{6,7}		ẽ:::˦˨
2D2	e4^87+~	ए॒ँ४ ^{5,6} / ए॒ँ४ ^{7}		ẽ:::˦˨
2D3	e4^86~	३ए॒ँ४ ^{5} / ए॒ँ४ ^{6}		ẽ:::˦˩
2D4	e*		ᵉ	ĕ
300	E	ऐ	ai	ɐɪ̯:
301	E~	ऐँ	aĩ	ɐɪ̯̃:
302	E/	ऐ $^{1-4}$ / ऐ॑ $^{5-7}$ / ऐ॑ ^{8}	aí	ɐɪ̯́:
303	E/~	ऐँ $^{1-4}$ / ऐ॑ँ $^{5-7}$ / ऐ॑ँ ^{8}	aĩ́	ɐɪ̯̃́:
304	E\	ऐ॒ $^{1-5}$ / ऐ ^{6,7} / ऐ ^{8}	ai/ai̱	ɐɪ̯̀:
305	E\~	ऐ॒ँ $^{1-5}$ / ऐँ ^{6,7} / ऐँ ^{8}	aĩ/aĩ̱	ɐɪ̯̃̀:
306	E^	ऐ॑ ^{1,3} / ऐ॒ ^{2} / ऐ॑ ^{8}	aì	ɐɪ̯̂:
307	E^~	ऐ॑ँ ^{1,3} / ऐ॒ँ ^{2} / ऐ॑ँ ^{8}	aĩ̀	ɐɪ̯̃̂:
308	E/8	ऐ $^{1-4}$ / ऐ॑ $^{5-7}$		ɐɪ̯:˥
309	E/8~	ऐँ $^{1-4}$ / ऐ॑ँ $^{5-7}$		ɐɪ̯̃:˥
30A	E\7	ऐ॒ $^{1-4}$ / ऐ $^{5-6}$ / ऐ ^{7}		ɐɪ̯:˧
30B	E\7~	ऐ॒ँ $^{1-4}$ / ऐँ $^{5-6}$ / ऐँ ^{7}		ɐɪ̯̃:˧
30C	E\6	ऐ॒ ^{5} / ऐ ^{6,7}		ɐɪ̯:˨
30D	E\6~	ऐ॒ँ ^{5} / ऐँ ^{6,7}		ɐɪ̯̃:˨

SLP2	SLP1	Devanāgarī	Roman	IPA
30E	E^98	ऐ॑ [1–4]		ɐ͜ɪː˥
30F	E^98~	ऐँ॑ [1–4]		ɐ͜ɪ̃ː˥
310	E^97	ऐ॒३॒॑ [1,4]		ɐ͜ɪː˥˦
311	E^97~	ऐँ॒३॒॑ [1,4]		ɐ͜ɪ̃ː˥˦
312	E^87	ऐ᳚ [5] / ऐ॑ [6,7]		ɐ͜ɪː˥˧
313	E^87~	ऐँ᳚ [5] / ऐँ॑ [6,7]		ɐ͜ɪ̃ː˥˧
314	E^87+	ऐ॒ [5,6] / ऐ॒ [7]		ɐ͜ɪː˦˧
315	E^87+~	ऐँ॒ [5,6] / ऐँ॒ [7]		ɐ͜ɪ̃ː˦˧
316	E^86	३ऐ॒ [5] / ऐ॒ [6]		ɐ͜ɪː˥˨
317	E^86~	३ऐँ॒ [5] / ऐँ॒ [6]		ɐ͜ɪ̃ː˥˨
318	E3	ऐ३	ai3	ɑ͜iːː
319	E3~	ऐँ३	aĩ3	ɑ͜ĩːː
31A	E3/	ऐ३॑ [1–4] / ऐ॑३ [5–7] / ऐ॑३ [8]	aí3	ɑ͜íːː
31B	E3/~	ऐँ३॑ [1–4] / ऐँ॑३ [5–7] / ऐँ॑३ [8]	aĩ́3	ɑ͜ĩ́ːː
31C	E3\	ऐ॒३ [1–7] / ऐ३ [8]	ai3/ai̱3	ɑ͜ìːː
31D	E3\~	ऐँ॒३ [1–7] / ऐँ३ [8]	aĩ3/aĩ̱3	ɑ͜ĩ̀ːː
31E	E3^	ऐ॑३ [1,3] / ऐ॒३ [2] / ऐ३ [8]	aì3	ɑ͜îːː
31F	E3^~	ऐँ॑३ [1,3] / ऐँ॒३ [2] / ऐँ३ [8]	aĩ̀3	ɑ͜ĩ̂ːː
320	E3/8	ऐ३ [1–4] / ऐ॑३ [5–7]		ɑ͜iːː˥
321	E3/8~	ऐँ३ [1–4] / ऐँ॑३ [5–7]		ɑ͜ĩːː˥
322	E3\7	ऐ॒३ [1–4] / ऐ३ [5–7]		ɑ͜iːː˧
323	E3\7~	ऐँ॒३ [1–4] / ऐँ३ [5–7]		ɑ͜ĩːː˧
324	E3\6	ऐ॒३ [5] / ऐ३ [6,7]		ɑ͜iːː˨

SLP2	SLP1	DEVANĀGARĪ	ROMAN	IPA
325	`E3\6~`	ऐँ॒३ [5] / ऐँ॒३ [6,7]		ɑ͜ĩ::˧
326	`E3^98`	ऐ॑३ [1–4]		ɑ͜i::˥
327	`E3^98~`	ऐँ॑३ [1–4]		ɑ͜ĩ::˥
328	`E3^97`	ऐ३॒॑ [1,4]		ɑ͜i::˥˦
329	`E3^97~`	ऐँ३॒॑ [1,4]		ɑ͜ĩ::˥˦
32A	`E3^87`	ऐ᳚३ [5] / ऐ॒३ [6,7]		ɑ͜i::˦˥
32B	`E3^87~`	ऐँ᳚३ [5] / ऐँ॒३ [6,7]		ɑ͜ĩ::˦˥
32C	`E3^87+`	ऐ३ [5,6] / ऐ॒३ [7]		ɑ͜i::˦˥
32D	`E3^87+~`	ऐँ३ [5,6] / ऐँ॒३ [7]		ɑ͜ĩ::˦˥
32E	`E3^86`	३ऐ३ [5] / ऐ॒३ [6]		ɑ͜i::˧˥
32F	`E3^86~`	३ऐँ३ [5] / ऐँ॒३ [6]		ɑ͜ĩ::˧˥
330	`E4~`	ऐँ४	aĩ4	ɑ͜ĩ:::
331	`E4/~`	ऐँ४ [1–4] / ऐँ॑४ [5–7] / ऐँ४ [8]	aĩ́4	ɑ͜ĩ́:::
332	`E4\~`	ऐँ॒४ [1–7] / ऐँ४ [8]	aĩ4/aĩ̱4	ɑ͜ĩ̀:::
333	`E4^~`	ऐँ॑४ [1,3] / ऐँ॒४ [2] / ऐँ४ [8]	aĩ̀4	ɑ͜ĩ̂:::
334	`E4/8~`	ऐँ४ [1–4] / ऐँ॑४ [5–7]		ɑ͜ĩ:::˥
335	`E4\7~`	ऐँ॒४ [1–4] / ऐँ४ [5–7]		ɑ͜ĩ:::˧
336	`E4\6~`	ऐँ॒४ [5] / ऐँ४ [6,7]		ɑ͜ĩ:::˧
337	`E4^98~`	ऐँ॑४ [1–4]		ɑ͜ĩ:::˥
338	`E4^97~`			ɑ͜ĩ:::˥˦
339	`E4^87~`	ऐँ᳚४ [5] / ऐँ४ [6,7]		ɑ͜ĩ:::˦˥
33A	`E4^87+~`	ऐँ॒४ [5,6] / ऐँ॒४ [7]		ɑ͜ĩ:::˦˥
33B	`E4^86~`	३ऐँ॒४ [5] / ऐँ॒४ [6]		ɑ͜ĩ:::˧˥

SLP2	SLP1	Devanāgarī	Roman	IPA
380	o1	ओ१	ŏ	o
381	o1~	ओँ१	ŏ̃	õ
382	o1/	ओ१[1–4] / ओ॑१[5–7] / ओ॑१[8]	ŏ́	ó
383	o1/~	ओँ१[1–4] / ओँ॑१[5–7] / ओँ॑१[8]	ŏ̃́	ṍ
384	o1\	ओ॒१[1–7] / ओ१[8]	ŏ̀/ŏ̱	ò
385	o1\~	ओँ॒१[1–7] / ओँ१[8]	ŏ̃̀/ŏ̱̃	õ̀
386	o1^	ओ१[1,3] / ओ॒१[2] / ओ१[8]	ŏ̏	ô
387	o1^~	ओँ१[1,3] / ओँ॒१[2] / ओँ१[8]	ŏ̃̏	õ̂
388	o1/8	ओ१[1–4] / ओ॑१[5–7]		o˥
389	o1/8~	ओँ१[1–4] / ओँ॑१[5–7]		õ˥
38A	o1\7	ओ॒१[1–4] / ओ१[5–7]		o˧
38B	o1\7~	ओँ॒१[1–4] / ओँ१[5–7]		õ˧
38C	o1\6	ओ॒१[5] / ओ१[6,7]		o˨
38D	o1\6~	ओँ॒१[5] / ओँ१[6,7]		õ˨
38E	o1^98	ओ१[1–4]		o˥˦
38F	o1^98~	ओँ१[1–4]		õ˥˦
390	o1^97	ओ१॒[1,4]		o˥˧
391	o1^97~	ओँ१॒[1,4]		õ˥˧
392	o1^87	ओ१[5] / ओ१[6,7]		o˦˧
393	o1^87~	ओँ१[5] / ओँ१[6,7]		õ˦˧
394	o1^87+	ओ॒१[5,6] / ओ॒१[7]		o˦˧
395	o1^87+~	ओँ॒१[5,6] / ओँ॒१[7]		õ˦˧
396	o1^86	३ओ॒१[5] / ओ॒१[6]		o˦˨

SLP2	SLP1	DEVANĀGARĪ	ROMAN	IPA
397	`o1^86~`	३ओँ॒१[5] / ओँ᳚१[6]		õ˦˨
398	`o`	ओ	o	oː
399	`o~`	ओँ	õ	õː
39A	`o/`	ओ[1–4] / ओ॑[5–7] / ओ॑[8]	ó	óː
39B	`o/~`	ओँ[1–4] / ओँ॑[5–7] / ओँ॑[8]	ṍ	ṍː
39C	`o\`	ओ॒[1–5] / ओ[6,7] / ओ[8]	o/o̱	òː
39D	`o\~`	ओँ॒[1–5] / ओँ[6,7] / ओँ[8]	õ/õ̱	õ̀ː
39E	`o^`	ओ॑[1,3] / ओ᳚[2] / ओ[8]	ȍ	ôː
39F	`o^~`	ओँ॑[1,3] / ओँ᳚[2] / ओँ[8]	ȍ̃	õ̂ː
3A0	`o/8`	ओ[1–4] / ओ॑[5–7]		oː˥
3A1	`o/8~`	ओँ[1–4] / ओँ॑[5–7]		õː˥
3A2	`o\7`	ओ॒[1–4] / ओ[5–6] / ओ[7]		oː˧
3A3	`o\7~`	ओँ॒[1–4] / ओँ[5–6] / ओँ[7]		õː˧
3A4	`o\6`	ओ॒[5] / ओ[6,7]		oː˨
3A5	`o\6~`	ओँ॒[5] / ओँ[6,7]		õː˨
3A6	`o^98`	ओ[1–4]		oː˥
3A7	`o^98~`	ओँ॑[1–4]		õː˥
3A8	`o^97`	ओ३॒[1,4]		oː˥˧
3A9	`o^97~`	ओँ३॒[1,4]		õː˥˧
3AA	`o^87`	ओ᳚[5] / ओ[6,7]		oː˦˧
3AB	`o^87~`	ओँ᳚[5] / ओँ[6,7]		õː˦˧
3AC	`o^87+`	ओ[5,6] / ओ[7]		oː˦˧
3AD	`o^87+~`	ओँ[5,6] / ओँ[7]		õː˦˧

SLP2	SLP1	DEVANĀGARĪ	ROMAN	IPA
3AE	o^86	३ओ॒[5] / ओ᳖[6]		o:˨˦
3AF	o^86~	३ओँ॒[5] / ओँ᳖[6]		õ:˨˦
3B0	o3	ओ३	o3	o::
3B1	o3~	ओँ३	õ3	õ::
3B2	o3/	ओ३[1–4] / ओ॑३[5–7] / ओ᳡३[8]	ó3	ó::
3B3	o3/~	ओँ३[1–4] / ओँ॑३[5–7] / ओँ᳡३[8]	ṍ3	ṍ::
3B4	o3\	ओ॒३[1–7] / ओ᳐३[8]	o3/o̱3	ò::
3B5	o3\~	ओँ॒३[1–7] / ओँ᳐३[8]	õ3/õ̱3	õ̀::
3B6	o3^	ओ॑३[1,3] / ओ᳚३[2] / ओ᳒३[8]	ò3	ô::
3B7	o3^~	ओँ॑३[1,3] / ओँ᳚३[2] / ओँ᳒३[8]	õ̀3	ỗ::
3B8	o3/8	ओ३[1–4] / ओ॑३[5–7]		o::˥
3B9	o3/8~	ओँ३[1–4] / ओँ॑३[5–7]		õ::˥
3BA	o3\7	ओ॒३[1–4] / ओ३[5–7]		o::˧
3BB	o3\7~	ओँ॒३[1–4] / ओँ३[5–7]		õ::˧
3BC	o3\6	ओ॒३[5] / ओ᳭३[6,7]		o::˨
3BD	o3\6~	ओँ॒३[5] / ओँ᳭३[6,7]		õ::˨
3BE	o3^98	ओ॑३[1–4]		o::˦
3BF	o3^98~	ओँ॑३[1–4]		õ::˦
3C0	o3^97	ओ॒३॒॑[1,4]		o::˥˧
3C1	o3^97~	ओँ॒३॒॑[1,4]		õ::˥˧
3C2	o3^87	ओ᳜३[5] / ओ़३[6,7]		o::˧˥
3C3	o3^87~	ओँ᳜३[5] / ओँ़३[6,7]		õ::˧˥
3C4	o3^87+	ओ᳚३[5,6] / ओ᳚३[7]		o::˧˥

SLP2	SLP1	DEVANĀGARĪ	ROMAN	IPA
3C5	o3^87+~	ओँ॒३ [5,6] / ओँ॒३ [7]		õ::˧˦
3C6	o3^86	३ओ॒३ [5] / ओ॒३ [6]		o::˨˦
3C7	o3^86~	३ओँ॒३ [5] / ओँ॒३ [6]		õ::˨˦
3C8	o4~	ओँ४	õ4	õ:::
3C9	o4/~	ओँ४ [1–4] / ओँ॑४ [5–7] / ओँ॑४ [8]	ṍ4	ṍ:::
3CA	o4\~	ओँ॒४ [1–7] / ओँ४ [8]	õ4/õ̱4	õ̀:::
3CB	o4^~	ओँ॑४ [1,3] / ओँ॒४ [2] / ओँ४ [8]	õ̀4	õ̂:::
3CC	o4/8~	ओँ४ [1–4] / ओँ॑४ [5–7]		õ:::˥
3CD	o4\7~	ओँ॒४ [1–4] / ओँ४ [5–7]		õ:::˧
3CE	o4\6~	ओँ॒४ [5] / ओँ४ [6,7]		õ:::˨
3CF	o4^98~	ओँ॑४ [1–4]		õ:::˥˦
3D0	o4^97~			õ:::˥˧
3D1	o4^87~	ओँ४ [5] / ओँ४ [6,7]		õ:::˦˧
3D2	o4^87+~	ओँ॒४ [5,6] / ओँ॒४ [7]		õ:::˧˦
3D3	o4^86~	३ओँ॒४ [5] / ओँ॒४ [6]		õ:::˨˦
400	O	औ	au	ɐʊ̯ː
401	O~	औँ	aũ	ɐʊ̯̃ː
402	O/	औ [1–4] / औ॑ [5–7] / औ॑ [8]	aú	ɐʊ̯́ː
403	O/~	औँ [1–4] / औँ॑ [5–7] / औँ॑ [8]	aṹ	ɐʊ̯̃́ː
404	O\	औ॒ [1–5] / औ [6,7] / औ [8]	au/au̱	ɐʊ̯̀ː
405	O\~	औँ॒ [1–5] / औँ [6,7] / औँ [8]	aũ/aũ̱	ɐʊ̯̃̀ː
406	O^	औ॑ [1,3] / औ॒ [2] / औ [8]	aù	ɐʊ̯̂ː
407	O^~	औँ॑ [1,3] / औँ॒ [2] / औँ [8]	aũ̀	ɐʊ̯̃̂ː

SLP2	SLP1	DEVANĀGARĪ	ROMAN	IPA
408	O/8	औ॑ [1–4] / औ॑ [5–7]		ɐ͜ʊː˥
409	O/8~	औँ॑ [1–4] / औँ॑ [5–7]		ɐ͜ʊ̃ː˥
40A	O\7	औ॒ [1–4] / औ [5–6] / औ꣡ [7]		ɐ͜ʊː˧
40B	O\7~	औँ॒ [1–4] / औँ [5–6] / औँ꣡ [7]		ɐ͜ʊ̃ː˧
40C	O\6	औ॒ [5] / औ꣡ [6,7]		ɐ͜ʊː˨
40D	O\6~	औँ॒ [5] / औँ꣡ [6,7]		ɐ͜ʊ̃ː˨
40E	O^98	औ॑ [1–4]		ɐ͜ʊː˥˦
40F	O^98~	औँ॑ [1–4]		ɐ͜ʊ̃ː˥˦
410	O^97	औ॒३॑ [1,4]		ɐ͜ʊː˥˧
411	O^97~	औँ॒३॑ [1,4]		ɐ͜ʊ̃ː˥˧
412	O^87	औ᳚ [5] / औ꣡ [6,7]		ɐ͜ʊː˦˧
413	O^87~	औँ᳚ [5] / औँ꣡ [6,7]		ɐ͜ʊ̃ː˦˧
414	O^87+	औ॒ [5,6] / औ॒ [7]		ɐ͜ʊː˦˨
415	O^87+~	औँ॒ [5,6] / औँ॒ [7]		ɐ͜ʊ̃ː˦˨
416	O^86	३औ॒ [5] / औ॒ [6]		ɐ͜ʊː˥˨
417	O^86~	३औँ॒ [5] / औँ॒ [6]		ɐ͜ʊ̃ː˥˨
418	O3	औ३	au3	ɑ͜uːː
419	O3~	औँ३	aũ3	ɑ͜ũːː
41A	O3/	औ३ [1–4] / औ॑३ [5–7] / औ॑३ [8]	aú3	ɑ͜úːː
41B	O3/~	औँ३ [1–4] / औँ॑३ [5–7] / औँ॑३ [8]	aű3	ɑ͜ű̃ːː
41C	O3\	औ॒३ [1–7] / औ॑३ [8]	au3/au̲3	ɑ͜ùːː
41D	O3\~	औँ॒३ [1–7] / औँ॑३ [8]	aũ3/aũ̲3	ɑ͜ũ̀ːː
41E	O3^	औ॑३ [1,3] / औ॒३ [2] / औ॑३ [8]	aù3	ɑ͜ûːː

SLP2	SLP1	Devanāgarī	Roman	IPA
41F	O3^~	औ॑ँ३ [1,3] / औ॒ँ३ [2] / औँ३ [8]	aũ̂3	ɑ͜ũ̂::
420	O3/8	औ३ [1–4] / औ॑३ [5–7]		ɑ͜u::˦
421	O3/8~	औँ३ [1–4] / औ॑ँ३ [5–7]		ɑ͜ũ::˦
422	O3\7	औ॒३ [1–4] / औ३ [5–7]		ɑ͜u::˧
423	O3\7~	औ॒ँ३ [1–4] / औँ३ [5–7]		ɑ͜ũ::˧
424	O3\6	औ॒३ [5] / औ३ [6,7]		ɑ͜u::˨
425	O3\6~	औ॒ँ३ [5] / औँ३ [6,7]		ɑ͜ũ::˨
426	O3^98	औ॑३ [1–4]		ɑ͜u::˥˧
427	O3^98~	औ॑ँ३ [1–4]		ɑ͜ũ::˥˧
428	O3^97	औ॒३॑ [1,4]		ɑ͜u::˥˨
429	O3^97~	औ॒ँ३॑ [1,4]		ɑ͜ũ::˥˨
42A	O3^87	औ᳚३ [5] / औ३ [6,7]		ɑ͜u::˦˧
42B	O3^87~	औ᳚ँ३ [5] / औँ३ [6,7]		ɑ͜ũ::˦˧
42C	O3^87+	औ३ [5,6] / औ३ [7]		ɑ͜u::˧˦
42D	O3^87+~	औँ३ [5,6] / औँ३ [7]		ɑ͜ũ::˧˦
42E	O3^86	३औ॒३ [5] / औ३ [6]		ɑ͜u::˨˦
42F	O3^86~	३औ॒ँ३ [5] / औँ३ [6]		ɑ͜ũ::˨˦
430	O4~	औँ४	aũ4	ɑ͜ũ:::
431	O4/~	औँ४ [1–4] / औ॑ँ४ [5–7] / औँ४ [8]	aű4	ɑ͜ű:::
432	O4\~	औ॒ँ४ [1–7] / औ॑ँ४ [8]	aũ̀4/aũ̱4	ɑ͜ũ̀:::
433	O4^~	औ॑ँ४ [1,3] / औ॒ँ४ [2] / औँ४ [8]	aũ̂4	ɑ͜ũ̂:::
434	O4/8~	औँ४ [1–4] / औ॑ँ४ [5–7]		ɑ͜ũ:::˦
435	O4\7~	औ॒ँ४ [1–4] / औँ४ [5–7]		ɑ͜ũ:::˧

SLP2	SLP1	DEVANĀGARĪ	ROMAN	IPA
436	O4\6~	औँ॒४[5] / औँ४[6,7]		ɑ͜ũ:::˧
437	O4^98~	औँ॑४[1–4]		ɑ͜ũ:::˥
438	O4^97~			ɑ͜ũ:::˦
439	O4^87~	औँ᳛४[5] / औँ़४[6,7]		ɑ͜ũ:::˦
43A	O4^87+~	औँ४[5,6] / औँ॒४[7]		ɑ͜ũ:::˦
43B	O4^86~	३औँ॒४[5] / औँ४[6]		ɑ͜ũ:::˥˧
480	k	क्	k	k
481	k!	क्	k	k˺
482	k~	कँ्	k̃	k^{n}
483	K	ख्	kh	k^{h}
484	K!	ख्	kh	$k^{h˺}$
485	K~	खँ्	kh̃	k^{hn}
486	g	ग्	g	g
487	g!	ग्	g	g˺
488	g~	गँ्	g̃	g^{n}
489	G	घ्	gh	g^{h}
48A	G!	घ्	gh	$g^{h˺}$
48B	G~	घँ्	gh̃	g^{hn}
48C	N	ङ्	ṅ	ŋ
48D	N!	ङ्	ṅ	ŋ˺
48E	c	च्	c	c
48F	c!	च्	c	c˺
490	c~	चँ्	c̃	c^{n}
491	C	छ्	ch	c^{h}

SLP2	SLP1	DEVANĀGARĪ	ROMAN	IPA
492	C!	छ्	ch	c$^{h˺}$
493	C~	छ्ँ	cĥ	c^{hn}
494	j	ज्	j	ɟ
495	j!	ज्	j	ɟ˺
496	j~	ज्ँ	j̃	ɟ^{n}
497	J	झ्	jh	ɟ^{h}
498	J!	झ्	jh	ɟ$^{h˺}$
499	J~	झ्ँ	jĥ	ɟ^{hn}
49A	Y	ञ्	ñ	ɲ
49B	Y!	ञ्	ñ	ɲ˺
49C	w	ट्	ṭ	ʈ
49D	w!	ट्	ṭ	ʈ˺
49E	w~	ट्ँ	ṭ̃	ʈ^{n}
49F	W	ठ्	ṭh	ʈ^{h}
4A0	W!	ठ्	ṭh	ʈ$^{h˺}$
4A1	W~	ठ्ँ	ṭĥ	ʈ^{hn}
4A2	q	ड्	ḍ	ɖ
4A3	q!	ड्	ḍ	ɖ˺
4A4	q~	ड्ँ	ḍ̃	ɖ^{n}
4A5	L	ळ्	ḷ	ɭ
4A6	Q	ढ्	ḍh	ɖ^{h}
4A7	Q!	ढ्	ḍh	ɖ$^{h˺}$
4A8	Q~	ढ्ँ	ḍĥ	ɖ^{hn}
4A9	|	ळ्ह्	ḷh	ɭ^{h}

SLP2	SLP1	DEVANĀGARI	ROMAN	IPA
4AA	R	ण्	ṇ	ɳ
4AB	R!	ण्	ṇ	ɳ˺
4AC	t	त्	t	t̪
4AD	t!	त्	t	t̪˺
4AE	t~	त्ँ	t̃	t̪^{n}
4AF	T	थ्	th	t̪^{h}
4B0	T!	थ्	th	$\text{t̪}^{\text{h˺}}$
4B1	T~	थ्ँ	th̃	t̪^{hn}
4B2	d	द्	d	d̪
4B3	d!	द्	d	d̪˺
4B4	d~	द्ँ	d̃	d̪^{n}
4B5	D	ध्	dh	d̪^{h}
4B6	D!	ध्	dh	$\text{d̪}^{\text{h˺}}$
4B7	D~	ध्ँ	dh̃	d̪^{hn}
4B8	n	न्	n	n̪
4B9	n!	न्	n	n̪˺
4BA	p	प्	p	p
4BB	p!	प्	p	p˺
4BC	p~	प्ँ	p̃	p^{n}
4BD	P	फ्	ph	p^{h}
4BE	P!	फ्	ph	$\text{p}^{\text{h˺}}$
4BF	P~	फ्ँ	ph̃	p^{hn}
4C0	b	ब्	b	b
4C1	b!	ब्	b	b˺

SLP2	SLP1	Devanāgarī	Roman	IPA
4C2	b~	बँ्	b̃	b^{n}
4C3	B	भ्	bh	b^{h}
4C4	B!	भ्	bh	b^{h}˺
4C5	B~	भँ्	bh̃	b^{hn}
4C6	m	म्	m	m
4C7	m!	म्	m	m˺
4C8	y	य्	y	j
4C9	y_	य्	y	ɟ͜j
4CA	y=	य्	y	
4CB	y!	य्	y	j˺
4CC	y~	यँ्	ỹ	j̃
4CD	r	र्	r	ɻ
4CE	l	ल्	l	l̺
4CF	l!	ल्	l	l̺˺
4D0	l~	लँ्	l̃	l̺̃
4D1	v	व्	v	w
4D2	v_	व्	v	β
4D3	v=	व्	v	
4D4	v!	व्	v	w˺
4D5	v~	वँ्	ṽ	w̃
4D6	S	श्	ś	ç
4D7	z	ष्	ṣ	ʂ
4D8	s	स्	s	s̺
4D9	h	ह्	h	ɦ

SLP2	SLP1	Devanāgarī	Roman	IPA
4DA	h~	हँ	h̃	ɦⁿ
4DB	H	ः	ḥ	h
4DC	H/8	ः[2,5]		
4DD	H\7	ᳲ[2]		
4DE	H\6	ᳲ[5]		
4DF	H^98	ᳳ[2]		
4E0	H^87	ᳳ[5]		
4E1	Z	ᳵ	ẖ	x
4E2	V	ᳶ	ḫ	ɸ
4E3	M	◌ं[9]	ṁ	
4E4	M#	ꣳ[2]		
4E5	M#/8	ꣳ[2]		
4E6	M#\7	ꣳ॒[2]		
4E7	M#\6			
4E8	M1	ꣴ[3]		
4E9	M1/8	ꣴ[3]		
4EA	M1\7	ꣴ॒[3]		
4EB	M1\6			
4EC	M1#	ꣵ[2]		
4ED	M1#/8	ꣵ[2]		
4EE	M1#\7	ꣵ॒[2]		
4EF	M1#\6			
4F0	M2	ꣶ[3]		
4F1	M2/8	ꣶ[3]		

SḶP2	SLP1	DEVANĀGARĪ	ROMAN	IPA
4F2	**M2\7**	ँ॒[3]		
4F3	**M2\6**			

Appendix D

Sanskrit Library Phonetic Featural

The Sanskrit Library Phonetic Featural encoding scheme (SLP3) creates a correspondence between codepoints numbered 1-242, selected SLP1 segments, and their features. Each SLP1 segment is associated with nineteen features each of which is assigned a value of plus, minus, or neutral. The latter applies if the feature is inapplicable to the segment in question. In addition true diphthongs are assigned pairs of featural values, one for each of the two constituent sounds. The SLP3 encoding is based upon phonetic features as described by Halle and shown in Table 4. In terms of the three axes of encoding described in Chapter 4, SLP3 encodes phonetics rather than graphics, and contrastive rather than complementary units. Although it encodes segments, these are explicitly associated with sets of features, each of which could be assigned a codepoint. Each segment could then be associated with sets of featural codepoints in a consistent and unambiguous featural encoding scheme. We have chosen instead to represent SLP3 in terms of phonetic segments associated with sets of phonetic features.

In column 1 the unique codepoints of SLP3 are shown in decimal notation. In column 2 the equivalent encoding in SLP1 is given. In columns 3 through 21 the value for each of nineteen features in Halle's system are given. Row four of the table header indicates terminal features. Rows one through three of the header show higher nodes in Halle's feature tree as shown in Table 12. 'GUTTRL' stands for GUTTERAL, 'SPal' and 'spal' for soft palate, and 'tblade' for tongue blade. The abbreviations shown in columns 3-21 in row four of the table header are given in the following table:

`G`	glottal
`Sp`	spread glottis
`St`	stiff vocal folds
`Sl`	slack vocal folds
`R`	rhinal
`N`	nasal
`Dr`	dorsal
`B`	back
`H`	high
`L`	low
`Cr`	coronal
`A`	anterior
`Dt`	distributed
`Lb`	labial
`Rd`	round
`Cn`	consonantal
`Sn`	sonorant
`Ct`	continuant
`Lt`	lateral

			GUTTRL				PLACE															
			Larynx				SPal		Dorsal				Coronal			Labial					
			glottis				*spal*		*tongue body*				*tblade*			*lips*					
SLP3	SLP2	SLP1	G	Sp	St	Sl	R	N	Dl	B	H	L	Cr	A	Dt	Lb	Rd	Cn	Sn	Ct	Lt
1	000	a		–	–	–		–	+	+	–	+						–			
2	001	a~		–	–	–		+	+	+	–	+						–			
3	002	a/		–	+	–		–	+	+	–	+						–			
4	003	a/~		–	+	–		+	+	+	–	+						–			
5	004	a\		–	–	+		–	+	+	–	+						–			
6	005	a\~		–	–	+		+	+	+	–	+						–			
7	006	a^		–	+	+		–	+	+	–	+						–			
8	007	a^~		–	+	+		+	+	+	–	+						–			
9	030	A		–	–	–		–	+	+	–	+						–			
10	031	A~		–	–	–		+	+	+	–	+						–			
11	032	A/		–	+	–		–	+	+	–	+						–			
12	033	A/~		–	+	–		+	+	+	–	+						–			
13	034	A\		–	–	+		–	+	+	–	+						–			
14	035	A\~		–	–	+		+	+	+	–	+						–			
15	036	A^		–	+	+		–	+	+	–	+						–			
16	037	A^~		–	+	+		+	+	+	–	+						–			
17	048	a3		–	–	–		–	+	+	–	+						–			
18	049	a3~		–	–	–		+	+	+	–	+						–			
19	04A	a3/		–	+	–		–	+	+	–	+						–			
20	04B	a3/~		–	+	–		+	+	+	–	+						–			
21	04C	a3\		–	–	+		–	+	+	–	+						–			
22	04D	a3\~		–	–	+		+	+	+	–	+						–			
23	04E	a3^		–	+	+		–	+	+	–	+						–			
24	04F	a3^~		–	+	+		+	+	+	–	+						–			
25	080	i		–	–	–		–	+	–	+	–						–			
26	081	i~		–	–	–		+	+	–	+	–						–			
27	082	i/		–	+	–		–	+	–	+	–						–			
28	083	i/~		–	+	–		+	+	–	+	–						–			
29	084	i\		–	–	+		–	+	–	+	–						–			
30	085	i\~		–	–	+		+	+	–	+	–						–			
31	086	i^		–	+	+		–	+	–	+	–						–			
32	087	i^~		–	+	+		+	+	–	+	–						–			
33	0B0	I		–	–	–		–	+	–	+	–						–			

			GUTTRL						PLACE												
			Larynx				SPal		Dorsal				Coronal			Labial					
			glottis				*spal*		*tongue body*				*tblade*			*lips*					
SLP3	SLP2	SLP1	G	Sp	St	Sl	R	N	Dl	B	H	L	Cr	A	Dt	Lb	Rd	Cn	Sn	Ct	Lt
34	0B1	I~		−	−	−		+	+	−	+	−						−			
35	0B2	I/		−	+	−		−	+	−	+	−						−			
36	0B3	I/~		−	+	−		+	+	−	+	−						−			
37	0B4	I\		−	−	+		−	+	−	+	−						−			
38	0B5	I\~		−	−	+		+	+	−	+	−						−			
39	0B6	I^		−	+	+		−	+	−	+	−						−			
40	0B7	I^~		−	+	+		+	+	−	+	−						−			
41	0C8	i3		−	−	−		−	+	−	+	−						−			
42	0C0	i3~		−	−	−		+	+	−	+	−						−			
43	0CA	i3/		−	+	−		−	+	−	+	−						−			
44	0CB	i3/~		−	+	−		+	+	−	+	−						−			
45	0CC	i3\		−	−	+		−	+	−	+	−						−			
46	0CD	i3\~		−	−	+		+	+	−	+	−						−			
47	0CE	i3^		−	+	+		−	+	−	+	−						−			
48	0CF	i3^~		−	+	+		+	+	−	+	−						−			
49	100	u		−	−	−		−	+	+	+	−				+	+	−			
50	101	u~		−	−	−		+	+	+	+	−				+	+	−			
51	102	u/		−	+	−		−	+	+	+	−				+	+	−			
52	103	u/~		−	+	−		+	+	+	+	−				+	+	−			
53	104	u\		−	−	+		−	+	+	+	−				+	+	−			
54	105	u\~		−	−	+		+	+	+	+	−				+	+	−			
55	106	u^		−	+	+		−	+	+	+	−				+	+	−			
56	107	u^~		−	+	+		+	+	+	+	−				+	+	−			
57	130	U		−	−	−		−	+	+	+	−				+	+	−			
58	131	U~		−	−	−		+	+	+	+	−				+	+	−			
59	132	U/		−	+	−		−	+	+	+	−				+	+	−			
60	133	U/~		−	+	−		+	+	+	+	−				+	+	−			
61	134	U\		−	−	+		−	+	+	+	−				+	+	−			
62	135	U\~		−	−	+		+	+	+	+	−				+	+	−			
63	136	U^		−	+	+		−	+	+	+	−				+	+	−			
64	137	U^~		−	+	+		+	+	+	+	−				+	+	−			
65	148	u3		−	−	−		−	+	+	+	−				+	+	−			
66	149	u3~		−	−	−		+	+	+	+	−				+	+	−			

			GUTTRL						PLACE												
			Larynx				SPal		Dorsal				Coronal			Labial					
			glottis				*spal*		*tongue body*				*tblade*			*lips*					
SLP3	SLP2	SLP1	G	Sp	St	Sl	R	N	Dl	B	H	L	Cr	A	Dt	Lb	Rd	Cn	Sn	Ct	Lt
67	14A	u3/		−	+	−		−	+	+	+	−				+	+	−			
68	14B	u3/~		−	+	−		+	+	+	+	−				+	+	−			
69	14C	u3\		−	−	+		−	+	+	+	−				+	+	−			
70	14D	u3\~		−	−	+		+	+	+	+	−				+	+	−			
71	14E	u3^		−	+	+		−	+	+	+	−				+	+	−			
72	14F	u3^~		−	+	+		+	+	+	+	−				+	+	−			
73	180	f		−	−	−		−										−			
74	181	f~		−	−	−		+										−			
75	182	f/		−	+	−		−										−			
76	183	f/~		−	+	−		+										−			
77	184	f\		−	−	+		−										−			
78	185	f\~		−	−	+		+										−			
79	186	f^		−	+	+		−										−			
80	187	f^~		−	+	+		+										−			
81	1B0	F		−	−	−		−										−			
82	1B1	F~		−	−	−		+										−			
83	1B2	F/		−	+	−		−										−			
84	1B3	F/~		−	+	−		+										−			
85	1B4	F\		−	−	+		−										−			
86	1B5	F\~		−	−	+		+										−			
87	1B6	F^		−	+	+		−										−			
88	1B7	F^~		−	+	+		+										−			
89	1C8	f3		−	−	−		−										−			
90	1C9	f3~		−	−	−		+										−			
91	1CA	f3/		−	+	−		−										−			
92	1CB	f3/~		−	+	−		+										−			
93	1CC	f3\		−	−	+		−										−			
94	1CD	f3\~		−	−	+		+										−			
95	1CE	f3^		−	+	+		−										−			
96	1CF	f3^~		−	+	+		+										−			
97	200	x		−	−	−		−										−			
98	201	x~		−	−	−		+										−			
99	202	x/		−	+	−		−										−			

			GUTTRL						PLACE												
			Larynx				SPal		Dorsal				Coronal			Labial					
			glottis				*spal*		*tongue body*				*tblade*			*lips*					
SLP3	SLP2	SLP1	G	Sp	St	Sl	R	N	Dl	B	H	L	Cr	A	Dt	Lb	Rd	Cn	Sn	Ct	Lt
100	203	x/~		–	+	–		+										–			
101	204	x\		–	–	+		–										–			
102	205	x\~		–	–	+		+										–			
103	206	x^		–	+	+		–										–			
104	207	x^~		–	+	+		+										–			
105	230	X		–	–	–		–										–			
106	231	X~		–	–	–		+										–			
107	232	X/		–	+	–		–										–			
108	233	X/~		–	+	–		+										–			
109	234	X\		–	–	+		–										–			
110	235	X\~		–	–	+		+										–			
111	236	X^		–	+	+		–										–			
112	237	X^~		–	+	+		+										–			
113	248	x3		–	–	–		–										–			
114	249	x3~		–	–	–		+										–			
115	24A	x3/		–	+	–		–										–			
116	24B	x3/~		–	+	–		+										–			
117	24C	x3\		–	–	+		–										–			
118	24D	x3\~		–	–	+		+										–			
119	24E	x3^		–	+	+		–										–			
120	24F	x3^~		–	+	+		+										–			
121	280	e1		–	–	–		–	+	–	–	–						–			
122	281	e1~		–	–	–		+	+	–	–	–						–			
123	282	e1/		–	+	–		–	+	–	–	–						–			
124	283	e1/~		–	+	–		+	+	–	–	–						–			
125	284	e1\		–	–	+		–	+	–	–	–						–			
126	285	e1\~		–	–	+		+	+	–	–	–						–			
127	286	e1^		–	+	+		–	+	–	–	–						–			
128	287	e1^~		–	+	+		+	+	–	–	–						–			
129	298	e		–	–	–		–	+	–	–	–						–			
130	299	e~		–	–	–		+	+	–	–	–						–			
131	29A	e/		–	+	–		–	+	–	–	–						–			
132	29B	e/~		–	+	–		+	+	–	–	–						–			

			GUTTRL						PLACE												
			Larynx				SPal		Dorsal				Coronal			Labial					
			glottis				*spal*		*tongue body*				*tblade*			*lips*					
SLP3	SLP2	SLP1	G	Sp	St	Sl	R	N	Dl	B	H	L	Cr	A	Dt	Lb	Rd	Cn	Sn	Ct	Lt
133	29C	e\		–	–	+		–	+	–	–	–						–			
134	29D	e\~		–	–	+		+	+	–	–	–						–			
135	29E	e^		–	+	+		–	+	–	–	–						–			
136	29F	e^~		–	+	+		+	+	–	–	–						–			
137	2B0	e3		–	–	–		–	+	–	–	–						–			
138	2B1	e3~		–	–	–		+	+	–	–	–						–			
139	2B2	e3/		–	+	–		–	+	–	–	–						–			
140	2B3	e3/~		–	+	–		+	+	–	–	–						–			
141	2B4	e3\		–	–	+		–	+	–	–	–						–			
142	2B5	e3\~		–	–	+		+	+	–	–	–						–			
143	2B6	e3^		–	+	+		–	+	–	–	–						–			
144	2B7	e3^~		–	+	+		+	+	–	–	–						–			
145	300	E		–	–	–		–	+	+/–	–/+	+/–						–			
146	301	E~		–	–	–		+	+	+/–	–/+	+/–						–			
147	302	E/		–	+	–		–	+	+/–	–/+	+/–						–			
148	303	E/~		–	+	–		+	+	+/–	–/+	+/–						–			
149	304	E\		–	–	+		–	+	+/–	–/+	+/–						–			
150	305	E\~		–	–	+		+	+	+/–	–/+	+/–						–			
151	306	E^		–	+	+		–	+	+/–	–/+	+/–						–			
152	307	E^~		–	+	+		+	+	+/–	–/+	+/–						–			
153	318	E3		–	–	–		–	+	+/–	–/+	+/–						–			
154	319	E3~		–	–	–		+	+	+/–	–/+	+/–						–			
155	31A	E3/		–	+	–		–	+	+/–	–/+	+/–						–			
156	31B	E3/~		–	+	–		+	+	+/–	–/+	+/–						–			
157	31C	E3\		–	–	+		–	+	+/–	–/+	+/–						–			
158	31D	E3\~		–	–	+		+	+	+/–	–/+	+/–						–			
159	31E	E3^		–	+	+		–	+	+/–	–/+	+/–						–			
160	31F	E3^~		–	+	+		+	+	+/–	–/+	+/–						–			
161	380	o1		–	–	–		–	+	+	–	–				+	+	–			
162	381	o1~		–	–	–		+	+	+	–	–				+	+	–			
163	382	o1/		–	+	–		–	+	+	–	–				+	+	–			
164	383	o1/~		–	+	–		+	+	+	–	–				+	+	–			
165	384	o1\		–	–	+		–	+	+	–	–				+	+	–			

			GUTTRL						PLACE											
			Larynx				SPal		Dorsal				Coronal			Labial					
			glottis				*spal*		*tongue body*				*tblade*			*lips*					
SLP3	SLP2	SLP1	G	Sp	St	Sl	R	N	Dl	B	H	L	Cr	A	Dt	Lb	Rd	Cn	Sn	Ct	Lt
166	385	o1\~		–	–	+		+	+	+	–	–				+	+	–			
167	386	o1^		–	+	+		–	+	+	–	–				+	+	–			
168	387	o1^~		–	+	+		+	+	+	–	–				+	+	–			
169	398	o		–	–	–		–	+	+	–	–				+	+	–			
170	399	o~		–	–	–		+	+	+	–	–				+	+	–			
171	39A	o/		–	+	–		–	+	+	–	–				+	+	–			
172	39B	o/~		–	+	–		+	+	+	–	–				+	+	–			
173	39C	o\		–	–	+		–	+	+	–	–				+	+	–			
174	39D	o\~		–	–	+		+	+	+	–	–				+	+	–			
175	39E	o^		–	+	+		–	+	+	–	–				+	+	–			
176	39F	o^~		–	+	+		+	+	+	–	–				+	+	–			
177	3B0	o3		–	–	–		–	+	+	–	–				+	+	–			
178	3B1	o3~		–	–	–		+	+	+	–	–				+	+	–			
179	3B2	o3/		–	+	–		–	+	+	–	–				+	+	–			
180	3B3	o3/~		–	+	–		+	+	+	–	–				+	+	–			
181	3B4	o3\		–	–	+		–	+	+	–	–				+	+	–			
182	3B5	o3\~		–	–	+		+	+	+	–	–				+	+	–			
183	3B6	o3^		–	+	+		–	+	+	–	–				+	+	–			
184	3B7	o3^~		–	+	+		+	+	+	–	–				+	+	–			
185	400	O		–	–	–		–	+	+/+	–/+	+/–				+	+	–			
186	401	O~		–	–	–		+	+	+/+	–/+	+/–				+	+	–			
187	402	O/		–	+	–		–	+	+/+	–/+	+/–				+	+	–			
188	403	O/~		–	+	–		+	+	+/+	–/+	+/–				+	+	–			
189	404	O\		–	–	+		–	+	+/+	–/+	+/–				+	+	–			
190	405	O\~		–	–	+		+	+	+/+	–/+	+/–				+	+	–			
191	406	O^		–	+	+		–	+	+/+	–/+	+/–				+	+	–			
192	407	O^~		–	+	+		+	+	+/+	–/+	+/–				+	+	–			
193	418	O3		–	–	–		–	+	+/+	–/+	+/–				+	+	–			
194	419	O3~		–	–	–		+	+	+/+	–/+	+/–				+	+	–			
195	41A	O3/		–	+	–		–	+	+/+	–/+	+/–				+	+	–			
196	41B	O3/~		–	+	–		+	+	+/+	–/+	+/–				+	+	–			
197	41C	O3\		–	–	+		–	+	+/+	–/+	+/–				+	+	–			
198	41D	O3\~		–	–	+		+	+	+/+	–/+	+/–				+	+	–			

			GUTTRL						PLACE												
			Larynx				SPal		Dorsal				Coronal			Labial					
			glottis				*spal*		*tongue body*				*tblade*			*lips*					
SLP3	SLP2	SLP1	G	Sp	St	Sl	R	N	Dl	B	H	L	Cr	A	Dt	Lb	Rd	Cn	Sn	Ct	Lt
199	41E	O3^		–	+	+		–	+	+/+	–/+	+/–				+	+	–			
200	41F	O3^~		–	+	+		+	+	+/+	–/+	+/–				+	+	–			
201	480	k		–	+	–		–	+									+	–	–	
202	483	K		+	+	–		–	+									+	–	–	
203	486	g		–	–	+		–	+									+	–	–	
204	489	G		+	–	+		–	+									+	–	–	
205	48C	N		–	–	+		+	+									+	+		–
206	48E	c		–	+	–		–					+	–	+			+	–	–	
207	491	C		+	+	–		–					+	–	+			+	–	–	
208	494	j		–	–	+		–					+	–	+			+	–	–	
209	497	J		+	–	+		–					+	–	+			+	–	–	
210	49A	Y		–	–	+		+					+	–	+			+	+		–
211	49C	w		–	+	–		–					+	–	–			+	–	–	
212	49F	W		+	+	–		–					+	–	–			+	–	–	
213	4A2	q		–	–	+		–					+	–	–			+	–	–	
214	4A5	L		–	–	+		–					+	–	–			+	+		+
215	4A6	Q		+	–	+		–					+	–	–			+	–	–	
216	4A9	l		+	–	+		–					+	–	–			+	+		+
217	4AA	R		–	–	+		+					+	–	–			+	+		–
218	4AC	t		–	+	–		–					+	+				+	–	–	
219	4AF	T		+	+	–		–					+	+				+	–	–	
220	4B2	d		–	–	+		–					+	+				+	–	–	
221	4B5	D		+	–	+		–					+	+				+	–	–	
222	4B8	n		–	–	+		+					+	+				+	+		–
223	4BA	p		–	+	–		–								+	–	+	–	–	
224	4BD	P		+	+	–		–								+	–	+	–	–	
225	4C0	b		–	–	+		–								+	–	+	–	–	
226	4C3	B		+	–	+		–								+	–	+	–	–	
227	4C6	m		–	–	+		+								+	–	+	+		–
228	4C8	y		–	–	+		–						–	+			–			
229	4CC	y~		–	–	+		+						–	+			–			
230	4CD	r		–	–	+		–					+	–	–			+	+		–
231	4CE	l		–	–	+		–					+	+				+	+		+

			GUTTRL						PLACE												
			Larynx				SPal		Dorsal				Coronal			Labial					
			glottis				*spal*		*tongue body*				*tblade*			*lips*					
SLP3	SLP2	SLP1	G	Sp	St	Sl	R	N	Dl	B	H	L	Cr	A	Dt	Lb	Rd	Cn	Sn	Ct	Lt
232	4D0	l~		–	–	+		+					+	+				+	+		+
233	4D1	v		–	–	+		–								+	+	–			
234	4D5	v~		–	–	+		+								+	+	–			
235	4D6	S		+	+	–		–					+	–	+			+	–	+	
236	4D7	z		+	+	–		–					+	–	–			+	–	+	
237	4D8	s		+	+	–		–					+	+				+	–	+	
238	4D9	h	+	+	–	+		–										–			
239	4DB	H	+	+	+	–		–										–			
240	4E1	Z		+	+	–		–	+									+	–	+	
241	4E2	V		+	+	–		–								+	–	+	–	+	
242	4E3	M		+	–	+	+	+										–			

Appendix E

Malcolm D. Hyman

12 November 1970 – 2 September 2009

E.1 *A Memoir* by Phoebe Pettingell

Malcolm could truthfully say, in the words of the John Cougar Mellencamp song, "I was born in a small town." It seems ironic that someone who became so much at home in the global intellectual community should have grown up in an isolated village in Northern Wisconsin – in the midst of the largest expanse of virgin timber in the United States. But perhaps the irony diminishes when one realizes that this part of Wisconsin is home to a diverse group of cultures, including three major Native Americans nations, immigrants from Middle and Eastern Europe, Scandinavia and the Balkans, Laos, Vietnam and Cambodia. Malcolm's own heritage was diverse. His father, the late literary critic, Stanley Edgar Hyman was descended from a Lithuanian rabbinic dynasty. My own family was predominantly Scottish, with one German great grandmother. The closeness of a small town that nonetheless possesses such diversity shaped Malcolm profoundly. Wherever he lived, he thought of Three Lakes as home.

His growing up there had not been anticipated. Stanley taught at Bennington College in Vermont. As writers, we both spent time in New York City, and lately had been living in Europe and England. However, Stanley's unexpected death three months before Malcolm's birth motivated me to join my mother at our former summer home in Three Lakes where she had been living permanently for several years. The atmosphere seemed congenial for the raising of a fatherless child, and we cooperated in his upbringing as long as he lived at home. Malcolm was rather shy as a child, though in college he became much more extroverted. From the beginning, he was deeply compassionate, with a respect for all living things. One could not so much as swat a mosquito in his presence. He was also a natural leader, one whose influence sprang from his generosity toward others and his having thought through what he had to say. All his life, Malcolm was his ideas, which, in turn, were imbued with his passionate convictions about the moral worth of creation.

Malcolm began talking late – he spoke a private language until kindergarten (this tendency ran in the male line in my family) which, in his case, may have influenced his fascination with grammar, syntax and language in general. Within a few months of entering first grade, he was reading on an adult level. One day, he mentioned the schwa to me. When I expressed ignorance, he asked with genuine surprise, "Don't you pay attention to the diacritical marks in the dictionary? In second grade, he brought home a book from the music library and, in a weekend, taught himself to read both treble and bass clef, not to mention alto and tenor. Shortly thereafter, he asked to take piano lessons, which he continued throughout high school. His musical gifts were significant enough to contemplate a career as a pianist or composer. By this time, he was spending every weekend in a city eighty miles from our home, working with a piano coach and studying harmony and composition.

He also brought home grammar text books throughout school, pouring over them and sometimes pointing out mistakes in the author's reasoning. At eleven, having never laid hands on a computer, he bought two books on programming. The following Monday, he walked into the high school computer lab and asked the teacher if he might try something. He then wrote a program that surpassed the teacher's skills. That summer, he enrolled in a graduate level computer course at The University of Wisconsin at LaCrosse. A year later, he began to attend the summer sessions in computing at Michigan Tech, where professors often asked him to assist in teaching the other students. At twelve, he was running his own software company, creating programs for local businesses.

Wisconsin devotes many of its resources to education from the primary grades through its excellent state university system, and the Three

Lakes school offered a particularly fine education, especially in the sciences. The teacher in charge of physics and advanced math courses had worked at the Fermi Lab. Everyone assumed Malcolm would choose to major in some branch of the sciences once he went to college, or else follow a musical career. However, he was fascinated by a wide range of fields. From age seven, he had won national children's poetry contests again and again. He proved to be quick at picking up languages – a gift from his rabbinic ancestors, but also from his grandmother who continued to teach herself new ones well into her 80s. By the time he applied to universities, Malcolm's interests had expanded to philosophy and theology. He had also fallen under the spell of James Joyce's A Portrait of the Artist as a Young Man, and imagined attending Trinity College in Dublin, Ireland, at some point. Knowing that this would require a background in Ancient Greek and Latin, at the last moment, he started entering his prospective major as Classics, and took a crash course in Latin with a local Episcopal priest. He ended up at Lawrence University in Appleton Wisconsin. They offered him a Merit Scholarship, and later awarded him the Wriston Fellowship on Academic merit. There, he met Professor Daniel J. Taylor, a scholar of the Roman grammarian and polymath, Marcus Terentius Varro (116-27 BCE). Dan became his mentor and friend, influencing the direction of his future academic career. Malcolm made the most of his college years, attending almost every lecture on campus, in addition to his course work, and making lasting friendships. The first semester of his senior year was spent at the Center for Classical Studies in Rome. In 1993, Malcolm graduated summa cum laude, the top student in his class.

Back at Lawrence, Malcolm had fallen under the spell of Martha Nussbaum when he read her The Fragility of Goodness. This influenced his decision to enter the Ph.D. program in Classics at Brown University in Providence, Rhode Island. An added incentive was that Dr. William Wyatt, Dan Taylor's own mentor, also taught in the department. With Nussbaum, Malcolm was able to pursue his interests in philosophy and ethics, while with Wyatt he continued to indulge his fascination with linguistic structures. With his colleague, Philip Thibodeau, he published several short papers. Over one summer, he took an intensive course in Sanskrit at Harvard, and while at Brown studied Akkadian. Though he never took a computer course after high school, his skills were such that he designed and maintained the highly sophisticated web site for the Brown Classics Department, and picked up design tips from the Rhode Island School of Design, next door. Some intellects keep their various interests in separate compartments. Malcolm, however, saw the relationships between different disciplines, and his vast knowledge in one area illuminated his understanding of others. His thirst for knowledge continued to expand as long as he lived. He read voraciously in literature, philosophy, psychology, history and the sciences. Popular culture was a longtime fascination for him, and music remained close to his heart.

Malcolm's dissertation concerned the way Latin grammarians treated barbarisms and solecisms. His first significant published paper, "Bad Grammar in Context," defined his philosophy in this regard: Let me conclude by sketching the "big picture," as I see it. Language is constituitive of institutions – such as religion and law – that serve to produce social cohesion. Given that spoken and written language are the media par excellence for communication, the importance of linguistic norms in maintaining group identity should be evident. Conservatism in language preserves the social status quo. But society is not a static entity; it must adjust continually to changing situations and modes of living. Revolutionary movements (such as Stoicism and early Christianity) aim toward an upheaval of traditional institutions; and so it is not surprising to see their depreciation of the prescriptive stance of the grammarians. These two linguistic attitudes – the prescriptive and the anti-prescriptive – exist in a dynamic that shapes, at any historical moment, the form of cultural life. Malcolm's own sympathies were generally against the prescriptivists, especially when their purpose was to define class barriers. Having grown up among people who worked with their hands, he fought the kind of genteel grammatical notions that look down on what they perceive as uneducated speech.

At the same time, he was intrigued with the ways in which culture is transmitted in writing, even when the writing does not communicate in conventional ways. His paper, "Of Glyphs and Glottography," written during his productive years at the Max Planck Institute for the History of Science in Berlin, examines proto-writing and the connection between written and spoken language. It begins with a typically whimsical epigraph, from Popeye the Sailor Man: "This writin' is wroten rotten, if you happen to ask me," and observes, It is ... evident that writing that is (or purports to be) glottographic may serve – as we learn from Greek nonsense inscriptions on vases or Japanese T-shirts with messages in dubious English (or non-English) – other functions: e.g. to communicate prestige directly or to connote cultural capital. Even writing that straightforwardly notates spoken language is overdetermined, in the sense that it can perform other functions besides. The paper goes on to point out that linguists and philologists tend to pay most attention to literary artifacts, whereas "calendars, tables of sines and cosines, architectural plans, recipes for foods and drugs, mathematical formulae, coins and banknotes, charts for navigation, computer programs – reflect highly sophisticated intellectual activity and serve as indispensable bearers of culture."

Malcolm's post-graduate career included positions at Harvard and Brown as a research fellow, and at the Max Planck Institute in their History of Science department. In the words of Dr. Jürgen Renn, the head of that department, Malcolm "was always there to give advice, to help out, to stimulate new ideas, or to clear the atmosphere with a subtle joke." His work led him more and more into computer programming as it pertained to making the worldwide Web more useful for scholars. As he pointed out, "Browsing the Web is scarcely more interactive than surfing television channels." He envisioned "not a browser but an interagent." His "Arboreal" program, developed in conjunction with the Max Planck Istitute, and used for the 2005 exhibition, "Albert Einstein: Chief Engineer of the Universe," as well as in his groundbreaking Sanskrit web projects with his Brown colleague and close friend, Dr. Peter Scharf, were two examples of his multiverse efforts to make the web ever more useful for intellectual pursuits. He and Dr. Renn envisioned a new epistemic Web: "Is it enough to create a digital library of Alexandria, with (perhaps) improved finding aids? We propose that the crucial question is how to structure knowledge on the Web to facilitate the construction of new knowledge, knowledge that will be critical in addressing the challenges of the emerging global society." Malcolm's work in Sanskrit on the web with Peter Scharf of Brown and with scholarly web programs with Dr. Mark Schifsky of Harvard continued to push these boundaries. But his primary interest in computing related to his fascination with linguistics itself and with human communication. Increasingly, he attempted to devise new models of thought for the various fields in which he worked: History of Science, Linguistics, Classics and Ancient Sumerian languages, and

Information Science.

It would seem that already Malcolm had set the course of a productive and happy life. He rejoiced in his many friends and colleagues who helped sustain his own productivity and with whom he was invariably and selflessly generous. In 2006, he married Dr. Ludmila Selemeneva, a Russian specialist in rhetoric, and on December 2, 2008, their son, Stanley William Hyman was born in Berlin. Malcolm was looking forward to dividing his time between there and Providence where his work at Brown had expanded. Yet he had always lived with such intensity and drive that periodically he succumbed to the temptation to push himself too far. Unfortunately, for some years he had also suffered from a complex of physical diseases which may well have had one underlying though undiagnosed root. Because he was such a selfless and warm person, convivial and happy to immerse himself in the fellowship of others, only those closest to him were aware that he suffered from several escalating and life-threatening conditions. His sudden death on September 4, 2009, left all who knew him bereft. It also deprived scholarship of the significant contributions he would surely have made had he lived longer. Fortunately, that aspect of him lives on in the continuing work of all whom he influenced, and not least in this book.

E.2 Curriculum Vitae

MALCOLM DONALD HYMAN
12 NOVEMBER 1970 – 2 SEPTEMBER 2009

EDUCATION

Ph. D. in Classics, May 2002
Brown University, Providence, RI
Thesis: "Barbarism and Solecism in Ancient Grammatical Thought"
Advisor: William F. Wyatt

B. A. in Classics, summa cum laude, June 1993
Lawrence University, Appleton, WI

RESEARCH INTERESTS

cognitive aspects of writing; ancient literacy

linguistic and scholarly computing

technical terminology and scientific concepts

Graeco-Roman language science

POSITIONS

Visiting Scholar, Department of Classics, Brown University, Providence, RI (2006–2009)

Wissenschaftlicher Mitarbeiter, Max-Planck-Institut für Wissenschaftsgeschichte, Berlin, Germany (2004–2009)

Research Fellow, Department of Classics, Harvard University (2001–2004)

GRANTS

Co-Principal Investigator, "Enhancing Access to Primary Cultural Heritage Materials of India," National Endowment for the Humanities ($301,540, 12 months, starting July 2009) (with PI: P. Scharf)

Co-Principal Investigator, "Collaborative Research: International Digital Sanskrit Library Integration," National Science Foundation ($225, 428, 36 months, starting January 2006) (with PIs: P. Scharf, V. Govindaraju)

Honors and Awards

NHC Young Scholar's Summer Institute, "The Concept of Language in the Academic Disciplines" (2003–2004)

Wilbour Fellowship in Latin, Brown University (1998, 1999)

Mellon Fellowship in the Humanities (1993–1994)

Governer J. T. Lewis Prize (senior with highest academic rank), Lawrence University (1993)

Phi Beta Kappa

Maurice P. Cunningham Prize in Greek (1993)

Wisconsin Association of Foreign Language Teachers Award (1993)

Peerenboom Prize Scholarship in the Field of Semantics, Lawrence University (1992)

Publications

"On the Tip of the Ancient Tongue: Failures of Lexical Access in Greek and Latin" (co-author: P. Thibodeau), in progress (2009)

"Studies in Cacemphaton" (co-author: P. Thibodeau), in progress (2009)

"Chomsky between Revolutions," in *Chomsky's Revolutions*, ed. D. Kibbee (forthcoming, 2009)

Linguistic Issues in Encoding Sanskrit (co-author: P. Scharf), Motilal Banarsidass (forthcoming, 2009)

"Toward an Epistemic Web" (co-author: J. Renn), in *Globalization of Knowledge and its Consequences*, ed. J. Renn (forthcoming, 2009)

"Euclid and Beyond: Towards a Long-term History of Deductivity" (co-author: M. Schiefsky), *Künstliche Intelligenz* 4/09 (2009)

"Enhancing Access to Primary Cultural Heritage Materials of India" (co-author: P. Scharf), in *Guide to OCR for Indic Scripts: Document Recognition and Retrieval,* edd. V. Govindaraju and S. Setlur, Advances in Pattern Recognition (2009)

"From Pāṇinian Sandhi to Finite State Calculus," in *Sanskrit Computational Linguistics: First and Second International Symposia,* edd. G. Huet, A. Kulkarni, P. Scharf, Lecture Notes in Artificial Intelligence (2007)

Review of Eleanor Dickey, *Ancient Greek Scholarship, Historiographia Linguistica* 35.3 (2008)

"Encoding Sāmaveda with Ruby," Sanskrit Library Technical Note 1 (2007)

"Semantic Networks: A Tool for Investigating Conceptual Change and Knowledge Transfer in the History of Science," in *Übersetzung und Transformation,* edd. H. Böhme, C. Rapp, and W. Rösler (2007)

"Of Glyphs and Glottography," *Language & Communication* 26.3/4 (2006)

"Terms for 'Word' in Roman Grammar," in *Antike Fachtexte*, ed. T. Fögen (2005)

Review of David Sedley, *Plato's* Cratylus, *Historiographia Linguistica* 32.1 (2005)

"One-Word Solecisms and the Limits of Syntax," in *Syntax in Antiquity,* edd. P. Swiggers and A. Wouters, Orbis Supplementa 23 (2003)

Review of Rachel Barney, *Names and Nature in Plato's* Cratylus, *Bryn Mawr Classical Review* 2003.03.35 (2003)

"Bad Grammar in Context," *New England Classical Journal* 29.2 (2002)

"The Hope of the Year: Virgil *Georgics* 1.224 and Hesiod *Opera et Dies* 617" (co-author: P. Thibodeau), *Classical Philology* 94.2 (1999)

Seven articles in *Bearers of Meaning: The Ottilia Buerger Collection of Ancient and Byzantine Coins at Lawrence University,* Lawrence University Press (1995)

Presentations and Papers

"Reflecting on Oral Traditions: Pāṇini's Grammar," Writing and the Transmission of Knowledge, Bibliothek Werner Oechslin, Einsiedeln, Switzerland, April 30–May 2, 2009

"Linguae Francae, Monetary Systems, and Economy," Multilingualism, Linguae Francae, and the Global History of Religious and Scientific Concepts, The Norwegian Institute at Athens, Greece, April 3–5, 2009

Commentary on P. Marthelot, "Bühler's Theory of Language as a Solution to the Crisis in Psychology," Crisis Debates in Psychology: International Workshop, Berlin, October 10–12, 2008

"The Globalisation of Knowledge and its Consequences" (with J. Renn), 4th HERA Annual Conference "European Diversities — European Identities," Strasbourg, October 8–9, 2008

"Term Discovery in an Early Modern Latin Scientific Corpus," ALLC/ACH, Oulu, Finland, June 24–28, 2008

Workshop on "Multilingualism," co-organizer (with J. Braarvig), Max Planck Institute for the History of Science, May 7, 2008

"Humanities Computing: Theoretical Challenges," invited lecture, Humanities Center, Harvard University, April 17, 2008

"The Epistemic Web," Epistemic Networks and GRID + Web 2.0 for Arts and Humanities, Imperial College, London, January 30–31, 2008

"Multilingualism and the Globalization of Knowledge," Universitet i Oslo, December 11, 2007

"On Glottography: Parallels between Ontogeny and History," Workshop on the Origin of Writing Systems, Max-Planck-Institut für Wissenschaftsgeschichte, Berlin, August 27–31, 2007

"Introduction: Modeling the Diffusion of Knowledge," Dahlem Konferenzen 97, Globalization of Knowledge and its Consequences, Program Advisory Committee Meeting, Berlin, May 22–25, 2007

"A Digital Library for Sanskrit and the Challenges of Non-Western Cultural Heritage" (with P. Scharf), Million Books Workshop, Tufts University, Medford, Massachusetts, May 22–24, 2007

"From Research Challenges of the Humanities to the Epistemic Web (Web 3.0)" (with J. Renn), NSF/JISC Digital Libraries Infrastructures, Phoenix, April 17–19, 2007

"What is the Next Step? A Humanities Perspective" (with J. Renn), Cyber-research Infrastructures and Data Management for Science and Communities — an ESF/BOREAS Workshop, Paris, February 19–20, 2007

"A Computational Approach to Sanskrit Morphology and Phonology," World Sanskrit Conference, Edinburgh, July 10–14, 2006

"Software para realizar exposiciones virtuales" (with J. Damerow), Workshop: Ciencia y Cultura entre dos mundos, La Orotava, Tenerife, May 31, 2006

"Towards a New Platform for Linguistic Analysis and Scholarly Annotation," Digital Philology: Problems and Perspectives, Universität Hamburg, January 20, 2006

Co-chair of roundtable discussion "Comparative Literacies of the Ancient World," American Historical Society (participants: S. Houston, M. Hyman, D. Lurie, R. Salomon), January 5, 2006

"Semantic Networks in Ancient and Early Modern Mechanics Texts: Development and Transformation," SFB 644 Jahrestagung: Übersetzung und Transformation, Humboldt-Universität, December 3, 2005

"Aristotle's Theory of the Syllable," ICHoLS, Champaign-Urbana, September 2, 2005

"Encoding Sanskrit Phonetics vs. Encoding Devanāgarī Script," Devanāgarī OCR Workshop, Brown University, Providence, Rhode Island, January 22–23, 2005

"The Challenges of the Humanities to the World Wide Web: Perspectives from the Archimedes Project" (with M. Schiefsky), ALLC/ACH, Göteborg, Sweden, June 11–16, 2004

"Interfaces for Parser and Dictionary Access," invited speaker, LDC Institute, University of Pennsylvania, January 26, 2004

Co-chair of panel "Linguistic Issues in the Text Encoding of Sanskrit," ALLC/ACH, Athens, Georgia, May 30, 2003

"Greek and Roman Grammarians on Motion Verbs and Place Adverbials," NAAHoLS, Atlanta, Georgia, January 4, 2003

"The Archimedes Project: Current Research" (with M. Schiefsky), NSDL Workshop, Dibner Institute, MIT, March 9, 2002

Conference organization

"Multilingualism, Linguae Francae, and the Global History of Religious and Scientific Concepts" (with J. Braarvig), The Norwegian Institute at Athens, Greece, April 3–5, 2009

"Viva Voce: Echoes of Performance in the Ancient Text" (with V. Panoussi, J. Rowley, P. Thibodeau, M. Sundahl), Brown University, February 7–8, 1997

Teaching

Teaching Fellow, Department of Classics, Brown University (1995–1997)

- Essentials of the Latin Language (two semesters)
- Introduction to Latin (intensive)

Teaching Assistant, Department of Classics, Brown University (1994)

- Reason and the Human Good in Ancient Ethical Thought (Instructor: Martha C. Nussbaum)

Professional affiliations

North American Association for the History of the Language Sciences
Linguistic Society of America
Henry Sweet Society for the History of Linguistic Ideas
Association for Literary and Linguistic Computing
Association for Computing in the Humanities

Professional Activities

Leader, Cross-Sectional Group III: The Spread of Knowledge through Cultures, TOPOI: The Formation and and Transformation of Space in

Ancient Civilizations (German Excellence Cluster 264) (2009)

Project Manager, XML Workflow and Presentation, project funded by the Max Planck Digital Library (2008–2009)

- Managed a team of three individuals to develop a standardized workflow for transcription of historical books into structured XML, a Relax NG schema for these texts, and software for online presentation and content-based access to historical sources

Program Committee member, Second International Sanskrit Computational Linguistics Symposium (Brown University, May 15–17, 2008); Third International Sanskrit Computational Linguistics Symposium (Hyderabad, January 12–14, 2009)

Expert consultant to ISO/IEC JTC1/SC2/WG2 "Universal Multiple-Octet Coded Character Set" (2007–2008)

- Proposed standards for encoding Vedic Characters in ISO 10646/ Unicode
- Co-author of working group documents N3235, N3235R, N3290

Exhibitor at the Wissenschaftssommer in Essen, Germany (theme: "Die Geisteswissenschaften: ABC der Menschheit") (2007)

- Developed exhibit on current research in linguistic computing and the decipherment of ancient Near Eastern writing

Member of Sonderforschungsbereich 644 "Transformationen der Antike," Berlin, Germany (2005–2008)

- Investigator in Teilprojekt A6, "Gewicht, Bewegung und Kraft: Begriffliche Strukturveränderungen antiken Wissens als Folge seiner Tradierung"

Chief technical architect for the interactive component of the German government-sponsored exhibition "Albert Einstein: Ingenieur des Universums: 100 Jahre Relativität, Atome und Quanten" (2004–2005)

- The interactive component — "an exhibition without walls" — is an original concept, with major financial support from the Heinz Nixdorf Foundation, Siemens, and BASF
- Development: distributed software system (Python/Zope) allows for content creation by scientists and template design by design professionals. About fifty interactive stations in the Kronprinzenpalais run the enviroment for the duration of the exhibition. The exibition has, in addition, a permanent home on the Web, which includes all digital content produced during the course of the exhibition
- The exhibition won a bronze medal in the "Exhibition Campaign" category of the International Museum Communication Award (2007)

Member, Board of Directors, The Sanskrit Library, Providence, Rhode Island (2004–2009)

Technical Consultant, CDLI (Cuneiform Digital Library Initiative), Berlin/Los Angeles (2002–2009)

Research Fellow, Archimedes Project, Harvard University (2001–2004)

- Collaborator with an international team of scholars to implement a digital research library of texts in the history of mechanics
- Chief developer of *Arboreal*, an XML-based scholarly working environment for texts in Greek, Latin, Arabic, Chinese, Akkadian, Sumerian, and modern European languages (Java, 45,000+ lines)

Technical and linguistic consultant for Sanskrit Library Project, Brown University (2000–2009)

- Implemented system for morphological analysis of Sanskrit
- Developed system for typesetting a book MS. in Sanskrit, using TeX (automatic hyphenation for Devanāgarī text; automatic index generation and formatting)

- Authored electronic index browser, with capabilities for lexical and grammatical analysis of word-forms (Java, 7000+ lines)

Prepared SGML-encoded text of Dyer-Seymour commentary on Plato's *Apology* and *Crito* for Perseus Project (1998)

Referee for John Benjamins, *Transactions of the American Philological Association, New England Classical Journal, Historiographia Linguistica, Harvard Studies in Classical Philology,* Association for Literary and Linguistic Computing, Association for Computing in the Humanities, Boston Studies in the Philosophy of Science, (1994–2009)

Computer Skills

Programming Languages: Java, Perl, Python
Other: XML, XSL, RDF, Relax NG, TEI, HTML, CGI, JavaScript, LaTeX, PostgreSQL, Zope, R, xfst
Linux system administration

Languages Read

Latin, Ancient Greek, Sanskrit, Italian, French, Spanish, German
some university study also of Akkadian

Other Skills

Copy-editing and indexing experience

Bibliography

Abercrombie, D. (1949), 'What is a "letter"?', *Lingua* **2**(1), 54–63.

—. (1981), Extending the Roman alphabet: Some orthographic experiments of the past four centuries, *in* Asher & Henderson (1981), pp. 207–224.

Abhyankar, K. V., ed. (1967), *Paribhāṣāṅgraha (A Collection of Original Works on Vyākaraṇa Paribhāṣās)*, Bhandarkar Oriental Research Institute, Pune.

AbiFarès, H. S. (2001), *Arabic Typography: A Comprehensive Sourcebook*, Saqi, London.

Abu-Rabia, S. & Taha, H. (2006), Reading in Arabic orthography: Characteristics, research findings, and assessment, *in* Joshi & Aaron (2006), pp. 321–338.

Agenbroad, J. E. (n.d.), 'Difficult characters: A collection of Devanagari conjunct consonants', International Association of Orientalist Librarians, Bulletin 38, pages 17–53.

Al-Nassir, A. A. (1993), *Sibawayh the Phonologist: A Critical Study of the Phonetic and Phonological Theory of Sibawayh as Presented in his Treatise Al-Kitab*, Vol. 10 of *Library of Arabic Linguistics*, Kegan Paul, London.

Allen, G. D. (1988), 'The PHONASCII system', *Journal of the International Phonetic Association* **18**(1), 9–25.

Allen, W. S. (1951), 'Some prosodic aspects of retroflexion and aspiration in Sanskrit', *Bulletin of the School of Oriental and African Studies, University of London* **13**(4), 939–946.

——. (1953), *Phonetics in Ancient India*, Oxford University Press, London.

Alpert, M. (1981), Speech and disturbances of affect, *in* Darby (1981), pp. 221–240.

Anderson, S. R. (1985), *Phonology in the Twentieth Century: Theories of Rules and Theories of Representations*, University of Chicago Press, Chicago.

Aronoff, M. (1992), Segmentalism in linguistics: The alphabetic basis of phonological theory, *in* P. Downing, S. D. Lima & M. Noonan, eds, 'The Linguistics of Literacy', Vol. 21 of *Typological Studies in Language*, John Benjamins, Amsterdam, pp. 71–82.

Asher, R. E. & Henderson, E. J. A., eds (1981), *Towards a History of Phonetics*, Edinburgh Univeristy Press, Edinburgh.

Baddeley, A. & Wilson, B. (1988), 'Comprehension and working memory: A single case neuropsychological study', *Journal of Memory and Language* **27**(5), 479–498.

Badecker, W. (1996), 'Representational properties common to phonological and orthographic output systems', *Lingua* **99**, 55–83.

Bailey, T. G., Firth, J. R. & Harley, A. H. (1956), *Teach Yourself Urdu*, English Universities Press, London.

Bakker, H. T., Barkhuis, R. & Velthuis, F. J. (1990), 'Printing Nāgarī script with TEX', *Newsletter of the International Association of Sanskrit Studies* **3**, 27–34.

Bansal, V. & Sinha, R. M. K. (1999), On how to describe shapes of Devanagari characters and use them for recognition, *in* 'Proceedings of the Fifth International Conference on Document Analysis and Recognition (ICDAR '99)', pp. 410–413.

——. (2000), 'Integrating knowledge sources in Devanagari text recognition system', *IEEE Transactions on Systems, Man, and Cybernetics—Part A: Systems and Humans* **30**(4), 500–505.

Bare, J. S. (1976), *Phonetics and Phonology in Pāṇini: The System of Features Implicit in the Aṣṭādhyāyī*, Vol. 21 of *Natural Language Studies*, Phonetics Laboratory, University of Michigan. PhD thesis, 1975.

Barlow, J. S. (1995), *A Chinese-Russian-English Dictionary*, University of Hawai'i Press, Honolulu.

Barry, R. K., ed. (1997), *ALA-LC Romanization Tables: Transliteration Schemes for Non-Roman Scripts*, Cataloging Distribution Service, Library of Congress, Washington.

Beech, J. R. & Mayall, K. A. (2007), The word shape hypothesis re-examined: Evidence for an external feature advantage in visual recognition, *in* P. L. Cornelissen & C. Singleton, eds, 'Visual Factors in Reading', Blackwell, Malden MA, pp. 87–103.

Beeching, W. A. (1990), *Century of the Typewriter*, 2d edn, British Typewriter Museum Publishing, New York.

Bell, A. M. (1870), *Explanatory Lecture on Visible Speech, The Science of Universal Alphabetics, Delivered before the College of Preceptors, Feb. 9, 1870*, Simpkin, Marshall, & Co., London.

Bemer, R. W. (1963), 'The American Standard Code for Information Interchange', *Datamation* **8–9**, 32–36, 39–44.

Benseler, G. E. (1841), *De Hiatu in Oratoribus Atticis et Historicis Graecis Libri Duo*, J. G. Engelhardt, Freiburg.

Bharati, A., Chaitanya, V. & Sangal, R. (1996), *Natural Language Processing: A Paninian Perspective*, Prentice-Hall of India, New Delhi.

Bhaskararao, P. & Mathur, R. (1991), 'Phonetic nature of anusvaara', *Bulletin of the Deccan College Post-graduate & Research Institute* **51–2**, 229–231.

Bhatia, T. K. (1974), 'The problems of programming Devanagari script on PLATO IV and a proposal for a revised Hindi typewriter', Language, Literature and Society: Occasional Papers, No. 1. Center for Southeast Asian Studies, Northern Illinois University, pages 52–64.

Bhatt, S. (n.d.), 'Character encoding standard for Indian scripts—a report', <http://www.cicc.or.jp/english/hyoujyunka/mlit4/7-3India/India.htm>.

Birnbaum, D. J. (1989), Issues in developing international standards for encoding non-Latin alphabets, *in* E. Johnson, ed., 'Proceedings of the Fourth International Conference on Symbolic and Logical Computing', Dakota State University, Madison SD, pp. 41–54.

Boltz, W. G. (2006), 'Pictographic myths', *Bochumer Jahrbuch zur Ostasienforschung* **30**, 39–54.

Bondy, J. A. (1972), The "graph theory" of the Greek alphabet, *in* Y. Alavi, D. R. Lick & A. T. White, eds, 'Graph Theory and Applications: Proceedings of the Conference at Western Michigan University, May 10–13, 1972', Vol. 303 of *Lecture Notes in Mathematics*, Springer, Berlin, pp. 43–54.

Brown, W. N. (1953), 'Script reform in modern India, Pakistan, and Ceylon', *Journal of the American Oriental Society* **73**(1), 1–6.

Bruce, V. & Young, A. (1998), *In the Eye of the Beholder*, Oxford University Press, Oxford.

Brugmann, K. (1906–1916), *Grundriss der vergleichende Grammatik der indo-germanischen Sprachen*, 2d edn, Trübner, Strassburg. 2 vols.

Bühler, G. (1896), *Indische Palaeographie: von circa 350 A. Chr.–circa 1300 P. Chr.*, Vol. 1. Bd., 11. Heft of *Grundriss der indo-arischen Philologie und Altertumskunde*, K. J. Trübner, Strassburg.

Bukatman, S. (1993), 'Gibson's typewriter', *South Atlantic Quarterly* **92**(4), 627–645.

Bureau of Indian Standards (1992), *Indian Script Code for Information Interchange—ISCII standard*, New Delhi.

Burk, M. G. (1976), An exposition and a relative chronology of the phonological transformations from Indo-European to Sanskrit, Master's thesis, The University of Texas at Austin. Jointly published with *Svātmaprakāśikā* 'Light on one's real self'.

Burrow, T. (1955), *The Sanskrit Language*, Faber & Faber, London. Reprinted, Motilal Banarsidass, 2001.

Busetto, L. (2003), 'Fonetica nell'India antica', *Studi Linguistici e Filologici Online* **1**, 191–226. <http://www.humnet.unipi.it/slifo/>.

Calabrese, A. (1998), On coronalization and affrication in palatalization processes: An inquiry into the nature of a sound change, *in* D. Chen, T.-H. Hsin & E. Shortt, eds, 'Papers in Phonology', Vol. 9 of *University of Connecticut Working Papers in Linguistics*, University of Connecticut Department of Linguistics, Storrs CN.

Caramazza, A. (2000), Aspects of lexical access: Evidence from aphasia, *in* Y. Grodzinsky, L. P. Shapiro & D. Swinney, eds, 'Language and the Brain: Representation and Processing', Academic Press, San Diego, chapter 11, pp. 203–228.

Caramazza, A. & Miceli, G. (1990), 'The structure of graphemic representations', *Cognition* **37**, 243–297.

Cardona, G. (1965), 'On Pāṇini's morphophonemic principles', *Language* **41**(2), 225–237.

——. (1977), 'A note on morphophonemic and phonetic rules in Sanskrit', *The Mysore Orientalist* **10**, 1–6.

——. (1980), On the Āpiśaliśikṣā, *in* A. L. Basham et al., eds, 'A Corpus of Indian Studies: Essays in Honor of Prof. Gaurināth Sastrī', Sanskrit Pustak Bhandar, Calcutta, pp. 245–256.

——. (1983), Phonetics and phonological rules in grammars, *in* 'Linguistic Analysis and Some Indian Traditions', Bhandarkar Oriental Research Institute, Pune, pp. 1–36.

——. (1987), 'Some neglected evidence concerning the development of abhinihita sandhi', *Studien zur Indologie und Iranistik* **13/14**, 59–68.

——. (1993), 'The *Bhāṣika* accentuation system', *Studien zur Indologie und Iranistik* **18**, 1–40.

——. (1997), *Pāṇini: His Work and its Traditions, Vol. I, Background and Introduction*, 2d edn, Motilal Banarsidass.

——. (2003), Sanskrit, *in* Cardona & Jain (2003), pp. 104–160.

——. (n.d.), Developments of nasals in early Indo-Aryan: anunāsika and anusvāra. Unpublished MS.

——. & Jain, D., eds (2003), *The Indo-Aryan Languages*, number 2 *in* 'Routledge Language Family Series', Routledge, London.

Carterette, E. C. & Friedman, M. P., eds (1978), *Handbook of Perception Volume IX: Perceptual Processing*, Academic Press, New York.

Chao, Y.-R. (1930), 'A system of tone-letters', *Le Maître Phonétique* **30**, 24–27.

Chomsky, N. & Halle, M. (1968), *The Sound Pattern of English*, MIT Press, Cambridge MA.

Clements, G. N. (1985), The geometry of phonological features, *in* 'Phonology Yearbook', Vol. 2, Cambridge University Press, Cambridge, pp. 225–252.

——. (1990), The role of the sonority cycle in core syllabification, *in* J. Kingston & M. E. Beckman, eds, 'Papers in Laboratory Phonology I: Between the Grammar and Physics of Speech', Cambridge University Press, Cambridge, pp. 283–333.

Clements, G. N. & Hume, E. V. (1995), The internal organization of speech sounds, *in* Goldsmith (1995*b*), pp. 245–306.

Cohen, L. & Dehaene, S. (2004), 'Specialization within the ventral stream: the case for the visual word form area', *NeuroImage* **22**, 466–476.

Cole, M., Levitin, K. & Luria, A. (2006), *The Autobiography of Alexander Luria: A Dialogue with The Making of Mind*, Lawrence Erlbaum, Mahwah NJ.

Cubelli, R. (1991), 'A selective deficit for writing vowels in acquired dysgraphia', *Nature* 353, 258–260.

Damerow, P. (1996), *Abstraction and Representation: Essays on the Cultural Evolution of Thinking*, Vol. 175 of *Boston Studies in the Philosophy of Science*, Kluwer, Dordrecht.

—. (1999), 'The origins of writing as a problem of historical epistemology', Max-Planck-Institut für Wissenschaftsgeschichte Preprint 114.

Dani, A. H. (1963), *Indian Palaeography*, Clarendon Press, Oxford.

Darby, J. K., ed. (1981), *Speech Evaluation in Psychiatry*, Grune & Stratton, New York.

Desbordes, F. (1990), *Idées romaines sur l'écriture*, Presses Universitaires de Lille.

Deshpande, M. M. (1997*a*), Pāṇini and the distinctive features, *in* I. Hegedus, P. A. Michalove & A. M. Ramer, eds, 'Indo-European, Nostratic, and Beyond: Festschrift for Vitalij V. Shevoroshkin', Vol. 22 of *Journal of Indo-European Studies Monographs*, Institute for the Study of Man, Washington DC, pp. 72–87.

—, ed. (1997*b*), *Śaunakīyā Caturādhyāyikā: a Prātiśākhya of the Śaunakīya Atharvaveda, with commentaries Caturādhyāyībhāṣya, Bhārgava-Bhāskara-Vṛtti and Pañcasandhi*, Dept. of Sanskrit and Indian Studies, Harvard University, Cambridge MA.

Diehl, K. S. (1968), 'Bengali types and their founders', *Journal of Asian Studies* 27(2), 335–338.

Dixon, R. M. W. & Aikhenvald, A. Y. (2002), Word: A typological framework, *in* R. M. W. Dixon & A. Y. Aikhenvald, eds, 'Word: A Cross-Linguistic Typology', Cambridge University Press, Cambridge, pp. 1–41.

Driver, G. R. (1976), *Semitic Writing: From Pictograph to Alphabet*, 3d edn, Oxford University Press, London. Edited by S. A. Hopkins.

Edgerton, F. (1946), *Sanskrit Historical Phonology: A Simplified Outline for Beginners in Sanskrit*, Vol. 5 of *Supplement to the Journal of the American Oriental Society*, American Oriental Society, Baltimore MD.

——. (1970), *Buddhist Hybrid Sanskrit Grammar and Dictionary, 2 vols.*, Motilal Banarsidass, Delhi. Facsimile of 1953 New Haven edition.

Edgerton, W. F. (1941), 'Ideograms in English writing', *Language* **17**(2), 148–150.

Eisenstein, E. L. (1980), *The Printing Press as an Agent of Change: Communications and Cultural Transformations in Early-Modern Europe*, Cambridge University Press, Cambridge.

Ellis, A. W. (1979), 'Slips of the pen', *Visible Language* **13**(3), 265–282.

Emeneau, M. B. (1946), 'The nasal phonemes of Sanskrit', *Language* **22**(2), 86–93.

Erduman, D., ed. (2004), *Geschriebene Welten: Arabische Kalligraphie und Literatur im Wandel der Zeit*, Dumont, Köln.

Esterman, M., Verstynen, T., Ivry, R. B. & Robertson, L. C. (2006), 'Coming unbound: Disrupting automatic integration of synesthetic color and graphemes by transcranial magnetic stimulation of the right parietal lobe', *Journal of Cognitive Neuroscience* **18**(9), 1570–1576.

Estes, W. K. (1978), Perceptual processing in letter recognition and reading, *in* Carterette & Friedman (1978), pp. 163–220.

Fano, R. M. (1966), *Transmission of Information: A Statistical Theory of Communications*, 2d edn, MIT Press, Cambridge MA.

Firth, J. R. (1936), 'Alphabets and phonology in India and Burma', *Bulletin of the School of Oriental Studies* **8**(2/3), 517–546.

—— (1946), 'The English school of phonetics', *Transactions of the Philological Society* pp. 92–132.

French, M. A. (1976), Observations on the Chinese script and the classification of writing-systems, *in* Haas (1976), pp. 101–129.

Frost, R. (1992), Orthography and phonology: The psychological reality of orthographic depth, *in* P. Downing, S. D. Lima & M. Noonan, eds, 'The Linguistics of Literacy', Vol. 21 of *Typological Studies in Language*, John Benjamins, Amsterdam, pp. 255–274.

Fry, A. H. (1941), 'A phonemic interpretation of visarga', *Language* **17**(3), 194–200.

Füssel, S. (2005), *Gutenberg and the Impact of Printing*, Ashgate, Burlington, VT. First published in 1999 as *Gutenberg und seine Wirkung*, Insel, Frankfurt am Main.

Gaylord, H. E. (1995), 'Character representation', *Computers and the Humanities* **29**, 51–73.

Geyer, L. H. (1970), A Two-Channel Theory of Short Term Visual Storage, PhD thesis, SUNY at Buffalo.

Geyer, L. H. & DeWald, C. G. (1973), 'Feature lists and confusion matrices', *Perception & Psychophysics* **14**(3), 471–482.

Ghosh, P. K. (1983), An approach to type design and text composition in Indian scripts, Technical Report STAN-CS-83-965, Department of Computer Science, Stanford University. <http://infolab.stanford.edu/TR/CS-TR-83-965.html>.

Gibson, E. J. (1969), *Principles of Perceptual Learning and Development*, Appleton-Century-Crofts, New York.

——. (1972), Reading for some purpose, *in* Kavanagh & Mattingly (1972), pp. 3–19.

Gill, E. (1936), *An Essay on Typography*, 2d edn, Sheed and Ward. Facsimile edition with new introduction by Christopher Skelton, David R. Godine, Boston, 2007.

Gillam, R. (2002), *Unicode Demystified: A Practical Programmer's Guide to the Encoding Standard*, Addison-Wesley, Boston.

Glaister, G. A. (1979), *Glaister's Glossary of the Book: Terms Used in Papermaking, Printing, Bookbinding, and Publishing with Notes on Illuminated Manuscripts and Private Presses*, 2d edn, University of California Press, Berkeley.

Goldin-Meadow, S. (2003), *Hearing Gesture: How Our Hands Help Us Think*, Belknap Press, Cambridge MA.

Goldsmith, J. A. (1995*a*), Phonological theory, in *The Handbook of Phonological Theory* (Goldsmith, 1995*b*), pp. 1–23.

—, ed. (1995*b*), *The Handbook of Phonological Theory*, Blackwell, Cambridge MA.

Goodglass, H. (1993), *Understanding Aphasia*, Academic Press, San Diego.

Govindaraju, V., Setlur, S., Khedekar, S., Kompalli, S., Farooq, F. & Vemulapati, R. (2004), Enabling digital access to multi-lingual Indian documents, *in* 'Proceedings of the First International Workshop on Document Image Analysis for Libraries'.

Griffen, T. D. (1976), 'Toward a nonsegmental phonology', *Lingua* **40**, 1–20.

Gupta, R. (2006), 'Technology for Indic scripts: A user perspective', *Language in India* **6**, 1–17. <http://www.languageinindia.com/july2006/indictechnology.pdf>.

Haas, W., ed. (1976), *Writing without Letters*, Vol. 4 of *Mont Follick Series*, Manchester University Press, Manchester.

Hadj-Salah, A. (1971), 'La notion de syllabe et la theorie cinetico-impulsionnelle des phoneticiens arabes', *Al-Lisāniyyāt* **1**, 63–83.

Halle, M. (1983), 'On distinctive features and their articulatory implementation', *Natural Language Theory* **1**, 91–105.

——. (1988), 'Remarques sur la révolution scientifique en phonologie, 1926/1930', *Actes de la recherche en sciences sociales* **74**, 89–96.

——. (1995), 'Feature geometry and feature spreading', *Linguistic Inquiry* **26**(1), 1–46.

——. (2002), *From Memory to Speech and Back: Papers on Phonetics and Phonology 1954–2002*, Vol. 3 of *Phonology and Phonetics*, De Gruyter, Berlin.

Halle, M., Vaux, B. & Wolfe, A. (2000), 'On feature spreading and the representation of place of articulation', *Linguistic Inquiry* **31**(3), 387–444.

Hamann, S. R. (2003), The Phonetics and Phonology of Retroflexes, PhD thesis, Universiteit Utrecht.

Hamp, E. P. (1959), 'Graphemics and paragraphemics', *Studies in Linguistics* **14**(1–2), 1–5.

Haralambous, Y. (2002), 'Unicode et typographie: un amour impossible', *Document Numérique* **6**(3/4), 107–139.

——. (2004), *Fontes & codages*, O'Reilly, Paris.

Haralambous, Y. & Plaice, J. (2002), 'Low-level Devanāgarī support for Omega—Adapting devnag', *TUGboat* **23**(1), 50–56. <http://www.tug.org/TUGboat/Articles/tb23-1/haralambous.pdf>.

Harley, A. H. (1955), *Colloquial Hindustani*, Routledge & Kegan Paul, London. With an introduction by J. R. Firth.

Harris, W. V. (1989), *Ancient Literacy*, Harvard University Press, Cambridge MA.

Hellingman, J. (1998), 'Indian scripts and Unicode', <http://ldc.upenn.edu/myl/IndianScriptsUnicode.html>.

Henderson, L. (1985), 'On the use of the term "grapheme"', *Language and Cognitive Processes* **1**(2), 135–148.

Hillenbrand, J. M. & Houde, R. A. (1996), 'The role of F_0 and amplitude in the perception of intervocalic glottal stops', *Journal of Speech & Hearing Research* **39**(6), 1182–1191.

Hixon, T. J. (1987), Respiratory function in speech, in *Respiratory Function in Speech and Song* (Hixon & Collaborators, 1987), chapter 1, pp. 1–54.

Hixon, T. J. & collaborators (1987), *Respiratory Function in Speech and Song*, College-Hill Press, Boston.

Hoberman, R. D. (1985), 'The phonology of pharyngeals and pharyngealization in Pre-Modern Aramaic', *Journal of the American Oriental Society* **105**(2), 221–231.

Hock, H. H. (1975), 'Substratum influence on (Rig-Vedic) Sanskrit?', *Studies in the Linguistic Sciences* **5**(2), 76–125.

——. (1979), 'Retroflexion rules in Sanskrit', *South Asian Languages Analysis* **1**, 47–62.

——. (1993), 'Subversion or convergence? the issue of pre-Vedic retroflexion reexamined', *Studies in the Linguistic Sciences* **23**(2), 73–115.

——. (n.d.), 'Devanagari made easy', Unpublished instructional materials.

Hockey, S. (2000), *Electronic Texts in the Humanities: Principles and Practice*, Oxford University Press, New York.

Hoenig, A. (1990), 'A constructed Duerer alphabet', *TUGboat* **11**(3), 435–438. <http://www.tug.org/TUGboat/Articles/tb11-3/tb29hoenig.pdf>.

Hofstadter, D. R. (1985), *Metamagical Themas: Questing for the Essence of Mind and Pattern*, Basic Books, New York.

Hubel, D. H. & Wiesel, T. N. (1968), 'Receptive fields and functional architecture of monkey striate cortex', *Journal of Physiology* **195**, 215–243.

Huet, G. (2005), 'A functional toolkit for morphological and phonological processing, application to a Sanskrit tagger', *Journal of Functional Programming* **15**(4), 573–614.

—. (2009), Formal structure of Sanskrit text: Requirements for a mechanical Sanskrit processor, *in* Huet, Kulkarni & Scharf (2009), pp. 162–199.

Huet, G., Kulkarni, A. & Scharf, P. M., eds (2009), *Sanskrit Computational Linguistics: First and Second International Symposia: Rocquencourt, France, October 2007; Providence, RI, USA, May 2008*, Vol. 5402 of *Lecture Notes in Artificial Intelligence*, Springer, Berlin.

Hyman, M. D. (2006), 'Of glyphs and glottography', *Language & Communication* **26**, 231–249.

Ingram, W. H. (1966), 'The ligatures of early printed Greek', *Greek, Roman and Byzantine Studies* **7**(4), 371–389.

Ishida, R. (2002), 'An introduction to Indic scripts', Paper delivered at 22nd Int. Unicode Conference, San José, CA, Sept. 2002. <http://www.w3.org/2002/Talks/09-ri-indic/indic-paper.pdf>.

Ivanov, V. V. & Toporov, V. N. (1968), *Sanskrit*, Nauka, Moscow. Originally published in Russian, 1960.

Jaffré, J.-P. & Fayol, M. (2006), Orthography and literacy in French, *in* Joshi & Aaron (2006), pp. 81–103.

Jakobson, R. ([1929] 1971), Remarques sur l'évolution phonologique du russe comparée à celle des autres langues slaves, *in* 'Selected Writings, Vol. 1: Phonological Studies', 2d edn, Mouton, The Hague, pp. 7–116.

Jakobson, R., Fant, C. G. M. & Halle, M. (1963), *Preliminaries to Speech Analysis: The Distinctive Features and their Correlates*, MIT Press, Cambridge MA. With additions and corrigenda to the 1952 edition.

Jenkins, J. H. (1999), 'The Unicode character-glyph model: Case studies', Paper delivered at 15th Int. Unicode Conference, San

José, CA, Aug./Sept. 1999. <http://developer.apple.com/fonts/WhitePapers/IUC15CG.pdf>.

Jones, D. (1942), *The Problem of a National Script for India*, Pioneer Press., Lucknow, U. P.

—— (1962), *The Phoneme: Its Nature and Use*, 2d edn, W. Heffer & Sons, Cambridge.

Joseph, J. E. (2000), *Limiting the Arbitrary: Linguistic Naturalism and its Opposites in Plato's Cratylus and Modern Theories of Language*, Vol. 96 of *Studies in the History of the Language Sciences*, John Benjamins, Amsterdam.

Joshi, A., Ganu, A., Chand, A., Parmar, V. & Mathur, G. (2004), 'Keylekh: A keyboard for text entry in Indic scripts', CHI 2004, April 24–29, Vienna.

Joshi, R. K. (2006), 'The phonemic model from India for bi-modal applications', Paper delivered at the Second Workshop on Internationalizing SSML, Heraklion, Crete, May 2006. <http://www.w3.org/2006/02/SSML/agenda.html>.

Joshi, R. K., Dharmadhikari, T. N. & Bedekar, V. V. (2007), 'The phonemic approach for Sanskrit text', <http://sanskrit.inria.fr/Symposium/Phonemics_CDAC.pdf>.

Joshi, R. M. & Aaron, P. G., eds (2006), *Handbook of Orthography and Literacy*, Erlbaum, Mahwaw NJ.

Kahan, B. (2000), *Ottmar Mergenthaler: The Man and his Machine; A Biographical Appreciation of the Inventor on his Centennial*, Oak Knoll Press, New Castle DE.

Kahn, D. (1996), *The Codebreakers: The Story of Secret Writing*, 2d edn, Scribner, New York.

Kapr, A. (1993), *Fraktur: Form und Geschichte der gebrochenen Schriften*, Hermann Schmidt, Mainz.

Katsoulidis, T. (1996), The physiognomy of the Greek typographical letter, *in* M. S. Macrakis, ed., 'Greek Letters: From Tablets to Pixels', Oak Knoll Press, New Castle DE, pp. 153–161.

Kaufman, S. A. (1984), 'On vowel reduction in Aramaic', *Journal of the American Oriental Society* **104**(1), 87–95.

Kavanagh, J. F. & Mattingly, I. G., eds (1972), *Language by Ear and by Eye: The Relationships between Speech and Reading*, MIT Press, Cambridge MA.

Keane, E. (2004), 'Tamil', *Journal of the International Phonetic Association* **34**(1), 111–116.

Kelly, J. (1981), The 1847 alphabet: an episode of phonotypy, *in* Asher & Henderson (1981), pp. 248–264.

Kemp, J. A. (1994), Phoneme, *in* R. E. Asher, ed., 'The Encyclopedia of Language and Linguistics', Vol. 6, Pergamon, New York, pp. 3029–3036.

Kenyon, F. G. (1951), *Books and Readers in Ancient Greece and Rome*, 2d edn, Clarendon, Oxford.

Kernighan, B. W. & Pike, R. (1984), *The UNIX Programming Environment*, Prentice-Hall, Englewood Cliffs NJ.

Kielhorn, L. F., ed. (1962, 1965, 1972), *The Vyākaraṇa-mahābhāṣya of Patañjali*, third edition revised and furnished with additional readings, references and select critical notes by k. v. abhyankar edn, Bhandarkar Oriental Research Institute, Pune. 3 vols.

Kim, C. W. (1997), The structure of phonological units in han'gŭl, *in* Y.-K. Kim-Renaud, ed., 'The Korean Alphabet: Its History and Structure', University of Hawai'i Press, Honolulu, pp. 145–160.

Kita, S., ed. (2003), *Pointing: Where Language, Culture, and Cognition Meet*, Erlbaum, Mahwaw NJ.

Klatt, D. H. (1976), 'Linguistic uses of segmental duration in English: Acoustic and perceptual evidence', *Journal of the Acoustical Society of America* **59**(5), 1208–1221.

Klima, E. S. (1972), How alphabets might reflect language, *in* Kavanagh & Mattingly (1972), pp. 57–80.

Kompalli, S. (2007), Design of a Stochastic Framework for Font-independent Devanagari OCR, PhD thesis, University of Buffalo.

Krampen, M. (1986), On the origins of visual literacy: Children's drawings as compositions of graphemes, *in* M. E. Wrolstad & D. F. Fisher, eds, 'Toward a New Understanding of Literacy', Praeger, New York, pp. 80–111.

Krishna, S. (1991), *India's Living Languages: The Critical Issues*, Allied Publishers, New Delhi.

Kropač, I. H. (1991), Medieval documents, *in* D. I. Greenstein, ed., 'Modelling Historical Data: Towards a Standard for Encoding and Exchanging Machine-Readable Texts', Vol. 11 of *Halbgraue Reihe zur Historischen Fachinformatik*, Max-Planck-Institut für Geschichte, St. Katharinen, pp. 117–127.

Ladefoged, P. (1971), *Preliminaries to Linguistic Phonetics*, University of Chicago Press, Chicago.

——. (2005), 'Features and parameters for different purposes', Department of Linguistics, UCLA. Working Papers in Phonetics. Paper No104_1. Pages 1–13, <http://repositories.cdlib.org/uclaling/wpp/No104_1>.

Lagally, K. (1999), '7-bit meta-transliterations for 8-bit Romanizations', <http://elib.uni-stuttgart.de/opus/volltexte/1999/421/pdf/421_1.pdf>.

—— (2004), 'ArabTeX: Typesetting Arabic and Hebrew, user manual version 4.00', <http://129.69.218.213/arabtex/doc/arabdoc.pdf>.

Laughery, K. R. (1971), Computer simulation of short-term memory: A component decay model, *in* G. T. Bower & J. T. Spence, eds, 'The Psychology of Learning and Motivation: Advances in Research and Theory', Vol. 6, Academic Press, New York.

Laver, J. (1994), *Principles of Phonetics*, Cambridge University Press, Cambridge.

Lunde, P. (1981), 'Arabic and the art of printing', *Aramco World* **32**(2), 20–25.

Lyytinen, H., Aro, M., Holopainen, L., Leiwo, M., Lyttinen, P. & Tolvanen, A. (2006), Children's language development and reading in a highly transparent orthography, *in* Joshi & Aaron (2006), pp. 47–62.

MacCarthy, P. A. D. (1969), The Bernard Shaw alphabet, *in* W. Haas, ed., 'Alphabets for English', number 1 *in* 'Mont Follick Series', Manchester University Press, Manchester, pp. 105–117.

Macdonell, A. A. (1910), *Vedic Grammar*, K. J. Trübner, Strassburg.

Mackenzie, C. E. (1980), *Coded Character Sets, History and Development*, The Systems Programming Series, Addison-Wesley, Reading MA.

MacMahon, M. K. C. (1981), Henry Sweet's system of shorthand, *in* Asher & Henderson (1981), pp. 265–281.

MacWhinney, B. (1991), *The CHILDES Project: Tools for Analyzing Talk*, Erlbaum, Hillsdale NJ.

Maddieson, I. (1984), *Patterns of Sounds*, Cambridge University Press, Cambridge. With a chapter contributed by Sandra Ferrari Disner.

Mahmoud, Y. (1979), The Arabic Writing System and the Sociolinguistics of Orthographic Reform, PhD thesis, Georgetown University.

Massaro, D. W. (1973), 'Perception of letters, words, and nonwords', *Journal of Experimental Psychology* **100**(2), 349–353.

McArthur, T., ed. (1992), *The Oxford Companion to the English Language*, Oxford University Press, Oxford.

McCarthy, J. (1994), The phonetics and phonology of Semitic pharyngeals, *in* P. Keating, ed., 'Papers in Laboratory Phonology III: Phonological Structure and Phonetic Form', Cambridge University Press, Cambridge, pp. 191–233.

McNeill, D. (1992), *Hand and Mind: What Gestures Reveal about Thought*, University of Chicago Press, Chicago.

Mermelstein, P. & Eden, M. (1964), 'Experiments on computer recognition of connected handwritten words', *Information and Control* 7, 255–270.

Mikami, Y., abu Bakar, A. Z., Sonlert-lamvanich, V., Vikas, O., Pavol, Z., abdul Rozan, M. Z., János, G. N. & Takahashi, T. (2005), Language diversity on the internet: An Asian view, *in* UNESCO Institute for Statistics, ed., 'Measuring Linguistic Diversity on the Internet', UNESCO, Paris, pp. 91–103.

Miller, D. G. (1994), *Ancient Scripts and Phonological Knowledge*, Vol. 116 of *Amsterdam Studies in the Theory and History of Linguistic Science*, John Benjamins, Amsterdam.

Mīmāṁsaka, Y. (1964), *Vaidika-vāṅmaya meṁ vividha svarāṅkana-prakāra*, Bharatiya Pracyavidya Pratisthan, Ajmer.

Mishra, V. (1972), *A Critical Study of Sanskrit Phonetics*, Chowkhamba Sanskrit Series Office, Vārānasī.

Mohanty, S. K. (1998), The formulation of parameters for type design of Indian scripts based on calligraphic studies, *in* R. D. Hersch, J. André & H. Brown, eds, 'Electronic Publishing, Artistic Imaging, and Digital Typography: 7th International Conference on Electronic Publishing, EP '98, St. Malo, France, March 30–April 3, 1998: Proceedings', pp. 157–166.

Monier-Williams, M. (1872), *A Sanskrit-English Dictionary Etymologically and Philologically Arranged with Special Reference to Greek, Latin, Gothic, German, Anglo-Saxon, and Other Cognate Indo-European Languages*, Clarendon, Oxford.

Morison, S. (1972), *Politics and Script: Aspects of Authority and Freedom in the Development of Graeco-Latin Script from the Sixth-Century BC*, Clarendon Press, Oxford.

Mujoo, A., Malviya, M. K., Moona, R. & Prabhakar, T. V. (2000), A search engine for Indian languages, *in* K. Bauknecht, S. K.

Madria & G. Pernul, eds, 'Electronic Commerce and Web Technologies: First International Conference, EC-Web 2000, London, UK, September 4–6, 2000, Proceedings', Vol. 1875 of *Lecture Notes in Computer Science*, Springer, Berlin, pp. 349–358.

Narasimhan, R. & Reddy, V. S. N. (1967), 'A generative model for handprinted English letters and its computer implementation', *ICC Bulletin* **6**, 275–287.

Naus, M. J. & Shillman, R. J. (1976), 'Why a Y is not a V: A new look at the distinctive features of letters', *Journal of Experimental Psychology: Human Perception and Performance* **2**(3), 394–400.

Nolan, F. (1997), Speaker recognition and forensic phonetics, *in* W. J. Hardcastle & J. Laver, eds, 'The Handbook of Phonetic Sciences', Blackwell, Oxford, pp. 744–767.

Oberlies, T. (2003), Aśokan Prakrit and Pāli, *in* Cardona & Jain (2003), pp. 161–203.

Ohala, M. (1983), *Aspects of Hindi Phonology*, Vol. 2 of *MLBD Series in Linguistics*, Motilal Banarsidass, Delhi.

Olivier, F. (1974), 'Le dessin enfantin est-il une écriture?', *Enfance* **22**, 183–216.

Oudeyer, P.-Y. (2006), *Self-Organization in the Evolution of Speech*, Vol. 6 of *Studies in the Evolution of Language*, Oxford University Press, Oxford.

Pāṭhaka, P. Y., ed. (1883), *Kātyāyana's Prātiśākhya of the White Yajur Veda [Vājasaneyi Prātiśākhya] with the Commentary of Uvaṭa*, Benares Sanskrit Series 8, Vārānasī.

Page, R. I. (1999), *An Introduction to English Runes*, 2d edn, Boydell, Woodbridge, UK.

Pandey, A. (1998), 'An overview of Indic fonts for TEX', *TUGboat* **19**(2), 115–120.

Parida, L. (1993), **Vinyas:** an interactive calligraphic type design system, *in* 'Proceedings of the International Conference on Computer Graphics (ICCG 93)', Bombay, pp. 355–368.

Patel, P. (1995), Brahmi scripts, orthographic units, and reading acquisition, *in* I. Taylor & D. Olson, eds, 'Scripts and Literacy: Reading and Learning to Read Alphabets, Syllabaries, and Characters', Kluwer, Dordrecht, pp. 265–276.

Pierce, J. (1999), Sound waves and sine waves, *in* P. R. Cook, ed., 'Music, Cognition, and Computerized Sound: An Introduction to Psychoacoustics', MIT Press, Cambridge MA, pp. 37–56.

Pitman, I. (1837), *Stenographic Sound-Hand*, Samuel Bagster, London.

Priolkar, A. K. (1958), *The Printing Press in India: Its Beginnings and Early Development: Being a Quatercentenary Commemoration Study of the Advent of Printing in India (in 1556)*, Marathi Samshodhana Mandala, Mumbai.

Pulgram, E. (1951), 'Phoneme and grapheme: A parallel', *Word* **7**, 15–20.

Pulgram, E. (1976), The typologies of writing-systems, *in* Haas (1976), pp. 1–28.

Pullum, G. K. & Ladusaw, W. A. (1986), *Phonetic Symbol Guide*, University of Chicago Press, Chicago.

Ramachandran, V. S. & Hubbard, E. M. (2001), 'Psychophysical investigations into the neural basis of synaesthesia', *Proceedings of the Royal Society of London, B* **268**, 979–983.

Ramachandran, V. S., Hubbard, E. M. & Butcher, P. A. (2004), Synesthesia, cross-activation, and the foundations of neuroepistemology, *in* G. A. Calvert, C. Spence & B. E. Stein, eds, 'The Handbook of Multisensory Processes', MIT Press, Cambridge MA, pp. 867–883.

Ramsey, S. R. (1989), *The Languages of China*, 2d edn, Princeton University Press, Princeton NJ.

Rastogi, S. L., ed. (1967), *The Śuklayajuḥ-prātiśākhya of Kātyāyana*, Vol. 179 of *Kashi Sanskrit Series*, Chowkhamba Sanskrit Series Office, Vārānasī. Forward by Mangal Deva Shastri (author's father).

Rath, T. M. & Manmatha, R. (2003), Features for word spotting in historical manuscripts, *in* 'Proceedings: Seventh International Conference on Document Analysis and Recognition: August 3 to 6, 2003, Edinburgh, Scotland, vol. 1', pp. 218–222.

Reed, S. K. (1978), Schemes and theories of pattern recognition, *in* Carterette & Friedman (1978), pp. 137–162.

Renou, L. (1952), *Grammaire de la langue védique*, IAC, Lyon.

Rich, A. N. & Mattingley, J. B. (2005), Can attention modulate color-graphemic synesthesia?, *in* Robertson & Sagiv (2005), chapter 7, pp. 108–123.

Robertson, L. C. & Sagiv, N., eds (2005), *Synesthesia: Perspectives from Cognitive Neuroscience*, Oxford University Press, New York.

Romani, C. & Calabrese, A. (1998), 'Syllabic constraints in the phonological errors of an aphasic patient', *Brain and Language* **64**, 83–121.

Roper, G. (2002), Early Arabic printing in Europe, *in* E. Hanebutt-Benz, D. Glass & G. Roper, eds, 'Sprachen des Nahen Ostens und die Druckrevolution: Eine interkulturelle Begegnung', WVA-Verlag Skulima, Westhofen, pp. 129–150.

Rosenberger, T. M. G. (1998), Prosodic font: The space between the spoken and the written, Master's thesis, MIT.

Ross, F. (2002), 'Non-Latin type design at Linotype', Paper delivered at the First annual Friends of St Bride conference, Twentieth Century Graphic Communication: Technology, Society, and Culture, London, 24–25 Sept. 2002. <http://stbride.org/friends/conference/twentiethcentury-graphiccommunication/NonLatin.html>.

Ryan, F. X. (1993), 'Some observations on the censorship of Claudius and Vitellus, A.D. 47–48', *American Journal of Philology* **114**(4), 611–618.

Saenger, P. (1991), The separation of words and the physiology of reading, *in* D. Olson & N. Torrance, eds, 'Literacy and Orality', Cambridge University Press, Cambridge, pp. 198–214.

Salomon, R. (1995), 'On the origin of the early Indian scripts', *Journal of the American Oriental Society* **115**(2), 271–279.

—. (1998), *Indian Epigraphy: A Guide to the Study of Inscriptions in Sanskrit, Prakrit, and The Other Indo-Aryan Languages*, Oxford University Press, New York.

Sampson, G. (1985), *Writing Systems: A Linguistic Introduction*, Stanford University Press, Stanford.

Sastri, B. (1987), *Śrīmadbhagavatpatañjalimuniviracitam Pātañjalam Mahābhāṣyaṃ Kaiyaṭopādhyāyapraṇītena Pradīpena, Nāgeśabhaṭṭaviracitena Mahābhāṣyapradīpoddyotena*, 2d edn, Vāṇīvilāsa Prakāśana, Varanasi. [Sanskrit]. = The *Mahābhāṣya* of Patañjali with Kaiyaṭa's *Pradīpa* and Nāgeśa's *Uddyota*. 8 vols. in 7. Original edition: Śrīguruprasādaśāstrī-granthamālā, no. 1.

Scharf, P. M. (2003), *Rāmopākhyāna: The Story of Rāma in the Mahābhārata: An Independent-Study Reader in Sanskrit*, RoutledgeCurzon, London.

—. (2009), Modeling Pāṇinian grammar, *in* Huet et al. (2009), pp. 95–126.

Scharfe, H. (1977), *Grammatical Literature*, Vol. 5 fasc. 2 of *A History of Indian Literature*, Harrassowitz, Wiesbaden. Jan Gonda, ed., pp. 72–216.

—. (2002), 'Kharoṣṭhī and Brāhmī', *Journal of the American Oriental Society* **122**(2), 391–393.

Schlesinger, C., ed. (1989), *The Biography of Ottmar Mergenthaler, Inventor of the Linotype: A New Edition, with Added Historical Notes Based on Recent Findings*, Oak Knoll Press, New Castle DE.

Schmidt, J. (1875), *Zur Geschichte des Indogermanischen Vocalismus*, Vol. 2, Hermann Böhlau, Weimar.

Shallice, T. (1981), 'Phonological agraphia and the lexical route in writing', *Brain* **104**, 413–429.

Shanbhag, S., Rao, D. & Joshi, R. K. (2002), An intelligent multi-layered input scheme for phonetic scripts, *in* 'Proceedings of the 2nd International Symposium on Smart Graphics', ACM Press, New York, pp. 35–38.

Shapiro, L. P., McNamara, P., Zurif, E., Lanzoni, S., & Cermak, L. (1992), 'Processing complexity and sentence memory: Evidence from amnesia', *Brain and Language* **42**(4), 431–453.

Sharma, R. (2002), *Brāhmī Script: Development in North-Western India and Central Asia*, B. R. Publishing, Delhi. 2 vols.

Sharma, V. V., ed. (1934), *Vājasaneyi Prātiśākhya of Kātyāyana: With the Commentaries of Uvaṭa and Anantabhaṭṭa*, Vol. 5 of *Madras University Sanskrit Series*, University of Madras. वाजसनेयिप्रातिशाख्यं कात्यायनप्रणीतं भाष्यद्वयोपेतम्.

Shastri, M. D., ed. (1931), *The Ṛgveda-prātiśākhya with the Commentary of Uvaṭa: Edited from Original Manuscripts, with Introduction, Critical and Additional Notes, English Translation of the Text, and Several Appendices*, Vol. 2: Text in Sūtra-Form and Commentary with Critical Apparatus, The Indian Press, Allahabad.

—, ed. (1937), *The Ṛgveda-prātiśākhya with the Commentary of Uvaṭa: Edited from Original Manuscripts, with Introduction, Critical and Additional Notes, English Translation of the Text, and Several Appendices*, Vol. 3: English Translation of the Text, Additional Notes, Several Appendices and Indices, Motlilal Banarsidass, Lahore.

—, ed. (1959), *The Ṛgveda-prātiśākhya with the Commentary of Uvaṭa: Edited from Original Manuscripts, with Introduction, Critical and Additional Notes, English Translation of the Text, and Several Appendices*, Vol. 1: Introduction, Original Text of the Ṛgveda-prātiśākhya in Stanza-Form, Supplementary Notes, and Several Appendices, Vaidika Svādhyāya Mandira, Vārānasī.

Shaw, G. B. (1962), *Androcles and the Lion: an Old Fable Renovated by Bernard Shaw; with a Parallel Text in Shaw's Alphabet, to be Read in Conjunction Showing its Economies in Writing and Reading*, Penguin, Harmondsworth.

Shaw, G. W. (1980), 'Printing in Devanagari: The evolution of types in Devanagari script', *The Monotype Recorder* **2 (n.s.)**, 28–32. देवनागरी लिपि के टाइपों का विकास.

Shimron, J. & Navon, D. (1980), 'The distribution of visual information in the vertical dimension of Roman and Hebrew letters', *Visible Language* **14**(1), 5–12.

Shoup, J. E. (1980), Phonological aspects of speech recognition, *in* W. Lea, ed., 'Trends in Speech Recognition', Prentice-Hall, Englewood Cliffs NJ, pp. 125–138.

Simner, J., Ward, J., Lanz, M., Hansari, A., Noonan, K., Glover, L. & Oakley, D. A. (2005), 'Non-random associates of graphemes to colours in synaesthetic and non-synaesthetic populations', *Cognitive Neuropsychology* **22**(8), 1069–1085.

Singh, A. K. (1991), *Development of Nagari Script*, Parimal Publications, Delhi.

—. (2006), 'A computational phonetic model for Indian language scripts', Constraints on Spelling Changes: Fifth International Workshop on Writing Systems. Nijmegen, The Netherlands, October, 2006.

Singh, K. S. (1997), *Languages and Scripts*, number 9 *in* 'People of India National Series', Oxford University Press, Delhi.

Skelton, C. (2008), 'Methods of using phylogenetic systematics to reconstruct the history of the Linear B script', *Archaeometry* **50**(1), 158–176.

Smilek, D., Dixon, M. J. & Merikle, P. M. (2005), Binding of graphemes and synesthetic colors in color-graphemic synesthesia, *in* Robertson & Sagiv (2005), chapter 5, pp. 74–89.

Smith, F., Lott, D. & Cronnell, B. (1969), 'The effect of type size and case alternation on word identification', *American Journal of Psychology* **82**(2), 248–253.

Smith, F. W. (1964), 'New American Standard Code for Information Interchange', *Western Union Technical Review* **18**(2), 50–61.

Smith, G. (1885), *The Life of William Carey, D. D.: Shoemaker and Missionary, Professor of Sanskrit, Bengali, and Marathi in the College of Fort William, Calcutta*, J. Murray, London.

Snowling, M. J. (2005), Dyslexia, *in* B. Hopkins, ed., 'The Cambridge Encyclopedia of Child Development', Cambridge University Press, Cambridge, pp. 433–436.

Snyman, J. W. (1970), *An Introduction to the !Xũ (!Kung) Language*, A. A. Balkema, Cape Town.

Sonka, M., Hlavac, V. & Boyle, R. (1999), *Image Processing, Analysis and Machine Vision*, 2d edn, PWS, Pacific Grove CA.

Sproat, R. (2006), 'Brahmi-derived scripts, script layout, and segmental analysis', *Written Language & Literacy* **9**(1), 45–65.

Srihari, S. N., Srinivasan, H., Huang, C. & Shetty, S. (2006), 'Spotting words in Latin, Devanagari and Arabic scripts', *Vivek: Indian Journal of Artificial Intelligence* **16**(3), 2–9.

Staal, J. F. (1972), *A Reader on the Sanskrit Grammarians*, Motilal Banarsidass, Delhi.

Steinberg, S. H. (1961), *Five Hundred Years of Printing*, 2d edn, Penguin, Harmondsworth.

Stemberger, J. P. (1982), 'The nature of segments in the lexicon: Evidence from speech errors', *Lingua* **56**, 235–259.

Strasser, G. F. (1988), *Lingua Universalis: Kryptologie und Theorie der Universalsprachen im 16. und 17. Jahrhundert*, Vol. 38 of *Wolfenbütteler Forschungen*, Harrasowitz, Wiesbaden.

Suen, C. Y., Mori, S., Kim, Ş. H. & Leung, C. H. (2003), Analysis and recognition of Asian scripts—the state of the art, *in* 'Proceedings of the 7th International Conference on Document Analysis and Recognition', pp. 866–878.

Sweet, H. (1892), *A Manual of Current Shorthand, Orthographic and Phonetic*, Clarendon, Oxford.

Syropoulos, A., Tsolomitis, A. & Sofroniou, N. (2003), *Digital Typography Using LaTeX*, Springer, New York.

Szemerényi, O. (1967), 'The new look of Indo-European: Reconstruction and typology', *Phonetica* **17**(2), 65–99.

Takakusu, J. (1896), *Record of the Buddhist Religion as Practised in India and the Malay Archipelago*, Clarendon, Oxford.

Tolchinsky, L. (2003), *The Cradle of Culture and What Children Know About Writing and Numbers Before Being Taught*, Erlbaum, Mahwaw NJ.

Tomasello, M. (1999), *The Cultural Origins of Human Cognition*, Harvard University Press, Cambridge MA.

Treiman, R. (2006), Knowledge about letters as a foundation for reading and spelling, *in* Joshi & Aaron (2006), pp. 581–599.

Trigger, B. G. (1998), 'Writing systems: A case study in cultural evolution', *Norwegian Archaeological Review* **31**(1), 39–62.

Trigo Ferre, R. L. (1988), The Phonological Derivation and Behavior of Nasal Glides, PhD thesis, MIT, Cambridge MA. MIT Dissertations in Linguistics TRIG01.

Tversky, A. (1977), 'Features of similarity', *Psychological Review* **84**(4), 327–352.

Unicode Consortium (2006), *The Unicode Standard, Version 5.0*, Addison-Wesley, Boston.

Vacek, J. (1976), 'The Sanskrit sibilants', *Wissenschaftliche Zeitschrift der Humboldt-Universität zu Berlin, Gesellschafts und sprachwissenschaftliche Reihe* **25**(3), 407–412.

Vachek, J. (1973), *Written Language: General Problems and Problems of English*, number 14 *in* 'Janua Linguarum Series Critica', Mouton, The Hague.

Vaid, J. (2002), 'Exploring word recognition in a semi-alphabetic script: The case of Devanagari', *Brain and Language* **81**, 679–690.

van den Bosch, A., Content, A., Daelemans, W. & de Gelder, B. (1994), 'Measuring the complexity of writing systems', *Journal of Quantitative Linguistics* **1**(3), 178–188.

van Nooten, B. A. (1973), The structure of a Sanskrit phonetic treatise, *in* I. Konks, P. Numerkund & L. Mall, eds, 'Oriental Studies', Toid Orientalistika Alalt; Trudy po Vostokovedeniju II 2, Tartu University, Tartu, pp. 408–436.

Varma, S. (1929), *Critical Studies in the Phonetic Observations of Indian Grammarians*, Royal Asiatic Society, London. Reprint: Delhi: Munshiram Manoharlal, 1961.

Vedavrata, ed. (1962–1963), *Patañjali's Vyākaraṇamahabhaṣya with Kaiyaṭa's Pradīpa and Nāgojībhaṭṭa's Uddyota*, Haryāṇā Sāhitya Saṁsthāna, Gurukula Jhajjar (Rohatak).

Velten, H. V. (1956), Hedgehogs *Versus* foxes in comparative linguistics, *in* M. Halle, H. G. Lunt, H. McLean & C. H. van Schooneveld, eds, 'For Roman Jakobson: Essays on the Occasion of His Sixtieth Birthday, 11 October 1956', Mouton, The Hague, pp. 585–587.

Vincent, D. (2000), *The Rise of Mass Literacy: Reading and Writing in Modern Europe*, Polity, Cambridge.

Voigt, R. (2005), 'Die Entwicklung der aramäischen zur Kharoṣṭhī- und Brāhmī-Schrift', *Zeitschrift der Deutschen Morgenländischen Gesellschaft* **155**, 25–50.

Vygotskii, L. S. (2005), *Pedagogicheskaia psikhologiia*, AST-Astrel-Liuks, Moscow.

Walden Font (1997), 'The Gutenberg press: Five centuries of German Fraktur', <http://www.waldenfont.com/downloads/gbpmanual.pdf>.

Waller, R. (1986), 'What electronic books will have to be better than', *Information Design Journal* **5**(1), 72–75.

—. (1988), The Typographic Contribution to Language: Towards a Model of Typographic Genres and Their Underlying Structures, PhD thesis, University of Reading.

Ward, J. & Romani, C. (2000), 'Consonant-vowel encoding and ortho-syllables in a case of acquired dysgraphia', *Cognitive Neuropsychology* **17**(7), 641–663.

Ward, J., Simner, J. & Auyeung, V. (2005), 'A comparison of lexical-gustatory and grapheme-colour synaesthesia', *Cognitive Neuropsychology* **22**(1), 28–41.

Watson, P. J. & Hixon, T. J. (1987), Respiratory kinematics in classical (opera) singers, in *Respiratory Function in Speech and Song* (Hixon & Collaborators, 1987), chapter 10, pp. 337–374.

Weir, R. H. (1967), Some thoughts on spelling, *in* W. M. Austin, ed., 'Papers in Linguistics in Honor of Léon Dostert', Mouton, The Hague, pp. 169–177.

Wennerstrom, A. (2001), *The Music of Everyday Speech: Prosody and Discourse Analysis*, Oxford University Press, New York.

White, A. (2002), 'The Unicode Standard for Scripts of India (TUSSI): A request to make the TUSSI specification compatible with the ISCII standard, and beyond', <http://www.exnet.btinternet.co.uk/uniprop/encoding.htm>.

Whitney, W. D. (1861), 'On Lepsius's standard alphabet', *Journal of the American Oriental Society* **7**, 299–332.

—. (1862), 'The Atharva-veda-prâtiçâkhya, or Çâunakîyâ catur-âdhyâyikâ: Text, translation, and notes', *Journal of the American Oriental Society* **7**, 333–615.

—. (1868), 'The Tâittirîya-Prâtiçâkhya, with its commentary, the Tribhâshyaratna: Text, translation, and notes', *Journal of the American Oriental Society* **9**, 1–469.

——. (1880), 'On the transliteration of Sanskrit', *Journal of the American Oriental Society* **11**(Proceedings of the American Oriental Society at New York, October, 1880), li–liv.

——. (1889), *Sanskrit Grammar: Including Both the Classical Language, and the Older Dialects, of Veda and Brahmana*, 2d edn, Harvard University Press, Cambridge MA.

Wikner, C. (2002), 'Sanskrit for $\LaTeX\,2_{\varepsilon}$, Version 2.2', <http://www.ctan.org/tex-archive/language/sanskrit/sktdoc.ps>.

Williams, C. E. & Stevens, K. N. (1981), Vocal correlates of emotional states, *in* Darby (1981), pp. 221–240.

Windisch, E. (1917), *Geschichte der Sanskrit-Philologie und indischen Altertumskunde*, Karl J. Trübner, Strassburg. Reprint: Berlin: De Gruyter, 1992.

Wissink, C. (2001), 'Issues in Indic language collation', Paper delivered at the 19th Int. Unicode Conference, San José, CA, Sept. 2001. <http://www.unicode.org/notes/tn1/Wissink-IndicCollation.pdf>. [= Unicode Technical Note #1].

Witzel, M. (1974), 'On some unknown systems of marking the Vedic accents', *Vishveshvaranand Indological Journal* **12**, 472–502. [= Vishvabandu Commemoration Volume].

——. (1999), 'Substrate languages in old Indo-Aryan (R̥gvedic, Middle and Late Vedic)', *Electronic Journal of Vedic Studies* **5**(1), 1–67. <http://www.ejvs.laurasianacademy.com/ejvs0501/ejvs0501article.pdf>.

Wollen, K. A. & Ruggiero, F. T. (1983), 'Colored-letter synesthesia', *Journal of Mental Imagery* **7**(2), 83–86.

Wujastyk, D. (1990), 'Standardization of Sanskrit for electronic data and screen representation', <http://www.tug.org/tex-archive/fonts/csx/docs/charset.ps>.

——. (1996), 'Transliteration of Devanāgarī', <http://www.ucl.ac.uk/~ucgadkw/members/transliteration/translit.pdf>.

Zwicky, A. M. (1965), Topics in Sanskrit Phonology, PhD thesis, MIT. MIT Working Papers in Linguistics.

Index